Sid Meier's
MEMOIR!

By the Creator
of Civilization!

Sid Meier's
MEMOIR!

A Life in
Computer Games

Sid Meier
written with Jennifer Lee Noonan

W. W. NORTON & COMPANY
Independent Publishers Since 1923

Copyright © 2020 by Sid Meier and Jennifer Lee Noonan

For information about permission to reproduce selections from this book, write to
Permissions, W. W. Norton & Company, Inc., 500 Fifth Avenue, New York, NY 10110

For information about special discounts for bulk purchases, please contact
W. W. Norton Special Sales at specialsales@wwnorton.com or 800-233-4830

Manufacturing by Lake Book
Book design by Lovedog Studio
Production manager: Anna Oler

Library of Congress Cataloging-in-Publication Data

Names: Meier, Sid, author. | Noonan, Jennifer Lee, author.
Title: Sid Meier's memoir! : a life in computer games / Sid Meier ;
written with Jennifer Lee Noonan.
Description: First edition. | New York : W.W. Norton & Company, 2020.
Identifiers: LCCN 2020015913 | ISBN 9781324005872 (hardcover) |
ISBN 9781324005889 (epub)
Subjects: LCSH: Meier, Sid. | Video game designers—United States—Biography. |
Video games—History. | Video games—Design. | Video gamers—Psychology.
Classification: LCC GV1469.3.M45 A3 2020 | DDC 794.8—dc23
LC record available at https://lccn.loc.gov/2020015913

W. W. Norton & Company, Inc., 500 Fifth Avenue, New York, N.Y. 10110
www.wwnorton.com

W. W. Norton & Company Ltd., 15 Carlisle Street, London W1D 3BS

1 2 3 4 5 6 7 8 9 0

To the worldwide community of
computer, console, and mobile gamers
(and their long-suffering spouses, parents,
and significant others).

CONTENTS

Sid Meier's
MEMOIR!

ONE BILLION HOURS
An Introduction

A BILLION HOURS AGO,
Neanderthals were making spearheads in the Stone Age. A billion hours from now, it will be the year 116,174 AD, assuming the calendar system holds up that long. With a billion hours to play with, you could make roughly 13,000 round trips to Alpha Centauri at the speed of light, or play a back-to-back marathon of every *Star Trek* movie ever made for every person in New York . . . twice.

Or, you could spend it all playing *Sid Meier's Civilization*. So I'm told.

One billion hours is the sort of number that is humbling to the point of incomprehensibility—and it's a wildly conservative estimate, at that. The game distribution service Steam only began collecting player data in earnest within the last decade, and one billion is actually the number of hours played on *Civilization V*, specifically, from its release in 2010 up through 2016. A six-year window into one game in a series that (as of this printing) spans twenty-nine years and twelve editions, not to mention the expansion packs.

To imagine the hours devoted to all the incarnations of *Civ* since 1991 is, well, incomprehensible. I wouldn't want to try. What's more, any fair assessment of *Civ*'s success would have to include all the other games I've crafted along the way—including titles like *Pirates!* and *Railroad Tycoon*, which were popular series*

---

* *Achievement Unlocked:* A Journey of 1,000 Miles—Read one page.

in their own right, but also overlooked gems like *C.P.U. Bach* and *SimGolf*. I'd even want to acknowledge projects that started strong but fizzled early, because sometimes it takes a misstep to figure out where you should be headed. Each game taught me something, each game was both painful and gratifying in its own way, and each game contributed to what came after it.

What follows is a largely chronological examination of all the games I've produced over my lifetime, from the wildly successful to the completely unheard of. It's a thorough list, including a few that were developed outside the traditional career model where you do things like "make money" and "get sued if you copy other people's ideas." Just as every sprawling empire can be traced back to a single settler, my reputation as a benevolent industry patriarch wasn't built in a day, and the truth is I was once a young kid who didn't know there were rules, making games out of not-so-original ideas for maximum fun and minimum (often nonexistent) profit. Fortunately, I've been told the statute of limitations has expired, so I'm ready to come clean. But whether they took a billion lines of code—not an impossible estimate for all of the *Civ* products combined—or less than a hundred, there is one thing every game in this book has in common. They are fundamentally comprised, as all games are, of a series of interesting decisions.

Like most sweeping definitions, this one requires a little unpacking, which I'll get into in Chapter 16. But the most important take-away is that it's a mindset that looks outward, rather than inward. We are surrounded by decisions, and therefore games, in everything we do. "Interesting" might be subject to personal taste to some degree, but the gift of agency—that is, the ability of players to exert free will over their surroundings rather than obediently following a narrative—is what sets games apart from other media, regardless of whether that agency is expressed through a computer keyboard, plastic tokens, physical movement, or entirely in the mind. Without a player's input, there can be no game; conversely, it takes only a single interaction to transform an observer into a participant, and thus a player.

Of course, it's still incumbent upon us as designers to make that decision-making enjoyable, and that's not always an easy task. I don't claim, for example, that the decision over what to have for lunch would necessarily make for a good game—only that it has the potential to be turned into one, or at least part of one. No subject is universally boring; everything contains a core of fascination somewhere, and the primary job of a game designer is not to *make* something fun, but to *find* the fun. I have a habit (some might call it a compulsion) of analyzing how things work, examining their effects on people, and parsing out which elements are fundamentally compelling and which are just window dressing. Once you isolate the most interesting part of any given decision, then you're ready to build an interactive experience for the player that feels fascinatingly new, yet comfortingly familiar. That's my philosophy, anyway. It seems to have worked out pretty well.

I'm often asked in interviews when I got interested in games, usually with the implied hope that I'll identify a prodigiously early moment in my childhood when I suddenly knew I was a game designer. Interviewers seem especially keen to discover some talismanic object of inspiration—perhaps it was the 630-page illustrated Civil War book that my father gave me in elementary school, or the train station I lived next to in Switzerland, or an Errol Flynn swashbuckling classic flickering on our tiny, black-and-white television—and they want me to say that in that instant, I felt the flash of destiny. How else can one explain the relatively uncommon path I've taken in life, if not in terms of sudden twists and critical junctures?

But from my perspective, there was no turning point. I never made the conscious decision to embrace gaming, because as far as I can tell gaming already *is* the default, straightforward path. Not only does it span a billion hours of history—ancient Sumerians were throwing dice as early as 5000 BC, and cruder games almost certainly go back as far as the Neanderthals—but it's a deeply embedded human instinct. A newborn baby will play tug-of-war with its own foot before it even understands who the foot belongs to. Everyone starts out life as a gamer, and I was no different. First, I laughed at peekaboo, then I lined up toy soldiers, then I played board games, then I made fun computer programs. To me, it seems like the most logical progression in the world. The question "When did you start?" would be better framed as "Why didn't you stop?"—but even then, I won't have a good answer. I find it mind-boggling that a life spent dedicated to gaming is the exception, rather than the rule.

If my gravestone reads "Sid Meier, creator of *Civilization*" and nothing else, I'll be fine with that. It's a good game to be known for, and I'm proud of the positive impact it's had on so many players' lives. But it won't be the whole story.

This is the whole story.

1

WHAT HAPPENS IN VEGAS

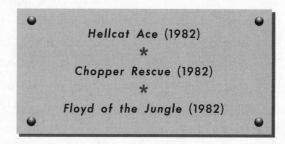

Hellcat Ace (1982)

*

Chopper Rescue (1982)

*

Floyd of the Jungle (1982)

THE STORY OF HOW I STARTED

my first videogame company has become almost legendary within the gaming community, but like most legends, the version you've heard has probably been inflated a bit along the way. Yes, it happened in Las Vegas. Yes, it was based on a dare of sorts. Alcohol may have been involved, at least for one of the participants. But the actual company wasn't formed until months later, and regardless, I'm not a fan of viewing the past as some inevitable march to destiny. At the time, it didn't feel that way at all.

I began my career as a systems analyst for General Instrument, installing networked cash register systems in retail stores throughout my home state of Michigan. Working with computers was satisfying, and I was grateful to have what amounted to a very good job for a recent graduate. I wasn't desperate to unleash my creativity on the world, or even thinking very hard about the future of the industry. At best, you could call it a state of ignorant bliss: there was no such thing as a retail computer game, only free bits of code passed between hobbyists, so it would have been difficult for me to harbor secret dreams of becoming a professional computer game designer. That's not to say I didn't know what cool was—I'd programmed my first game just a few months after entering college—but cool was cool, and work was work, and the two never overlapped.

Actually, that's not entirely true. There was one slightly cool division at GI called AmTote, which made electronic scoreboards. Rumor has it they designed all of the original game show equipment for *The Price Is Right*, but their main product was a vertical gambling odds tracker called the Mighty Totalizator. Despite sounding like a bad sci-fi weapon, the totalizator was invented (and presumably named) by the Australian Sir George Julius, back in 1913. Gambling riots were a regular problem in those days, usually in response to low payouts on what should have been a long-odds pick. If, for example, a hot tip ran through the crowd about a last-minute injury to the champion, then extra bets would be placed on the underdog, potentially eliminating his underdog status. A bookie's odds are only a reflection of where everyone else's money is, and the faster those numbers could be updated and displayed to the crowd, the safer the men inside the ticket booths would be.

Julius's invention was one of the earliest examples of a mechanized computer, and contained enough bicycle gears and piano wire to fill an entire stable at the horse track where it was first installed. Fortunately, totalizators had become less spacious by the 1970s, but they were still no less fun to say out loud.

In any case, one of the side benefits of working for a company that makes gambling machines is corporate functions tend to take place in Las Vegas. It took several years and a few promotions, but finally, I was sent to my first major conference. Games of random chance weren't my thing, and I certainly didn't relish sitting through three days of meetings, but unlike many fellow introverts I do enjoy the sensory onslaught of the Vegas experience—and, perhaps more in line with my nerd reputation, I love blackjack. Most casinos offered low stakes games for just two dollars a hand in those days, and this seemed like a reasonable risk to take against my ability to work the odds with my own biological totalizator.

It also didn't hurt that Vegas had more videogame arcades than anywhere in the world.

Before any of that could happen, though, I would have to grind through several literal boss encounters in the convention hall each day. Things were already looking bleak by the first afternoon, and I wasn't sure I'd survive the closing seminar on business strategy, or market growth, or whatever tedious thing it was. So in a last ditch effort to stay awake, I turned and struck up a quiet conversation with the coworker seated next to me, a man named Bill Stealey.

He was in a different department, so we had never really met, but we had a passing recognition of each other as employees of the same large company. We had probably even been on the same flight out from Maryland, though I couldn't really picture Bill sitting passively in coach—much easier to imagine him knocking on the cockpit door to give the crew a few pointers. Bill was a reserve Air Force pilot who had fought his way into the program despite wearing glasses, and he was so proud of his training that he'd printed "Fighter Pilot Supreme" on all his business cards.

True to form, Bill began regaling me in hushed tones with stories from his flying days. I could see the overlap of our life experiences was slim at best, but the topic wasn't completely foreign to me, and I managed to offer up the fact that I'd been programming an airplane game in my spare time.

Bill nodded, as much to himself as to me. He, too, had recently purchased an Atari 800 home computer, which he confided was only nominally for work. Mostly, he'd gotten it to play a new game called *Star Raiders*. "I really want to get into selling games," he said. "This is the future!"

I told him that I had just sold my first game, actually, to a small publisher named Acorn Software.

"Oh?" Suddenly Bill looked very keen. "We should start a business!"

"That's an interesting idea," I deflected politely. It wasn't a bad suggestion, necessarily, but this was a man known for his gregarious enthusiasm. Even if he sincerely meant it in the moment, I thought, it was probably the kind of thing people said but never really pursued.

After the conference wrapped up for the day, Bill and I decided to stroll around Las Vegas together in search of arcades, and eventually we came upon the MGM Grand. I didn't keep score as we challenged each other on one flashing, beeping cabinet after another, but the way Bill tells it, I beat him at practically every game. Finally, he found his redemption: a World War I flight simulator called *Red Baron*.

"All right, young man, now I'll show you how it's done," he said, settling into the molded plastic seat.

I watched over his shoulder as he concentrated a decade of actual piloting experience toward the slightly less perilous task of shooting down stick-figure biplanes among zigzag mountains. He scored well, though exactly how well is up for debate—I recall a score of around 3,000, compared to his memory of 75,000. This is a fair ratio, as I generally tend to remember things being about one-twenty-fifth as sensational as Bill does. In this case, the evidence is on my side, as modern emulators show that ten minutes of perfect *Red Baron* gameplay leads to a score of just over 10,000. At roughly a thousand points per minute, I would have had to stand in witness of his flying skill for over an hour. But whatever the raw numbers were, it was a solid performance.

Then it was my turn to play.

"How did you do that?" Bill sputtered, staring wide-eyed at a final score that was roughly double his own (on that part we agree). "I'm an actual pilot! How could you possibly have beaten me?"

I shrugged. "While you were playing, I memorized the algorithms."

"You did what?"

"I'm a programmer," I reminded him. "The AI of the enemy

planes is very predictable, the only trick is to never let them get behind you. I could design a better game in two weeks."

"Then do it," he insisted, his wounded pride already forgotten. "If you can do it, I can sell it."

And so we began. At the time it felt like a fun project, but not any sort of life-changing decision. The big moments rarely do, I think, and the danger of retroactive mythologizing is that it makes people want to hold out for something dramatic, rather than throwing themselves into every opportunity. The reality is I'd been fiddling around with game programming for years by then, and like I told Bill, I'd already sold one game—technically four, but we'll get to that—before he and I ever talked. The first step is almost always to sit down and start working, and it's almost never to fly to Vegas and wait for somebody to offer you a business venture.

I had several prototypes in progress on my home computer, including a helicopter game that was almost finished, but I had promised Bill airplanes. So I focused the rest of that summer on *Hellcat Ace*, named after the Grumman F6F Hellcat used by the Navy in World War II. It wasn't an exaggeration to say I could create a better AI in two weeks, but there's a pretty big gulf between better and best, and I always wanted to be on the far side of it.

When I finally decided the game was as ready as it could be, I handed it over to Bill, and a day later he returned it to me with a list of bugs and military inaccuracies. That was when I knew that this partnership could really go somewhere. Bill wasn't looking to make a quick buck on something he didn't understand; he was as invested in the game quality as I was. I'm not sure he was as confident about me at that point, even after I took his suggestions in stride and updated the game. But he wasn't the type of person who could back down once I'd answered his challenge. I'd proven I could design a better game, and now he had no choice but to prove that he could sell it.

So with $1,500 in savings, we bought a stack of floppy disks, a package of label stickers, and a box of plastic baggies to put them in. This was standard packaging back then, even for professional releases—no one would have thought to waste an entire cardboard box on just a disk and a half-sheet of instructions. Meanwhile, printer technology was new enough that there was no such thing as a cheap consumer model. A printer was a printer, and the dot matrix in Bill's basement could create labels just as fancy as any moderate-size company's. All we needed was a logo.

Bill wanted to name our new company Smuggers, the culmination of a joke he'd made up after I had invited him to join my users' group. Though this phrase is often associated with the early chat rooms of the internet, a users' group originally referred to a physical group of computer users meeting in the real world. Gatherings would take place in a local store, or occasionally someone's living room, and we would all lug our giant computers and monitors with us so we could trade software in a true peer-to-peer fashion. I was not the founder or even the leader of our particular group, but Bill always called it "Sid Meier's Users' Group" so that he could impishly shorten it to SMUG. Fortunately, the other guys had a sense of humor about it, but it's fair to say that Smuggers was not my first choice for our company name.

I suggested MicroProse instead, because it seemed to me that computer code was just as elegant as any literary prose, and it made a nice double entendre with the word "pros." Bill thought it was a little hard to pronounce, but agreed that it was distinctive enough to be remembered. Turns out it wasn't quite as distinctive as we'd originally thought, because years later we would be sued over the name by a company called MicroPro, makers of the WordStar word processing program. Though we were arguably better known, their company slightly predated ours, and it was looking like we were going to have no choice but to change the name—eventually. Bill, being just as tenacious as he was enthusiastic, managed to affably drag on negotiations for years, until the plaintiffs suddenly changed their own name to WordStar International instead, and the whole issue was dropped. I'm not sure anyone but Bill could have done it, but that was just one of his many talents. Somehow he could stonewall a person in a way that made them feel glad for the opportunity.*

In the beginning, the sales calls Bill made were based mostly on convenience. If he had a business trip out of town, he'd walk from the train to the nearest computer store to try to sell a few copies. On weekends, he'd load a box of disks into the trunk of his car and drive as far as he could get down I-95, coming back just in time for Monday morning meetings at General Instrument.

Then late one evening, my phone rang.

"Sid, I think we might be onto something here."

"Bill? Where are you?"

"New Jersey. We just sold fifty copies of *Hellcat Ace.*"

"Hey, that's great!"

"Yeah," he said. "*So start copying,*" was the unspoken implication.

Every individual sale back then translated to about sixty seconds of boredom in front of my matched pair of floppy drives, making copies of the game one by one. I could try to read a book, but getting work done was impossible—multitasking wouldn't be a feature in home computers until about a decade after I needed it. Outsourcing, on the other hand, was just making its debut, and it didn't take long before I hired one of the younger members of our users' group to make copies for me at twenty-five cents a disk. He and I were close because he was too young to drive and I was giving him rides, so it's possible his first job ever was making the modern-day equivalent of thirty-nine dollars an hour at a video-game company. Not a bad gig.

In the meantime, I finished my helicopter game, *Chopper Rescue,* as well as another game I'd been working on called *Floyd of the Jungle.* At Bill's suggestion, I added an opening screen to all

---

* **Achievement Unlocked:** Books Don't Come with a Demo Mode—Time to buy this thing.

Floyd of the Jungle
box art.
© 1982 MicroProse,
www.microprose.com

three games that advertised the rest of the MicroProse "catalog," and copied the new version over whatever disks we already had in stock. Several more tweaks went in over time as Bill received feedback from store managers, so if any of our originals still survive, they're probably all different from one another.

Even though it wasn't an aircraft game, *Floyd of the Jungle* was usually the hook Bill used to get the attention of store employees. It offered multiplayer competition against their coworkers, which few could resist, and had elements of what would eventually be known as the platformer genre. Similar to bestselling arcade titles like *Space Panic* (1980) and *Donkey Kong* (1981), this style seemed to resonate with players on a deeper, more intuitive level: somehow, everyone knows that being at the top of the screen is better than being at the bottom, and if there's a damsel in distress, you have to rescue her. Flying the Grumman F6F took a little practice, but *Floyd* made sense immediately, and didn't require the players to be especially good—they only had to be on par with each other to have fun. With two or three employees crowded around the screen, shoppers would soon become curious, and once Bill handed his joystick over to a customer, the store was almost guaranteed to buy.

Other games had multiplayer, of course, including *Hellcat Ace* and *Chopper Rescue*, but only for two people. *Floyd* was special because it allowed all four joysticks to be used at once, something very few small-market games could boast in 1982. The one major release with four-player capability was *Asteroids,* which had been developed by Atari to showcase their own machine's capabilities. Technology manufacturers often had to take a "build it, and they will come" approach, and they never really knew if a feature would prove popular with developers until they'd already invested a few million in providing it. Sadly, four-player functionality would remain on the fringe for a long time to come, appearing in only a handful of arcade titles like *Gauntlet* (1985) and *Teenage Mutant Ninja Turtles* (1989), and no mainstream computer games until *Doom* exploded onto the scene in 1993.

Chopper Rescue's multiplayer was unique in its own way, though, because instead of controlling two identical characters, the joysticks were linked to different aspects of the same helicopter. Just like in many real-life military vehicles, one player navigated while the other fired weapons, which required plenty of cooperation and communication. A lot has been lost from those early years of technology, but I'm willing to claim this was the first videogame to give simultaneous players different tasks, at least until someone says otherwise.

Chopper Rescue was also when I figured out how to scroll in all directions. Most of my early games were inspired by new programming tricks—either learned, or developed from scratch—that I then found a way to build a game around. The big advancement in *Hellcat Ace*, for example, was a way to tilt the horizon more efficiently and accurately than other games. Changing the angle of a line may not seem like much in today's terms, but it's a lot harder when you're doing it on a computer whose entire memory could hold roughly three chapters of this book in plain text format.

Meanwhile, *Floyd of the Jungle* contained several advancements in one. Aside from managing four active players on the screen, it also included a new technique for animation that involved switching back and forth between slightly different versions of the same character. The hottest game on the market that year, *Space Invaders*, had used this approach to display a total of six alien types, wiggling their legs in a loop of just two positions each. But the code left room for considerably more, and I wanted to test its limits with as many creatures moving in as many different ways as possible. Aliens had been done already, so I settled on a rainforest backdrop instead, and only then did I think back to the countless Saturday mornings I'd spent watching *George of the Jungle* cartoons. Unlike later in my career, topic was still secondary to technique—I was making games *for* the computer, not games that could be put on a computer if necessary, and I wanted to utilize every available feature.

Part of the experiment was seeing how much I could cram on the screen without slowing down the game, and part of it was practicing my illustration skills, since most designers in those days had to be a one-stop shop. I maxed out the code with four-stage images of birds, elephants, crocodiles, snakes, lions, monkeys, and Pygmies (a peaceful set of tribes, in reality, but stereotypes of the day presented them as a formidable challenge for explorers, and it didn't occur to me at the time to question this received wisdom). Then there was the lovely damsel in distress, Janice, and of course Floyd himself, who had a separate resting animation in addition to all of his running, jumping, climbing, and dying moves. My monkey was a little lumpy, like those animal crackers you can never quite identify, but the crocodile and elephant were downright artistic. This was good news for MicroProse, because it would be another three years before we could afford to hire a real artist.

We started running ads in October 1982, and six months later we finally received our first review, in which the Atari-themed *Antic* magazine declared *Floyd of the Jungle* to be both "enjoyable," and "very good." Reviews back then were pretty light on adjectives in general. The next month, they covered *Hellcat Ace*, which was "effective" but "could be improved."

Bill didn't mind the lukewarm assessment, though. For one thing, the writer repeated one of his favorite promotional lines, "playtested by members of an Air National Guard Wing," which was just a slick way of referring to Bill and a couple of his friends. But the truth was his plan never really hinged on the review's content anyway. He just needed it to exist.

As soon as the articles were published, Bill began placing calls to hobby stores that were farther than driving distance away.

"Hello, I'm looking to buy a copy of *Hellcat Ace*."

"Hmm, I don't think we carry that one—"

"What?" he would fume. "What kind of computer store are you? Didn't you see the review in *Antic*?" Then he would hang up in a huff, muttering about taking his business elsewhere.

A week later he would call again, pretending to be somebody else. And a third time a week after that. He didn't even have to call from different numbers, since caller ID was still as imaginary as Dick Tracy's Apple Watch.

Finally, on the fourth week, he'd use his professional voice. "Good afternoon, I'm a representative from MicroProse Software, and I'd like to show you our latest game, *Hellcat Ace*." Spurred by the imaginary demand, they would invite him in.

It seems utterly transparent in today's marketing-savvy world, but in the era of mom-and-pop computer stores, it worked. Bill may very well have placed a call to every single outlet in the nation at that time, charming them with his energy and enthusiasm. He and I were the perfect combination, because I had no interest in sales, and he had no interest in the creative side. I could sit at home and program all night, he could get out every weekend and sell, and we never got in each other's way.

2

ADAPTATION

> Tic-Tac-Toe (1975) * The Star
> Trek Game (1979) * Hostage
> Rescue (1980) * Bank Game I
> (1981) * Bank Game II: The
> Revenge (1981) * Faux Space
> Invaders (1981) * Faux Pac-Man
> (1981) * Formula 1 Racing (1982)

"ADAPTATION" IS SUCH A
flattering word. So much nicer than "copyright infringement."
For 63 percent of these titles it really was an honest adaptation,
sometimes even at the request of the property owner. The other
37 percent, okay, I was maybe slightly infringing on an existing
trademark. But all it got me was a few bucks' worth of sales and
some free skeptical looks. Crime doesn't pay, kids. (Unless it serves
as inspiration and practice for a lifelong career in one of the most
rewarding industries on the planet, in which case it pays fine, both
monetarily and spiritually.) My well-intentioned plagiarism also
earned me a mild reprimand at General Instrument, where the
words "game designer" were decidedly absent from my job title.
But long before I was getting in trouble at work for making games,
I was getting in trouble at college for making games.

When I entered the University of Michigan in 1971, I had never
even seen a computer in person before, but the ultra-logical nature

of them was intriguing to me. So, on a whim, I signed up for a programming class alongside my physics and math double major, and by the end of the year, I was a computer science major instead. This decision greatly improved my employment prospects, I realize now, but that didn't factor in much at the time. Mostly, I did it because computers felt empowering. I couldn't calculate pi to 10,000 digits—or at the very least it would take me a long, long time—but I could write a program that could. The ability to say, in relatively few words, "Do something cool," and then have that cool thing pop out the other side, was unbelievably exciting. I wouldn't even say it was magical. It was technological, and that was better than magic.

Our class learned on an IBM 360 mainframe, programming in FORTRAN on eighty-column punch cards. We would prepare our deck of cards, bring them to the room that held the computer, and watch a staff member feed them into the card reader one by one. Then maybe ten minutes later, we'd walk up to a different desk to collect our results. The good old days were yet to come; these were still very much the bad old days.

Part of my scholarship at the university involved a work-study program to offset tuition costs, and after completing my one programming class, I boldly took a job with a professor who wanted some computer work done. It was a bit of a gamble to claim I was qualified for it, but not many students were in those days, and fortunately the work turned out to be pretty simple. Most of it was early explorations of educational software, like multiple-choice tests that could branch into different questions depending on your answers. But the equipment that Dr. Noah Sherman had in his lab was far more advanced than the stuff offered to second-year students like me. I now had access to a real teletype terminal, which allowed programs to be entered directly into the system without any punch cards acting as middleman. I could examine my broken output, correct the code, and verify the improved output on a much shorter cycle than before. Dr. Sherman could sense my enthusiasm, and he encouraged me to try out my own experiments on the machine after my work was done each day. He even left me with a key to the lab while he was away in Italy one summer.

By then, I was immersing myself in every computer-related topic I could find, most especially this new thing they were calling artificial intelligence. Precise instructions for a computer could be complicated enough to plan out, but teaching a computer how to make its own decisions, maybe even to learn from its mistakes, was on another level entirely. Alan Turing had famously called for an imitation of social behavior as the ultimate goal for a thinking computer, but I thought the more interesting prospect was a computer that could outsmart a human. Not just a math workhorse, but one that could predict my behavior, and be clever about what to do with that information. I wanted a computer that could model complex future possibilities, and eliminate undesirable outcomes until it had settled on the ideal course of action. In short, I wanted a computer that could game.

The classic starting point, I thought, would be tic-tac-toe—and history backed me up on this, though I didn't know it at the time. In 1950, just two years after Turing's invention of the stored-program computer, a man named Josef Kates had built a twelve-foot-tall behemoth he called "Bertie the Brain," which stood on display at the Canadian National Exhibition and beat all comers at tic-tac-toe. (Historians often distinguish between this and the first videogame, *Tennis for Two*, because the latter used a video screen for its display rather than simple lightbulbs.) Other engineers created independent versions of tic-tac-toe during the 1950s, and eventually followed them with operational renditions of checkers, blackjack, and even chess. Most recently, in 1975—the same year I was attempting to teach myself the tenets of gaming AI—a group of students at MIT had built a mechanical tic-tac-toe machine out of Tinkertoys, which was surprisingly similar to the original totalizator with its gears and piano wire. It would have been super helpful to know all this, but without the advent of the internet, I was largely isolated in my educational pursuits. So I plowed ahead on my own, without the benefit of others' wisdom.

The lab was mine as long as Dr. Sherman explored the Italian hilltops, so I put the hours to good use and worked every day on my self-assigned project. First, I created a simple text input scheme that allowed you to enter one move at a time. I hadn't figured out how to get the computer to display its next move on the screen yet, so instead I instructed it to send the grid to the nearest printer, which was stored in a separate room and shared by everyone in the building. I'd go over, collect my printout, come back to my desk, and enter my next move. It was slow, but at least I got some exercise. (If only I had known that games forcing you to walk around would be all the rage forty years later.)

After the third or fourth document containing nothing but Xs and Os, the woman running the output desk was on to me.

"Wait a minute!" she said, snatching back the paper she'd just handed over. "What do you think you're doing? Computers are not for games!"

I had no satisfactory answer to give her, since it seemed clear to me that was exactly what they were for.

"I'm going to have to report you," she scolded, already looking up the details of my account on her own terminal. She located the name and contact information of my supervising professor, and for a while I was afraid that my dream of a gaming computer would be cut short before it could even finish one round of tic-tac-toe. Dr. Sherman hadn't given me specific permission to do what I was doing, and maybe he would agree that it was frivolous. I might even be banished back to the world of punch cards.

Fortunately, he vouched for me, once they located him by phone on the other side of the Atlantic, and graciously told the staff that I had blanket permission to continue for the rest of the summer in whatever capacity I saw fit. I doubt he had any idea what he was setting in motion, but I was grateful.

After graduation, I began working for General Instrument,

and was once again given access to technology I could never have afforded on my own. The sixteen-bit Nova minicomputer—"mini" being relative, in this context—was considered a top-of-the-line machine because its processor was contained on a single printed circuit board, with no spaghetti wiring coming off the back. It was housed in a cabinet the height of an eighth-grader and cost more than a new car, and not only did I have one for my own personal use, but so did most of my coworkers. In addition, all of the mini-computers in our office could talk to each other directly, rather than being hobbled en masse to a central mainframe. We had a network.

Like the university teletype, GI's business machines only supported plain text, no graphics. But I wasn't the first to face this dilemma. As far back as 1865, even before the invention of the typewriter, Lewis Carroll was giving the publisher of *Alice in Wonderland* instructions on how to lay out their movable type-face in a way that drew pictures with the story itself. After the typewriter became widespread, so-called "artyping" exploded as a hobby, and newspapers around the country paid cash to reprint complex portraits and landscapes drawn one character at a time. In 1963, the practice went digital, after the publication of an official binary code for text known as the American Standard Code for Information Interchange, or ASCII. Typewriters hung around for another two decades, but the new acronym took hold, and from that point on pictures made with text characters were commonly known as ASCII art.

For me, the potential of this technology wasn't in the complexity of the drawing, but in the speed at which the computer could display what it thought of as plain text. Maybe that column of numbers was a list of grocery store sales data, refreshing every time somebody bought a banana somewhere on the East Coast—or maybe it was a fortress of cobblestone number 3s, aiming hyphens at the enemy sales data on the other side of the screen. The computer didn't know the difference. With the right layout of text, I realized, I could transform it from ASCII art into ASCII animation.

Perhaps there was something subconsciously inspiring about a black computer screen dotted with white characters, or perhaps it was just a case of paralyzing fandom, but I decided I would make a game based on *Star Trek*. There's actually a somewhat famous *Star Trek* ASCII game from the same era, created by Mike Mayfield in 1971. It was turn-based, with Klingons and asteroids plotted out on an overhead grid, and proved so popular that the code was reprinted in several books and nostalgically modified by fans to play on every computer system since. There's even a modern version that can play on Android smartphones. This widespread and well-documented program was not my game, and I am in no way taking credit for it. To the best of my knowledge, my *Star Trek* ASCII game never left the confines of the General Instrument network.

In contrast to Mayfield's turn-based program, mine was designed to run in real time, like an arcade game. First, I outlined the *Enterprise*'s viewscreen with underscores, slashes, and pipes (the vertical line in the upper-right-hand corner of your keyboard). These remained static throughout the game, while everything inside them moved around several times a second, animating the enemy ships and space debris flying toward you in mock-3D. Missiles and phasers had to be timed just right, and when you took out an enemy, you were rewarded with a little texty explosion. I even added small beeping sound effects, which turned out to be the beginning of the game's downfall.

Initially, I posted it for only a few interested coworkers, but within a few days it seemed like everyone had heard of it. The company network began to drag, and small beeps ricocheted through the halls as a sort of work-abandonment klaxon of shame. Nobody seemed especially apologetic, though, since it was easy to hear that they weren't alone.

Eventually, the drain on productivity became too significant to ignore, and I was told to delete the game. But the instruction was delivered with only a knowing shrug, since not even management could cast the first stone when it came to playing on company time.

My coworkers were understandably disappointed, but personally, I wore the ban with pride. It was an objective measure of how good the game must have been.

It did leave me with a problem, however. My appetite for making games was growing stronger. If I couldn't program them in the office anymore, where could I do it? Like a lot of fledgling industries, the home computer market in the late seventies was crowded and nonstandardized. There were a few major players like the Apple II and the TRS-80, but also many less popular machines like the Commodore PET, the Texas Instruments 99/4, and the Heathkit, which arrived as loose components you had to solder together yourself. But all of these seemed geared toward the engineer, rather than the programmer, and none took into account the needs of gaming at all. The TRS-80 didn't have a color screen, and several of the others didn't have plugs for joysticks. There were dedicated gaming systems, including the Magnavox Odyssey and the classic Atari 2600, but they were just passive readers. You couldn't make a game on one any more than you could make a TV show with a television set. Arcade machines could be programmed directly, but their hardware was well beyond my price range. All I could do was wait.

Finally, in late 1979, Atari released a pair of systems known as the 400 and the 800. They were code-named Candy and Colleen during production, supposedly in honor of two secretaries in the Atari offices, and these names live on in the emulator programs you can still find on the internet today. Candy, the 400, was marketed exclusively as a machine that could play games, and didn't include plugs for a traditional keyboard or a non-television monitor. It was little more than an upgrade to the Atari 2600. Colleen, on the other hand, was a real computer: bigger, heavier, with top-of-the-line graphics and sound capability, a real keyboard, expansion slots for added memory, and no fewer than four separate joystick ports.

Even better, the data output could be stored magnetically instead of on long paper tape riddled with holes. The magnetic tape was only a few millimeters wide, and rolled up neatly into what most people today would recognize as an audiocassette. Aside from being vastly more convenient, this meant that anyone who saw your stash of Atari tapes might assume you were carrying around the latest Billy Joel singles instead of a bunch of nerdy computer gear.

Other computers on the market could in theory make games, but here was a machine that had been designed for it, by the company that knew games better than anyone. I clipped out the mail-order form, and enclosed a check representing almost all of my savings. Several weeks later, the distinctive silver Atari box arrived on my doorstep, and within hours I was programming.

Not that I could make much at first. The Atari came with a single cartridge containing the BASIC computer language, and no additional instructions to speak of. But between my users' group, several magazine subscriptions, and diligent experimentation, I soon completed my first truly original work, if not exactly my most exceptional one. I named it *Hostage Rescue*. On the left side of the screen, a small green helicopter hovered, not much different than the one I would later use in *Chopper Rescue*. On the right was an array of face-ish-looking objects, colored blue for bad guys, or white for the hostages awaiting rescue as the title implied. Behind them was a single, oversized face that I very subtly referred to as "the Ayatollah." It was a timely game.

The Ayatollah shot missiles at you, you shot missiles at him, and whenever you could, you scooped up exposed hostages and returned them to safety on the left side of the screen. Touching a bad guy sacrificed the lives of all the hostages currently in your helicopter, and their headcount remained accusingly at the bottom of the screen for the rest of the game. Simple graphics, I thought, didn't have to mean pulled punches.

The next time I went back home to Detroit for a visit, I brought my new creative outlet with me. Both of my parents were European immigrants—my father from Switzerland, my mother from

Holland—who had come to America in part because of the modern, cosmopolitan life it offered. My father, especially, was a connoisseur of machinery and gadgets, so I had assumed he would find programming as interesting as I did. Instead, I received a terse reminder that his own career as a professional typesetter was being phased out of existence by this newfangled thing I'd brought into their living room. He was not impressed. But he stayed in the room, at least, watching with languid wariness as I connected the Atari to the television and handed my mother the unfamiliar joystick.

She was excited in the way that all mothers are excited for their children's accomplishments, and she admired the title screen graphics as if she might find a way to hang them on the refrigerator. Soon, however, my four-color rendition of the Iran hostage crisis had her frowning in concentration, and letting out small cries of "Oh no!" at each new threat that headed her way. As the game progressed, she became more and more rapt, clenching her jaw and dodging missiles with her whole body. Suddenly, she dropped the controller and turned her face away.

She couldn't play anymore, she told me. Her heart was racing and it was all too much.

We moved on and enjoyed the rest of the afternoon, but I never forgot that moment. My mother had become emotionally invested in this little game, so profoundly that she'd had to abandon it entirely. A few rugged blobs on the screen had given her palpitations, and she had felt a genuine stab of guilt over each dead hostage. If she'd made it to the end, no doubt her triumph would have been wholehearted as well.

Games were not just a diversion, I realized. Games could make you feel. If great literature could wield its power through nothing but black squiggles on a page, how much more could be done with movement, sound, and color? The potential for emotional interaction through this medium struck me as both fascinating and enticing.

Shortly afterward, I experienced a second major turning point in my relationship with games, this time through my Not Yet Inaccurately Nicknamed Users' Group (NYINUG). We were gathered at the back of the shop one evening, trading tips, stories, and pirated software in equal amounts, when someone new approached us. He wasn't a big computer guy himself, he explained, but he was looking for someone who was. A local bank had hired him to help with youth outreach, which apparently meant convincing teenagers that nothing was more hip than fiscal responsibility. One pillar of their plan, therefore, was to create money-themed videogames that they could set up in the bank's lobby. Even more baffling, they were willing to pay.

I took the job, a word I couldn't help but inspect over and over again in my mind. Were there people who got paid for making games? Could I be one of those people? I knew by now that I was a person who would make games, probably for the rest of my life, but it had never occurred to me that it could be a source of income. If that were true, then being a game designer seemed like the ideal job.

As with everything, I began to pick apart this puzzle in search of repeatable results, and the more I analyzed how this opportunity had come about, the more I began to appreciate the role the advertising consultant had played. Here was someone who, like most people, couldn't program computers himself, but who understood enough about them to see their potential. I was neither a boisterous salesman nor a self-promoter, and though I knew it was counterproductive to my own goals, I instinctively didn't want to deal with people who were blind to how incredibly cool these machines were. I had useful knowledge that others didn't have, but I would have to rely on those who had *knowledge of* my knowledge, who could be my link to the non-programming world. People, in other words, like my future partner Bill Stealey.

The money games were fun to make, despite being destined for failure in their role as "extreme banking" ambassadors. I designed one with a little piggy bank walking back and forth to catch falling coins, and another as a take on this brand-new arcade game called *Frogger,* in which you had to get your money across the street to the bank without getting run over. Maybe the cars were supposed to be symbolic of impulse purchases? I don't know how much I tried to justify my design choices. It was a weird gig.

At the same time, I began working in earnest on a new game that I could sell myself, to test out this professional game designer thing I'd set my sights on. Keeping my focus on marketability for the time being, I decided to build on an already successful formula, namely the smash hit from Taito known as *Space Invaders.* I don't even remember what my knockoff was called, but it was probably something obvious like *Alien Invasion* or *Planet Defenders.* I was still immersed in hacker culture at the time—which back then looked like a guy in a tucked-in polo shirt deciding between two circuit boards, not a shadowy figure crouched over a laptop in a secret hideout whispering "I'm in"—and I didn't consider for a moment whether I could get into trouble for selling such an unmistakable clone. To be fair, no version of *Space Invaders* had been released yet for the Atari 800, so I was still converting the game from scratch to a new system—another thing I didn't yet know they would pay people to do. If I'd been a Taito employee, they would have called it "porting" the game, instead of "stealing" it.

Once I was satisfied with my hand-assembled *Invaders* game, I put a small number of cassettes into plastic baggies and carried them down to the local electronics store. The manager indulgently listened to my pitch and bought maybe half a dozen for resale, though I imagine he was trying to keep me as a customer more than anything else. I'm not sure if they ever sold, but he didn't buy any more after that. Commercial failure was probably for the best, given the copyright concerns, and it did strike me eventually that I would need original ideas. But I went ahead and made a version of *Pac-Man,* too, just for the practice. The time to flex my creative muscle would be later, I figured, after I had mastered the basics.

My users' group enjoyed the free copy of *Pac-Man* I'd given

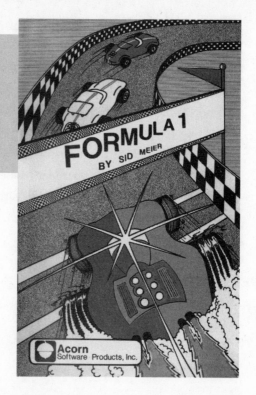

them, and in return, somebody tipped me off to a new technology called Player-Missile Graphics, which had to do with how quickly you could redraw an item as it moved freely around the screen. Though most examples involved spaceships and missiles, as the name implied, it occurred to me that the code could also lend itself nicely to a top-down racing game. From that I created *Formula 1 Racing*, which was the game I successfully sold to Acorn just before the trip to Las Vegas.

"Formula 1" was yet another trademark that I never paid to use, but at least the game itself was not especially similar to any of the racing games already on the shelves. Then again, it's kind of difficult for anyone to claim ownership of the premise "travel quickly in a circle." Like many games I made later in my career, *Formula 1 Racing* was fundamentally based on reality, which remains, at least for now, uncopyrightable. A racing game doesn't need a fictional driver with a predetermined back story; it needs that unique combination of emotional and psychological hooks that make you believe, however fleetingly, that you yourself are the driver.

Gaming, in turn, had its hooks embedded in me. I now believed, and not even fleetingly, that I myself could be a game designer. According to my short autobiography at the end of the *Formula 1 Racing* manual, this enterprising twenty-eight-year-old with exactly one professional title under his belt had two dreams in life.

One was "to develop a music composition system," which I eventually did. The other was "to write the ultimate strategy game."

3

CRUISING ALTITUDE

> Spitfire Ace (1982) * Wingman
> (1983) * Floyd of the Jungle II
> (1983) * Solo Flight (1983) *
> Air Rescue I (1984)

BY OUR FIRST CHRISTMAS,
Bill and I were selling almost five hundred games a month. I had
just churned out my fourth title, *Spitfire Ace*, which was the kind
of game we'd probably call an expansion pack today. It used the
same code base as *Hellcat Ace*, but moved the battle scenarios
from the Pacific to the European theater. The next step, as Bill saw
it, was to broaden our audience by porting all of our games onto
other systems, and at the top of his wish list was the hot new computer appearing in homes across America: the Commodore 64.

I was not particularly enthusiastic about this plan. For one
thing, converting our games to the Commodore would be a purely
financial move for the company, and I kind of felt like that was
Bill's problem, not mine. The work wouldn't involve anything
new or interesting; it was just a way to sell more of what we'd
already made. I had developed a lot of time-saving tools for myself
on the Atari, and I had a lot of ideas for new games that I didn't
want to derail. Digital gaming had already peaked, as far as I was

concerned—I mean, could the human eye even *see* more than 128 colors?—and if I hoped to establish myself in this obviously mature industry, then I didn't have time to rehash old code.

Bill agreed that a company is only as good as its latest product, and he did want me to keep producing. So instead, we hired two friends of mine named Grant Irani and Andy Hollis. They were both programmers at General Instrument as well as members of my Atari users' group, but despite this, computers were not our primary social outlet. Billy Joel wasn't giving up that easily, and being a rock 'n' roller was still far cooler for young guys like us than being a game designer. So most of our evenings together were spent noodling around in a basement band—similar to a garage band, but in Michigan, where the garage is too cold for nine months out of the year. Andy played drums, Grant was on vocals and guitar, and I played keyboard.

Though we'd technically doubled our workforce, MicroProse was still a nights-and-weekends operation out of our own homes, so it didn't feel like much had changed. Grant got busy porting *Floyd of the Jungle* to the Commodore 64, and Andy began altering the *Ace* conflict scenarios once again to create a version set in the Korean War. Meanwhile, Bill and I compromised on our respective interests with *Wingman*, a new style of flying game that would attempt to display independent, third-person multiplayer.

Usually multiplayer worked by showing the entire level on the screen at once, like *Floyd,* or else forcing the players to remain together, as in *Chopper Rescue.* But Bill wanted a game where two freely flying pilots could either team up or compete across a widespread level, and not necessarily be viewing the same section of the world at the same time. He may have seen the concept demonstrated in an arcade game, but nothing like it had ever been created on home computers. So I figured out a way to split the screen horizontally, keeping each player centered in their own half, but also visible in the other person's side of the screen when their paths overlapped. Even better, the code was finished with enough

Wingman screenshot.

time for Andy to add a first-person version of it to his game, *MiG Alley Ace*, transforming the third title of the trilogy into something unique from its predecessors.

With two more games in the catalog, and a foot in the door on a second platform, Bill decided it was time for him to leave General Instrument and work full-time at MicroProse. There was no realistic way for him to increase his efforts at the company otherwise, but I was more cautious about giving up my steady paycheck, and still not convinced that this dream was going to last. Our philosophy had always been to avoid loans and venture capital, and it would only take a couple months of slow sales to drag us under. I decided it would be more prudent for me to go half-time, spending two days a week at the new MicroProse office space and three at General Instrument.

Fortunately, my managers at GI were happy to keep me around in whatever capacity I was willing, especially since my gaming experiments served as a form of ongoing education that directly benefited them. As just one example, my recent proposal for a new operating system for GI had been based largely on the Atari

800 architecture I had become so familiar with. I doubt anyone at Atari could have predicted that their ideas would end up in cash registers throughout the Northeast, but the design worked well for our purposes and was approved. Most of my coworkers understood I'd be jumping ship eventually, and many of them were hoping for jobs at MicroProse themselves, so there was no animosity when I started splitting my time. Bill and I were the technological version of hometown heroes, and they were rooting for our success as much as we were.

Now fully dedicated to sales and promotion, Bill began touting his piloting experience even more heavily than before, and calling himself "Wild Bill" in press releases—a nickname from his Air Force days that might have been his call sign, or might have just been something he made up himself. At one point he managed to get the attention of a local TV station, and on the day the reporter was scheduled to arrive, he came to work in a full flight suit, marching around the office as if this were the way he always dressed. After the news crew left, he suggested in an "I'm kidding but not really" kind of way that from now on, we should salute him whenever the press was around.

Later, we found out that he'd had flight suits made for us as well, each bearing a custom shoulder patch with our company's new slogan, "The action is simulated, the excitement is real!" At first, I thought it was only a costume, but Bill proved its legitimacy by taking me to Martin State Airport for a personal flying experience. It was a clever way to write off his hobby as a business expense, along with the suits themselves, but his motives were not entirely self-serving. Now that *Wingman* was out the door, Bill's next big plan was to go head-to-head against Microsoft's wildly popular *Flight Simulator*, and he wanted me to have the most accurate inspiration possible.

Even with a pilot's license, Bill had to pass an initial skills test before they would let us rent one of their small two-seater Cessnas. I waited in the control tower, which at the municipal level was just a building facing the runway, while a pilot on staff took Bill up in the air to do a series of "touch and goes." They would take off, circle around gently, land again, and then accelerate directly into another takeoff. After several demonstrations of these two most important parts of flying, the staff member would turn over his seat to me, and Bill and I could go wherever we wanted.

I'm not sure if flying a Cessna is dramatically different from a fighter jet, or if Bill was just showing off and pushing the plane to its limits, but something in the way he was flying caused the employee next to me to mutter cheerfully, "Oh, that guy has no idea what he's doing."

I hadn't been nervous before, but I was definitely reconsidering now. *In ten minutes I'm going to be on that plane*, I reminded myself. If I ran, did I stand a chance? Probably not. Bill would find a way to get me back here.

Obviously, I survived. It wasn't even particularly terrifying, though I declined to take over the controls once we were safely in the air. Bill had taught many young pilots at the National Guard base in Pennsylvania, and a standard part of their training involved recovering from problems he had deliberately caused, such as aiming the plane toward the ground or stalling one engine. So on an intellectual level, I knew that I couldn't do anything too catastrophic for him to save us from. I guess I chickened out. I do wish I had put my hands on the controls at least once, just so I could say I'd done it.

Though Cessnas were an acceptable substitute, what Bill really wanted was a game featuring the F-15 fighter jet. The main reason we stuck to old-fashioned aircraft was they had old-fashioned technology. If the plane had simple instrumentation and topped out at 117 miles per hour, then we didn't have to worry about how fast we could draw the landscape, or how much flight data we could store. Never mind the compression algorithms; there simply wasn't enough physical space in the lower half of the screen to draw an F-15's panel full of gauges, at least not at current reso-

lutions. Promises of better graphics and higher processing speeds may have been just over the accurately tilting horizon, but for now, Bill's dream would have to wait.

Our official debut in the flying sim genre—as opposed to the arcade genre, which offered unrealistic maneuverability and unlimited fuel—was going to be called *Solo Flight*. I introduced the idea of a movable camera that could cover the plane from different perspectives, so the player could switch back and forth between views within the cockpit and behind the plane mid-flight. We also came up with the subtle but effective detail of showing your plane's shadow on the ground to help you estimate altitude, the first flight sim to do this as far as I know. Finally, I turned my focus to three-dimensional graphics, a beast I would continue to slay in small increments for years to come.

3D gets taken for granted now, but there is a ton of trigonometry involved, and I can't express enough how relatively powerless these computers were. If you have children, you probably have a pile of toys in your house with more processing speed than what we were working with. In any case, I manipulated something called a *linedraw* algorithm to make the mountains and runways project outward in a more 3D fashion than ever before, and you'll have to trust me when I say that it was really cool, and your mind would have been blown if you had been there at the time.

But all of these code improvements were outshined by one critical design choice: we didn't eliminate the concept of play. Even though "games" like the *Ace* titles and "simulators" like this one were considered isolated markets, we saw no reason why the plane nerds shouldn't have fun like the gaming nerds did. As long as we were careful not to cross the sacred line of realism, Bill and I could be the royal marriage that brought peace between our two nations. So we included a simple mail delivery challenge, suggesting deadlines and destinations that our pilots could attempt if they wanted to, no pressure.

The feature was a hit, and successfully distinguished us from Microsoft's *Flight Simulator*—even stealing the crown, in many reviewers' opinions. The circulation of these reviews was small, though, and there was no middle ground in the retail market. At the bottom were the mom-and-pop stores, and directly above them were national outlets like Sears, which in those days was even more profitable than Walmart. Upward mobility came all at once, or not at all.

The secret, Bill told me, was that the national chains didn't decide for themselves what products to carry. Instead, they leased out their shelf space to professional distributors, who would sign their own contracts with individual game companies, like recording agents looking for the next big act. A distributor stumbling upon our game at a local shop was about as likely as a major record producer scouting out karaoke night at the dive bar. To get the attention we needed, Bill said, we had to get ourselves to CES in Chicago.

In 1984, the Consumer Electronics Show was about half the size it is today, meaning it hosted a mere 90,000 attendees split between three massive floors of one of the largest convention halls in downtown Chicago. The plan was for us to go together, so that I could demonstrate the game and answer technical questions, while Bill would be free to grab everyone who walked by and convince them what a financial boon we could provide for their company. We also brought along George Geary, an all-around useful guy at the office who could hold down the fort if Bill and I were stretched too thin.

Room reservations at the McCormick conference center were beyond our budget, so we settled on a place a few blocks away. It had been over $11,000 just to secure a basic 10' × 10' booth, which was still a bargain considering that today's vendors spend closer to $150,000. I didn't know at the time how much it was costing us, but I would have gone along with it regardless. I always left the money decisions up to Bill, and he was sure that if we could just get *Solo Flight* in front of the right people, we would be picked up by a distributor before the end of the conference.

Even in its half-constructed state, the vendors' hall was exhilarating. I had never imagined the gaming industry could take up this much square footage, or be this diverse. Each booth represented a unique building block of our trade, and the surrounding disarray of cardboard boxes and black fabric did nothing to hide their potential. Here one person was selling a new and improved joystick, while across the aisle another had designed a hard drive that was faster than the others. Neither had to meddle with or even understand each other's specialties in order to collaborate. They just had to agree that games were worth it. I only hoped our own offering could live up to the rest.

Our booth itself, sadly, did not, and CES was an instructive experience in that regard. It wasn't until we saw the other companies unpacking that it dawned on us how little we'd brought. Where they had electric flashing signs, we had one vinyl banner. Lucasfilm and Electronic Arts had rows of demo stations, while we had a single Atari hooked up to a monitor swiped from someone's desk, probably my own.

Bill became oddly anxious to get what equipment we did have up and running. Better to act like this was our plan all along than to appear both unprepared *and* slow, I guess. But the tables we'd reserved were not in our booth when we arrived, and no one could promise when they would be delivered. Muttering about the evils of unionized operations, Bill strode off to take care of the problem, and returned a short while later with our three tables—or someone's three tables, at any rate. They were mismatched in both color and size, and did not exactly enhance the professionalism of our booth. But I knew better than to ask where he'd found them. "Do we, or do we not, have tables?" he would have replied. So we set them up.

A little while later, some workers came by with our nice, matching tables, but when they saw that we already had some, they shrugged and left again. Bill watched them go with triumphantly crossed arms. He was in his element, he had the energy of five people, and he was going to rule this corner of the convention hall like no warrior salesman ever had before.

And he did. By the end of the conference, we had multiple offers on our game.

Most were standard distributorship deals, and Bill was prepared to spend months aggressively negotiating those terms, should we decide to go in that direction. But one unusual offer had come from HesWare, a competing software developer that had taken the kind of venture capital money we had steadfastly turned down. It wasn't necessarily a bad thing to be a company with more money than games—a similar description could apply to the distributors we were hoping to partner up with at this convention, after all—but partnership was not the same as ownership, and Bill and I had always been clear about staying on our side of the equation. Rather than a stake in the company or ongoing royalties, however,

HesWare wanted to pay us a flat $250,000 to buy the game in its entirety and sell it as their own. The decision was big enough that Bill thought I should at least weigh in.

On the one hand, long-term sales of *Solo Flight* might surpass HesWare's offer, especially now that we had distributor deals on the table. On the other, we were still running on a very tight budget, with me not even able to work full-time yet. A large injection of cash would help us significantly, and keep us afloat if the game turned out to be a bust.

I gave Bill the only advice I had to offer: if you believe you have something special, then you should treat it that way. "I heard you shouldn't sell the family jewels," I said.

It turned out to be the right decision. Unbeknownst to us, Hes-Ware was going through significant financial problems, and they declared bankruptcy just a few months later. If we'd sold our game to them, we would have lost the rights and likely never been paid.

Instead, *Solo Flight* brought in steady sales from the moment it hit store shelves, and with our new status as a distributable company, we were able to update a few old games for national release as well. First, I honed my AI skills with a new version of *Floyd of the Jungle* that allowed the computer to play any character not in use by a real person. Taken to its logical conclusion, we now had a demo mode that could tantalize customers just like the arcades did. While I was at it, I tweaked the enemy AI in *Chopper Rescue*, and converted all of the code for both games into SidTran, a more efficient programming language that I had created myself. SidTran's main advantage over other languages was the same one provided by Dr. Sherman's teletype over the punch card system: instant gratification. You could see the results of your code changes faster, and make twice as many corrections in half the time.

Our distributor did require one major revision to *Chopper Rescue*, which was the title itself. There was another game with a somewhat similar premise called *Choplifter*, and we were now at a level where that sort of thing mattered, so the national re-release was named *Air Rescue I* instead. (Though I guess the distributor didn't worry about being liable for our company name, because no one ever brought that up until the day the injunction arrived.)

A few months after signing the *Solo Flight* deal, Bill said the words I'd been waiting to hear ever since the ad consultant had walked into our users' group four years earlier.

"Sid, we're making enough money. You can quit your day job."

I wasn't the only one he said it to, either. Almost overnight, we became a real office, with conversations at the water cooler and conference tables that had never been in anyone's kitchen. We were still more like a family than a corporation—most of our employees were old friends, Bill's wife had been doing our administrative work from the very beginning, and it wouldn't be long before I proposed to a young woman named Gigi, whom I'd predictably met at the office since that was where I spent all of my time. But what had started out as a labor of love now finally qualified as a legitimate labor that we all happened to love.

The expansion was a financially aggressive move with the potential to backfire, but to his great credit, Bill never lost sight of the fact that quality content was the driving force behind it all. Selling multiple games at once could not continue unless we also had the same number in development, so his next order of business was to advertise that we were hiring.

In order to lure the smartest and most creative talent in the industry, Bill told me, he wanted to promote the message that we treated our designers with the admiration and respect they deserved. He had already made himself an icon to the players and the press, marching around in uniform and loosely implying that the US Air Force had mobilized a game-testing division on our behalf, but that kind of grandstanding wouldn't appeal to the programmer types. They would only accept a folk hero, he said, one of their own. Therefore, he had decided that the two stars of his new ad campaign were going to be me and a giant pile of money.

I'm not sure if the photo ever made it into a magazine, but I

thought the concept was so bizarrely funny that I kept a copy for myself. In it, I am sitting at my desk with *Solo Flight* proudly displayed on the screen. Beside me are two drawstring bags straight out of a comic book—dollar signs painted on the side, and a bouquet of cash bursting from the top—while I hold a spread of bills in front of a well-coached expression of pleasant surprise. But Bill had decided that even this was too subtle, and just before the photo was taken, he had climbed onto my desk to hang glittering golden dollar signs from the ceiling. He never told me what kind of caption he had in mind, but I'm confident it didn't include the phrase "only recently quit his day job."

Even if we had been rolling in cash, flaunting it was not my style, to say the least. Bill himself is fond of telling an anecdote about how I once forgot to deposit a paycheck until Accounting called to investigate. I'm sure it was the result of a busy schedule rather than carelessness, but it's true that my checks were never earmarked for immediate spending on whatever the 1980s version of "bling" was. I'm usually a saver, and always a planner. But I was happy to go along with whatever Bill thought would help the company, up to and including outlandish photo ops. All that mattered to me was that I got to make games for a living.

The steady march of technology was bringing other industries to prominence in those days as well. In 1975, a French company named Sextant Avionique had developed the first "heads-up display," or HUD, for the Dassault Mercure aircraft. The idea was to project information onto a clear screen directly in the pilot's view, instead of forcing his eyes down to the instruments and back up again to the horizon. It was a big success, and aircraft manufacturers had quickly adapted the idea for both military and commercial applications, while science fiction writers fantasized about displays inside our own eyeballs (cue Arnold Schwarzenegger in *The Terminator*).

Then, in February 1984, the US Air Force announced their new fleet of F-15E fighter jets, which included a larger and more detailed HUD than ever before. The pilot's field of vision was to be filled from one edge to the other with glowing text, aiming guides, and highlights of the terrain for precision maneuvers. The runway was no longer a runway, but two digital lines. The enemy was overlaid with luminous crosshairs.

For the first time, flying a plane had become more like playing a videogame, instead of the other way around. I couldn't cram any more instrument data into the bottom half of the computer screen, so the military had helpfully moved it up into the top half for me. The mountain had come to Mohammed.

Now it was my turn to deliver the news that Bill had been waiting for years to hear: I was ready to make an F-15 flight simulator. He grinned like a kid on Christmas morning.

4

D-DAY

NATO Commander (1983) *
F-15 Strike Eagle (1984) * Silent
Service (1985) * Crusade in
Europe (1985) * Decision
in the Desert (1985) *
Conflict in Vietnam (1986)

ONE OF THE THINGS MICRO-
Prose was famous for was our game manuals, which over time
became as long and informative as textbooks. In the beginning,
though, they weren't especially tangential. Sometimes we had to
explain to novice computer owners—everyone, basically—that
the computer was working as intended, such as *Spitfire Ace*'s reassurance that the game would finish loading "in about 4 minutes."
Other times we were establishing gameplay conventions that are
taken for granted today, like "The screen will flash red when you
are hit" from *Hellcat Ace*, or *Chopper Rescue*'s promise that
"More points are awarded in the more difficult levels."

Mostly, though, we just wanted to be helpful, because nobody
likes a game they can't win at least some of the time. *Formula 1
Racing* advised players to "be careful taking the corners in fifth
gear: fourth is recommended," while *Hellcat Ace* encouraged you
to "Line up your next shot immediately, don't wait!" The manual

for *Spitfire Ace* even let you know that "The sky and ground are light blue and green respectively." Maybe we went a little overboard with that one.

The flying games, in particular, had pages full of information on special aerobatic maneuvers, partly because Bill had the knowledge and loved sharing it, but also perhaps because he was afraid the neat tricks we'd put in might go unnoticed if we didn't point them out. As each game added more details, each manual got longer. By the time we released *Solo Flight,* we were including narratives about the experience of flying that were well beyond what the game could simulate.

"Losing your attitude indicator in instrument conditions can be one of the most frightening occurrences in real flying. Combine this emergency with engine failure and smoke in the cockpit, and the pilot would be happy to use his silk elevator (parachute) to get his body back on the ground in one piece!"

What had taken sixteen pages with *Solo Flight* now stretched into thirty-six with *F-15 Strike Eagle.* We taught players that a speed of Mach 0.9 was actually a variable threshold, equivalent to "661 knots at sea level" but significantly less at higher altitudes. We provided complex graphs outlining the G-force difference between a seventy-, seventy-eight-, and eighty-two-degree turn. We listed the stall speed, service ceiling, and armaments of each completely accurate enemy aircraft, as well as the slant range of their surface-to-air missiles. The manual's centerfold diagram identified all twenty-nine indicators on the cockpit screen, followed by the ten different actions that could be accomplished with the joystick, before launching into a lengthy section on the difference between ailerons and rudders—even though the simulator "automatically interconnects these control surface movements to apply the correct amount of up elevator." We thought of everything.

Well, almost everything. Nowhere in the thirty-six-page manual did we mention how to land the plane.

This was critical information; it was impossible to land the plane on your own. We had never found the right balance between accuracy and playability. Landing the aircraft is the most difficult part in reality, but killing the player at the last moment of an otherwise successful mission was not a way to earn fans. So the compromise we came up with was to have the computer take over and automatically land the plane whenever you approached your home base from a reasonable distance and altitude. Unfortunately, we took it for granted that people who didn't make airplane games for a living would know what counted as reasonable in that situation. Oh, well. It still sold pretty well.

Omission of vital game mechanics aside, the manual for *F-15 Strike Eagle* was special in another way: it was our first game to attempt manual-based copy protection. Digital rights management, as it's known today, remains the eternal battle between creator and user. We come up with a way to protect a game; someone figures out how to break in. Rinse and repeat. Of course, Bill was adamantly against any practice that took money out of our pockets, but given the amount of software pirating I may have done in my younger days, I didn't have a peg leg to stand on when it came to casual sharing. There is something, however slight, to the argument that pirated games are a form of advertising to people who wouldn't otherwise have bought them. I purchased games on several occasions in the early days after being exposed to free versions, and I wouldn't have learned nearly as much or as fast about programming if I hadn't had real, unencrypted data to play around with. (Back in those days, the player's computer did the compiling on the fly as the game loaded, so the data on the disk was not only visible, but completely editable given the right tools.)

That being said, there are plenty of habitual pirates whose motives go beyond curiosity. I can't condone profiteers, and no one's a fan of the actively hostile users who hide malware inside

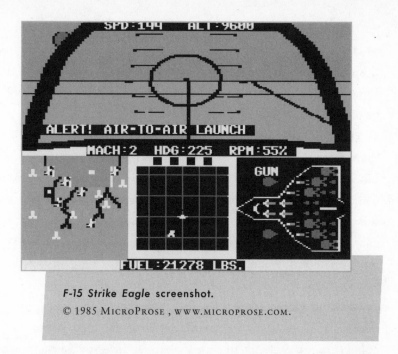

F-15 Strike Eagle screenshot.
© 1985 MicroProse , www.microprose.com.

the tempting download they've provided. Fortunately, we didn't
have to worry about the latter back then, since the first computer
virus wouldn't appear in the wild for another year or so after *F-15
Strike Eagle* was released. Ironically, that virus was originally
intended to be an aggressive form of copy protection itself: when
the program detected what it thought was a pirated version of
the authors' software, it would begin erasing critical parts of the
user's hard drive in retaliation. Occasionally, it targeted the innocent. Nicknamed "Brain," this well-intentioned but poorly executed virus included the full names and contact information of its
creators, because they saw no need to hide from the pirates they
thought they were targeting.

But even if we were too virtuous to conceive of malware in 1984,
unauthorized sharing was rampant. The science fiction novelist
Orson Scott Card once wrote that a particular MicroProse game
was so good that "even people who drive 55 mph might consider
stealing it." Sometimes, a game of middling popularity would end

up with more legitimate sales than a big hit, because it was harder to connect with someone else who owned it. Widely celebrated titles were easy to find on local bulletin boards, and according to some estimates, up to 80 percent of the copies being played might be pirated.

Videogames were considered artistic works under copyright law, thanks to the 1982 court case *Stern Electronics Inc. v. Kaufman*, but in reality there was no enforcement. Entire businesses were dedicated to breaking software protections, and they conducted themselves openly without fear of reprisal. Softkey Publishing, for example, was so successful that they could afford to circulate two separate monthly magazines full of code-breaking instructions just for software on the Apple II computer.

Working against us was the fact that data storage was limited, making the programs so small that a determined pirate could comb through each line of code by hand. The term "open-source" only had to be created after companies figured out how to make things closed-sourced, and genuine encryption belonged only to the military. There were a few data layout tricks we could use, like storing the information in a skewed spiral on the disk instead of in straight lines, but these were never too hard to figure out, and they sometimes made legitimate copies of the games unreadable.

Working in our favor, however, was the equally limited pace of data transfer. The fastest modem on the market in those days cost about $600 (over twice as much in today's dollars), and could transfer data at the blindingly slow speed of 1,200 bits per second. This meant that a typical 48K game (that is, roughly one-third the size of the Wikipedia page explaining what a kilobyte is) would take five or six minutes to download—not too bad for the potential game thief. But a single digital image, made from a real drawing and not ragged pixel art, could easily be as large as the game itself, making our manual full of pictures effectively impossible to send over a phone line.

The manual was a minor loss if it contained only instructions on how to play—games were expected to be intuitive, and many players just figured it out as they went along. But if the manual contained crucial information that the player couldn't progress without, then its absence would break the game without altering one bit of data. It's hard to pinpoint exactly whose idea it was, but there are several examples of "manual lookup" copy protection in games from 1984, and none from 1983, so clearly it caught on fast.

Many of the early examples were just tedious, along the lines of "what is the 12th word on the 17th page of the manual?" The better ones tied the information into the game somehow, presenting it as the words to a magic spell, or the answer to a riddle put forth by a tricksy enemy. For the decidedly non-fantasy setting of *F-15 Strike Eagle*, we went with top secret weapons authentication codes. Though we scattered them throughout the manual to avoid easy photocopying, our attempt was still too simplistic. There were only fifteen codes you might be asked to choose from, each consisting of a single letter. It was too many options for a player to guess randomly, but not too much information to copy by hand and include as a small text file along with the pirated data.

By our next game, we got smarter. Instead of providing codes, the manual for *Silent Service* required the player to visually match silhouettes of imaginary destroyers. The squared-off, black and white shapes were simple enough to store in the game's memory, but nonetheless too complex to describe verbally or convert into text.

Even after home scanners entered the market in the late 1980s, and data speeds increased to the point that images could be easily shared, the hassle of it all was enough to deter most casual copiers. I think people in general are honest, as long as the dishonest choice isn't ridiculously easy. When it comes to elite hackers, the biggest roadblock in the world isn't going to stop them anyway, so

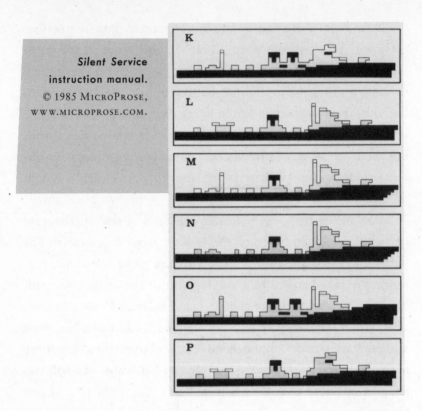

Silent Service instruction manual. © 1985 MicroProse, www.microprose.com.

we don't sweat them too much. It's not great that it's happening, but every copy protection scheme has been broken eventually, and somehow, game creators have survived.

Though the destroyer silhouettes took up only a few more inches than the weapons codes, the manual for *Silent Service* expanded again, proving that there was more to our compulsive writing than just the obstruction of thieves. The discussion mostly covered the tactics of real submarine missions—this was my first game based on stealth, rather than speed and firepower, and the fact that aiming torpedoes involved lots of trigonometry made it even better. Bill, however, subscribed to the old military joke that the acronym for anti-submarine warfare stood for "awfully slow warfare," and he was not satisfied even after we added options for speeding up the game clock and automatic aiming. Bill preferred to do battle at Mach 0.9, and the careful strategizing needed to win in *Silent Service* bored him immensely.

"Can't you just get on the surface and shoot it out with guns?" he complained.

"That's not really the point of this game," I'd remind him, again and again. But he wouldn't let up, and finally, I added a deck gun to the main submarine model just to appease him.

Not long after that, Bill was demonstrating the game to a major buyer, and it looked as if the AI would get the better of him, which is a bad thing when you're trying to sell your game. Retail executives are not interested in how clever or intricate your programming is. Most of them never play games at all, relying instead on their ability to read others' emotional states. If you're defeated during a demo, the whole room feels the letdown with you, and it's almost impossible to erase that first impression of disappointment. Of course the game shouldn't always be easy, but the time for losing comes later, after the rewards have been firmly established. In those first crucial minutes, the player absolutely must win, whether it's a kid alone on his computer or a gaggle of salespeople around a conference table.

Bill, ever the showman and still not a fan of slow tension, had chosen to take on multiple enemy ships at once, and all of them were lumbering toward him in what passed for a terrifying charge at submarine speeds. He fought and dodged as best he could, but eventually the last one had him blown to the surface and out of torpedoes. With seconds remaining before his doom, he switched to the deck gun and obliterated his enemy in a spray of gray and white seawater squares. The whole room cheered, according to Bill, and possibly put him up on their shoulders for an impromptu parade. More importantly, they bought the game.

From that moment on, Bill was a designer, and any time he felt one of our games was lacking in excitement or cheap thrills, he would yell "deck gun!" to argue his point. It became a running joke that lasted for years.

Artillery wasn't the only area where Bill stepped in to improve *Silent Service* against my instincts. He also decided that it was time for MicroProse to hire an artist.

I was, to be honest, a little offended. Sure, I was no Van Gogh, but I had been doing our game art for years and felt like I was pretty good—more than sufficient for sixteen-color graphics on a sprite grid, at any rate. Heck, I was so good, I didn't even have to plot my pictures out on graph paper like some designers did. I just visualized what I wanted, and entered it straight into the computer! I was especially proud of the graphical menu I had designed for *Silent Service*, where instead of choosing from a list of things the captain could interact with—radar, periscope, damage reports, and so on—I had drawn a full-screen interior of a submarine conning tower, and a little human-esque captain that you could move back and forth between the different areas of the room. I was *good*, darn it.

Then I saw the conning tower screen created by our new artist, Michael Haire. His 3D perspective was truer, his color contrast was livelier, and his captain looked human, without any need for an *-esque*. It was better in basically every possible way a work of art could be better.

Oh, I thought to myself. *I guess we did need a real artist.*

Painful revelations about my own skill aside, I couldn't help but be happy with the improvement to the game, and I consoled myself with the thought that this would leave me more time to spend on other aspects of programming. At some point, I had gotten it into my head that what *Silent Service* needed was a realistic map of the entire Pacific Ocean, including all the tiny islands no one knew the names of, and accurate water depths throughout. Now that art had been taken from me, I was even more determined to make the map special, and soon I worked out a programming trick based on fractals that allowed nearly infinite zoom, from a global view down to a rectangle of ocean just eight miles across. It wasn't exactly "open world" by the modern standards of *Minecraft* or the *Fallout* series,

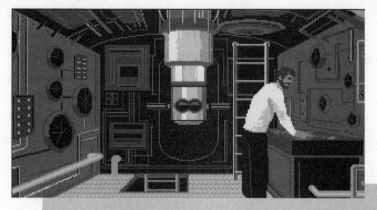

Silent Service screenshot.
© 1985 MicroProse, www.microprose.com.

because there was still only one thing you could go around doing, but it offered as much freedom as you could realistically get in a submarine game without attaching wheels and rolling it up onto dry land.

Meanwhile, *F-15 Strike Eagle* was defying all expectations, selling hundreds of thousands of copies and winning "Action Game of the Year" in a readers' poll from *Computer Gaming World*. This only made Bill's hunger for aircraft games more intense, but I was ready to move on. It wasn't burnout as much as I was just out of ideas. *F-15* had included every type of missile and bomb in the American arsenal, and our mechanics were as close to the real thing as we could get without security clearance. The radar was top notch, and so was the chaff you could deploy to confuse the radar. Every item on the screen was rendered in 3D, from the landscape to the projectiles to the enemy aircraft. I saw nothing left to improve.

Fortunately, other folks at the company were keeping a steady pace for now, with solid genre entries like *Kennedy* Approach*

* **Achievement Unlocked:** We Didn't Start the Fire—Collect Billy Joel, the Ayatollah, and Kennedy.

and *Acrojet*. They afforded me a certain freedom to explore, without making Bill worry too much that we were breaking the formula for success.

"Sid'll figure it out," he always said. Whether he meant I'd find new inspiration, or come to my senses, I wasn't sure.

His reluctance to diversify was not completely unwarranted. Before *Solo Flight*, I had made a brief foray into new territory with a game called *NATO Commander*, and it was, to put it politely, not my best work. Or, as I described it to one journalist many years later, "It was not even fun to play. It was just bad."

The idea had been to create a wargame on the computer that would eliminate all the drawbacks of the traditional tabletop versions. Wargames had developed out of the strategic planning done by actual generals, pushing around miniature platoons on a giant map of the battlefront. Training scenarios were developed for the officers who would eventually be playing with real lives, and later these fictional setups evolved into games made available to the public. Often, wargames are historically accurate reproductions of specific battles—giving you the option to play out Custer's last stand differently, for example—and they never stray beyond the military technology contemporary to their setting. Other key features include dozens of easy-to-lose miniatures instead of a single player piece, a map that takes up the entire table and requires hours to set up, and a complicated rulebook that you and your friends can argue over for at least as much time as you spend playing the game.

It was deficits like these that convinced me a computer could do it better. Along with instant setup of the board and a rulebook that never lost track of the exceptions, computers had the important ability to hide information from the player. Modern satellites may have nearly eliminated the fog of war, but for most of history, military commanders were blindly guessing about rival troop movements. Many battles took place only because of accidental encounters, and sometimes not even with the enemy. During World

War I, for example, the British submarine HMS *G9* stumbled upon the British destroyer HMS *Pasley*, and the two exchanged fire until the *G9* split in half and sank, leaving only one survivor to inform the *Pasley*'s captain of their mistake.

But when your opponent's pieces are right in front of you on the table, it's easy to guess where they are. Board game designers often tried to solve the problem with a complex system of fake pieces known as dummy counters, but these were awkward at best. By comparison, it was actually less work for a computer programmer to leave items unrendered on the screen. We didn't have to hide anything; we just chose not to draw it in the first place. Cardboard had served its purpose admirably when it was all we had, I thought, but transistors were obviously superior.

The problem was that *Nato Commander* was boring. For one thing, the limited scope of the map stole a surprising amount of momentum. There was some indefinable quality about seeing the world spread out before you, ripe for the conquering, but scrolling slowly back and forth across multiple screens sucked the energy right out of that experience. It turned out the game did need to take up an entire table, after all. This may have been the reason I became fixated on a zoom-able map for *Silent Service,* I can't remember. Frankly, though, the map wasn't the biggest issue.

When I played games like Risk as a child, my friends and I would crowd around the board, sharing our triumphs and good-natured taunts together. Invade our country, and we would take it personally; help stop the invader, and we would remember the favor. When one of us came too close to winning, the rest would team up to bring him down, and no computer would ever threaten to thumb wrestle me over who got to play Australia. Each player brought their own personality to the interaction, and even their own mood on a given day, and my algorithms simply could not replicate the camaraderie of friends around a table, egging each other on and learning from each other's strategies. My coworkers and I still regularly played board games together in the company break room, in fact—proof that even people who made computer games for a living understood the value of the in-person gaming experience. I'm admittedly biased, but I'd love to see someone crunch the numbers on productivity and job satisfaction in companies that choose gaming over other forms of team building.

Perhaps Turing had been right after all, with his belief that good AI had to involve social skills. Up to this point, I hadn't realized that community was such an important part of the fun when it came to wargames—nor, unfortunately, did I realize it now. Instead, after wrapping up *Silent Service*, I went back to the wargame genre, and persisted in banging my head against it for the next three projects in a row.

Crusade in Europe, Decision in the Desert, and *Conflict in Vietnam* were, like the original *Ace* series, closer to what would one day be called a game plus two expansion packs. All three were based on an engine I developed for *Crusade in Europe*, which was itself a reworking of the original *NATO Commander* code. With each successive release, we tried to add more historical depth, which is where I mistakenly thought we were going wrong. It didn't fix the gameplay issues, but it did lead to some moving narratives, at least.

To help us, we hired a historian and former Princeton professor named Ed Bever, who happened to write strategy game reviews for *Antic* magazine in his spare time. In addition to his deep understanding of military scenarios both past and present, he had once written that *NATO Commander* was "exciting and exacting," so obviously we thought he had good taste in games as well.

Among other talents, Ed was masterful at navigating the dichotomy between fun and solemnity. Real battles could be sensitive subjects, and it wouldn't be appropriate to put in quite the same level of destructive joy that we could get away with in other titles. This was especially true for *Conflict in Vietnam*, and the problem reared its head in a surprising number of places.

"One issue which aroused strong feelings was what to call losses on the status display screen," Ed wrote in the designers' notes.

"We reverted to total casualties for two reasons. One was to avoid offending those who lost relatives in Vietnam and therefore might find it offensive to count bodies, even in simulation. Second, the body count creates a misleading impression of the casualty ratios, because many Americans survived wounds that would have killed Vietnamese."

This was the first time we'd ever put disclaimers alongside the historical information in our manual, and it never quite sat right with me. Not because I thought we should have been less delicate, but because I realized that I would rather create things that didn't require disclaimers in the first place. All three of the *Command Series*, as the wargame trilogy came to be known, provided a solid simulation experience and profound historical lessons—but I don't think they necessarily counted as games.

The most elementary, defining feature of gaming is its interactivity. Players may not be rewarded for every choice, but the control over the outcome must be primarily in their hands, otherwise they're just watching a movie that demands occasional button jabs. In this case, there were not only too many historically predetermined parameters, but I had also introduced too much AI into the units. My hope had been to eliminate pesky micromanaging, but instead players had ended up with very little to do. They could even choose to do nothing at all, instead watching the game play out entire simulations against itself. Many reviewers were impressed with this—or at least they thought they were. But in reality, it wasn't fun to watch more than a couple of times. Like a computer endlessly calculating pi, it was conceptually neat, but not really all that interesting long-term.

These problems were only compounded by the fact that the conflicts were too recent to make any ending feel particularly happy. Even a swift, decisive victory still left the player asking, "But at what cost?" I've always felt that our role as game designers is to suspend reality, not examine the pain of real moral dilemmas. There's a place for that in art, certainly—and videogames do count as art—but it's generally not a place where people want to spend their time after a long day at the office. Even setting aside the added intensity of first-person engagement vs. passive observation, games are expected to sustain their audience far longer than any other art form. A trip to a museum or a tragic film might demand up to three hours of uncomfortable soul-searching, but game designers are asking you to commit somewhere between twenty and a billion hours with us. Not many people are willing to wallow in life's toughest moments for that long, and at the very least, I didn't want to wallow in them myself for an entire year of development. It had taken longer than usual for me to learn this lesson, but finally, I broke free of the wargame obsession, and returned to the skies.

5

COLLECTIVE
EFFORT

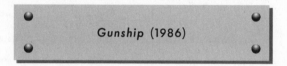

Gunship (1986)

AS I WAS SEARCHING FOR WHAT
to work on next, several years' worth of drama was coming to a
head in the computer hardware world, where Atari and Commodore had entered a war that was at least as much personal as it was
business. The dispute was complicated, involving hostile takeovers,
ex-employees of both companies defecting into new ventures, and
financial contracts being physically lost and then discovered again.
The end result was that each company was claiming ownership of
a technology that neither one had developed, and both had filed
multiple suits against the other in court. At the center of it all
was the latest holy grail of processor technology: the 68K chipset,
code-named Lorraine.

For the record, I always felt like code-naming projects was self-
aggrandizing, and we never did it at MicroProse. My games were
always just "the submarine game" or "the D-Day game" until we
came up with a real title just before launch. But to be fair, our
products already came with a sense of anticipation built in—the
word "game" alone implied something exciting was in store. If
you're designing hardware, I suppose "the faster gray box" doesn't
work that well as a code name. These days, our publisher does

make us use code names, as project teams have expanded and corporate espionage has become a real issue for the industry. Emails are all too easy to leak, and I understand the need for secrecy. But it does sometimes lead to a "Who's on first?" kind of conversation when someone isn't sure which off-the-wall code name goes with which project. Personally, if I don't want to tell people what I'm working on, I just don't tell people what I'm working on.

In any case, the ownership of Lorraine would take years for Atari and Commodore to finally settle, but in the short term, neither one could stop the other from using it in their next generation of hardware. I didn't care one way or the other about the corporate politics. A technology arms race was a great thing from our perspective, and having the 68K processor in both the Atari ST and the Commodore Amiga just meant we could deliver superior games to twice as many people.

Without a specific topic in mind, I went to work on a new 3D engine for the Amiga, which would end up being my only project on that machine before it bit the dust. The Amiga wasn't a bad computer by any means, but it failed to live up to its promise in sales numbers, and to a small business like ours, that mattered. We'd spend up to a year fine-tuning a game on whatever computer we started with—tweaking the visual layout for a particular screen resolution, optimizing sound effects with a certain audio chip in mind, and so on. Then when it was done, we'd spend only a few months shoehorning the code onto the other major systems. Our initial release was always going to be the best version of a game, so it made sense to maximize the experience for the greatest number of customers by developing on whatever was most popular at the time. The Amiga had a dedicated cult following, but it never rose to the top, either in homes or in our offices.

This trend wouldn't become apparent for at least a year, though, because developers were given prototypes of new hardware to work with long before they were sold to the public. So I tinkered away on my new 3D engine, imagining what kind of games we might someday make with it, while down the hall, the rest of the company continued to work on the established platforms.

One of these titles in progress was a helicopter game for the Commodore 64 called *Gunship*, which was created by Andy Hollis and a new designer named Arnold Hendrick. It had a heavy influence from the pen-and-paper role-playing games that Arnold had started his career making, including the somewhat radical concept of permanent death. You could save your progress and continue accruing victories at a later date, but *Gunship* gave no option to reload from a saved game after a failed mission. If you died, you died—although some players pulled off a deus ex machina rescue by quickly ejecting the floppy disk before their data could be overwritten. Other atypical features of the game included naming your character, and choosing your helicopter's weaponry while staying under maximum weight requirements, similar to allocating skill points in a traditional RPG. A level-20 wizard in a Dungeons & Dragons campaign could run from a battle or spend a night sleeping at the inn to replenish his stats, while the *Gunship* helicopter pilot could sit out a mission under the guise of sick leave, or take some needed R&R off-base. These character mechanics had been tested for more than a decade by board gaming veterans, and *Gunship* would be one of the first to successfully bring them into the digital realm.

Notably, players could also choose whether to automate helicopter landings or manage them personally, a process we made sure to explain in the manual this time.

But while the design mechanics were breaking boundaries, the flight mechanics were just breaking. We knew there would be an issue with unfamiliarity, since this was one of the first helicopter simulations ever to go on the market, and we planned to flatten the learning curve with a colorful frame of reminders called a keyboard overlay—a lost relic in today's world of ergonomic peripherals that are barely thicker than cardboard themselves. But our playtesters assured us that the collective, as a helicopter's control stick was known, operated intuitively enough. The main problem, they reported, was speed.

Despite flying slower than their winged cousins, helicopters are also more responsive side-to-side, and for a game programmer, rotating the world is harder than zooming by it horizontally. It would take several seconds for a plane to bank around from one position to the next, but a helicopter could turn sharply and even spin in place, which meant we had to render 360 degrees of landscape in a three-dimensional arc faster than we ever had before.

I offered up my new 3D engine, and the team eagerly took it, even though it would require a complete overhaul of *Gunship*'s underlying program. The Commodore 64 was less powerful than the Amiga that I'd been creating it for, but the new engine was still more efficient than anything else we had. Together, Andy Hollis and I spent months retrofitting the code and attempting to make the old computer perform like a new one.

Everything came down to frame rate, or the number of times per second that the computer could redraw the screen. Change one tiny thing in the foreground, like the pointer on an altitude gauge, and the computer could do it quickly. But change the entire background, and things got a lot choppier.

We set our sights on four frames per second, which wasn't so lofty. Even my original *Star Trek* game on the servers at General Instrument had run that fast, though of course moving text wasn't a fair comparison to a swerving hillside. Other games we'd made at MicroProse had run faster, but four was the bare minimum. Anything less would leave the game unplayable.

So far, we had three.

"I need one more optimization run," Andy would lament late into the evening, begging me to find a calculation that didn't need to be performed, or a piece of information that didn't need to be stored at that exact moment. "I know you can come up with one more idea."

The schedule had already been delayed significantly by swapping out the engine, and if we couldn't get the speed up soon, it would be time to start throwing out parts of the game like loose ballast, until whatever was left could stay in the air.

Fortunately, we managed, and the game went on to sell over 250,000 copies and win "Action Game of the Year" from *Computer Gaming World*. I wish I could sum up how we fixed it, but the math is long, complicated, and (I've been assured) boring. The important thing to note is that it wasn't one lightning-bolt solution, but dozens of incremental changes, many of which we couldn't take credit for. We had to find ways to do our job better, but we also had to take advantage of other people who were doing their jobs better: new technology, new compression algorithms, new ways to implement standard subroutines. Gaming is a collaborative effort, and it's silly to think that any one person can claim all the glory. As my first experience in the CES vendors' hall had proven, our industry was not made from one peerless, monolithic booth, but tens of thousands of small ones—some with mismatched tables, perhaps, but all with something to contribute.

The only place that gave me that warm and fuzzy collaborative feeling more than CES was the Computer Game Developers Conference. I didn't attend the very first CGDC, which was founded by designer Chris Crawford—best known at that point for a game called *Balance of Power* and a book titled *The Art of Computer Game Design*—and consisted of twenty-seven people sitting on the floor in his house. But I did make it to the second gathering six months later, at a Holiday Inn outside San Jose in September 1988. By that time, attendance had quintupled and lunch was catered, though we still ate standing up, doubling our paper plates so they wouldn't spill. Entrance fees were nominal, and organizers had to race to the bank with at-the-door proceeds in order to prevent the check they'd given the hotel from bouncing. I'm pretty sure that was also the year that Chris began delivering keynote speeches in costume. One year he cracked a whip at us to illustrate the power of subconscious creative urges; another year he delivered an impassioned theatrical performance comparing game design to *Don Quixote*, which he ended by grabbing a heavy metal sword and galloping through the audience.

"For truth!" he roared at us. "For beauty! For art! *Charge!*"

Toward the end of my first conference, the organizers surprised Chris with an award for being "Zee Greatest Game Designer in Zee Universe," illustrated by a large plastic light bulb trophy. Other awards were given out, but in general the organizers made a point to give them only to publishers, not individual designers, because they felt competition would fracture the community and create bad blood. MicroProse won an award for our playtesting department. I guess at the time we must have been shipping with fewer bugs than everyone else. Mostly I think we were just ahead of the curve in having a quality assurance team at all—one discussion at the conference centered around whether professional testers were even capable of providing unbiased feedback, with their paychecks coming in the form of dollars instead of fun. Fortunately, the topic quickly evaporated, perhaps after everyone realized that this line of thinking could logically extend to our own compensation, as well.

By the second or third year, I was giving presentations myself, and by the tenth I was on a "Legends of Game Design" panel with industry mainstays like Ron Gilbert, who had been programming for HesWare just before they went under and went on to design the revolutionary new SCUMM engine for LucasArts, which delighted programmers with its improved efficiency but perhaps raised some eyebrows with its thematic acronyms (the accompanying program tools were named SPUTM, SPIT, FLEM, MMUCAS, BYLE, and CYST). But even sitting on a dais in front of hundreds of people, I never felt removed from the other attendees. CGDC was the one place where we were all friends and equals, and everyone had something to talk about even if they weren't given a podium. Design in the 1980s was a largely independent activity, so no one was passing business cards or networking in the modern, rung-climbing sense. No one was protective of their status. We were just excited to have a community, and to be around others who understood our love for gaming in a way that our friends, and sometimes even our families, didn't. It wasn't that gaming was looked down on by the rest of the* world, necessarily, but it was sometimes glanced at sideways in confusion. Later decades would give rise to new flavors of mainstream fear about gamers and their obsessions, but back then the worst accusation an outsider would have leveled at us was that gaming was a frivolous pastime with minimal benefits—not as long as a book, not as pretty as a TV show, not as healthy as a sport. But in that respect, I don't think it was much different than other niche interests. Surely jazz musicians would have an equally hard time explaining just what's so special to them about riffing on a piano for hours on end, while architects would thrill at the chance to finally geek out with someone over the geometric peculiarities of Frank Gehry. There are lots of rare breeds in the world, and CGDC just happened to be the place where my rare breed gathered. I don't think any of us could have imagined back then the kind of cultural domination that gaming would someday achieve. We simply shared ideas, and turned each other on to games we might not have heard of yet, and ate a whole lot of cookies.

But of course the conference did eventually outgrow this youthful phase, as did the industry as a whole. In 1999, they dropped "Computer" from the name in order to include console games, then formally added mobile gaming in 2002. They split entry fees to provide different levels of access, and subdivided major presen-

* *Achievement Unlocked:* **My Country 'Tis of—Read the word "the" 1,000 times.**

·tation tracks like "art" and "design" into increasingly nuanced series like "localization" and "community management." By the early 2000s, they had graduated into venues too large to comfortably walk across, and in 2018, they welcomed a record-breaking 28,000 attendees. But it's never stopped being fun. Games are still the heart of it, and as long as that's the case, I think it can go on beating forever.

Though MicroProse accepted many more awards over the years, there were some distinctions that even CGDC couldn't offer. Shortly after *Gunship* was released, it received the rare but by no means desirable honor of being banned. Once upon a time, I had been flattered by GI's clampdown on ASCII spaceships, but this prohibition covered an entire country, and the accusation was a little more serious than loss of productivity. According to the West German government, *Gunship* was guilty of "promoting militarism," which made it "particularly suited to disorient youths socially and ethically."

Germany has a complicated relationship with its last hundred years of history. In 1986, a sizeable percentage of the population still held the horrors of World War II in living memory. There was—and still is—a profound sense that the cultural conditions leading up to it must never be allowed to happen again, and many corrective measures were imposed both internally and externally during the postwar years. One of the longest-lasting has been a media oversight committee known as the *Bundesprüfstelle für jugendgefährdende Medien*, or BPjM.

The BPjM maintained the "Youth Dangerous Publications List" (a name that has been retranslated at least once over the years, so it is often referred to as simply "the index"), and it had the power to censor any material that was deemed "morally corrupting and coarsening for the young user." This included themes of anti-Semitism and extreme violence, of course, but also less obvious subjects like alcohol abuse and suicide. More to the point, they rejected anything thought to be glorifying military action.

With the exception of this last aversion, it was a pretty standard list, the kinds of things that would earn a game a "Mature" rating in the United States today. In Germany, however, it was not just a question of refusing to sell to minors, as retailers do here. Media on the index could not be sold or advertised anywhere that children could potentially see it at all. If a store in Germany wanted to carry our game, they would now be required to have a separate "adults only" section of their store, including its own entrance out of sight from the main doors. Generally speaking, there was only one type of material sold that way, and it's fair to say those shoppers were not our usual customer base.

Having noticed *Gunship*, the BPjM was inspired to look back at the rest of our catalog, and retroactively blacklisted *Silent Service* and *F-15 Strike Eagle* as well, which had by then been selling for years without incident. It was a significant financial hit, as well as a personal one, since Germany accounted for about $1.5 million in sales for MicroProse, and we had planned to use it as a toehold to expand our distribution across the rest of Europe.

Bill harbored suspicions, in fact, that the complaint raised against us was purely a business move by more established European distributors, since other well-known military games by our competitors had somehow passed muster and remained off the index, such as *Gato*, *Sub Battle Simulator*, and *Up Periscope*. He filed a vigorous appeal and held press conferences to increase public outcry, but our hearings were inexplicably delayed more than once, and years passed before the games were finally removed from the index. By then, they were technologically obsolete, and wouldn't be selling many more copies anyway.

The one consolation in all of it was that the conversation about computer game censorship had been raised to the international level. At the same time that Bill was fighting our battle with the BPjM, Dungeons & Dragons came under fire in America from a number of religious groups, and a Massachusetts woman managed to get a novelization of a *Zork* game banned from her local school library. Meanwhile, a US postal worker refused to deliver copies of *Boy's Life* magazine because they contained an ad for the *Enchanter* trilogy of games. The UK newspaper the *Independent* ran a front-page story on censorship in gaming that mentioned us specifically, and some believe that the high-profile nature of our case played a part in the eventual creation of the US self-regulatory group the Entertainment Software Rating Board.

These days, Germany has softened its stance a little, and considers media harmful to minors only if it "tends to endanger their process of developing a socially responsible and self-reliant personality." World War II content is examined on a case-by-case basis for artistic merit, as well as a clear statement of opposition—players can fight against the Nazis as the Allied Forces, for example, but *Call of Duty: Black Ops* still had to remove the Rolling Stones' song "Sympathy for the Devil" from its German soundtrack because of a passing lyrical reference that placed the singer on the wrong side of a blitzkrieg. And though the ban on militarism in general has been lifted, a relatively conservative definition of violence remains, so publishers often choose to create a modified version of their game for the German market rather than risk being locked out. Killing aliens or robots is considered less inflammatory than killing humans, for instance, and it doesn't take much to change the bad guys' blood from red to green, or switch their skin tones to gray and toss in a few electric sparks.

Personally, I never had any intention of making the kind of game that needed alteration, which is probably why the banning of my three titles stung as much as it did. But it opened my eyes to the fact that not every culture viewed games the same way, and that there was definitely such a thing as an American game. What would a truly international game look like, I wondered, with no cultural bias, and universal appeal? It was an interesting idea to ponder.

Bill had been glad to see me drifting back toward familiar themes with *Gunship*, and felt that now was the time for my triumphant return to the flight simulator genre. It just made sense:

Sid and Wild Bill, the greatest maker and the greatest purveyor of airplane games, fresh off the helicopter and ready to blow everyone's minds once again.

"So, when's your next flight simulator going to be ready?" he asked.

I told him it didn't really interest me. There was something else I wanted to work on.

He frowned. "Another wargame?"

Oh no, I assured him. Definitely not. "I have this idea for a game about pirates."

6

AHOY!

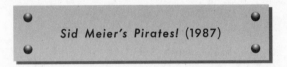

Sid Meier's Pirates! (1987)

THE IDEA FOR A PIRATE GAME
had actually been floated in a meeting a couple of months earlier by Arnold Hendrick, as one of several backdrops that could be used to flavor our steady stream of combat titles. I liked the idea in general, and could easily program ship battles with black flags and cannons instead of deck guns and radar. But that wasn't enough to excite me anymore. The Sid who cofounded MicroProse four years earlier would never have believed it was possible, but I was growing bored.

Mostly I was tired of hyperrealism. If real life were that exciting, who would need videogames in the first place? The flight simulator genre, especially, was forever clamoring for more dials to watch, more flaps to control, more accurate wind speed and wheel friction calculations—and no one seemed to notice that it had turned into work. Games weren't supposed to train you to be a real pilot; they were supposed to let you pretend for an hour that you could be one if you wanted to. It wasn't escapism if you didn't actually get anywhere.

Likewise, it wasn't enough to paint a seventeenth-century veneer over an otherwise straightforward boat simulator. When I thought of pirates, I didn't think of arduous ship maneuvers. I thought of sword fights, and swinging from ropes, and billowy white shirts with little string ties at the neckline for no reason. I thought of evil mustachioed Spaniards kidnapping damsels, and guys with peg legs singing about rum. I thought of swashbuckling, whatever that actually meant.

Pirates didn't spend all day fighting one another, I told Bill. Pirates had adventures.

Unfortunately, the "adventure" moniker had already been co-opted by a certain type of game that was traditionally text-based, and involved approximately zero adventuring. Instead, most of the player's time was spent arguing with the computer. The progression generally went something like this:

You are standing in a log cabin. There is a window to the north and a door to the east.

Look at the room.

I don't understand.

Look at the cabin.

You see a bed and a desk.

Look at the desk.

It is a desk.

Open the desk.

The desk is locked.

Look at the window.

It is a window.

Open the window.

You can't open the window.

Look at the bed.

It is a bed.

Look under the bed.

You see nothing of interest under the bed.

"Nothing of interest" was about right. These so-called adventure games weren't a test of your wits; they were a test to see how long the designer could hide something in plain sight until you thought to ask about it directly. Around the office, we referred to them as "pick up the stick" games, and no one had any desire to make one—but I didn't see why they should be given a monopoly, either. Adventuring didn't have to mean blindly groping for a set path. It could mean making up your own story, being in charge of your fate just like a pirate would be. I wanted a game that only hit the high points, taking you from one exciting scene to the next and leaving out all the walking around, looking at, and picking up.

Bill tried to talk me out of it. "That's crazy," he said. "We've never made anything like that before."

"I know," I said. That was one of the best things about the idea.

"Nobody will buy it."

I shrugged. I thought they would buy it, actually, but that was never my main motivation. I wanted to play a pirate game, which meant I was going to have to make a pirate game, since no one else had yet.

Bill could tell he wasn't going to change my mind. "Well, we should at least put your name on it," he muttered, throwing up one hand in surrender. "Sid Meier's pirate-whatever. Then maybe the people who liked *F-15* will recognize it's you, and buy it anyway."

I should mention that Bill has a much more glamorous version of this story, which starts long before the conversation he and I had. According to him, the idea to put my name on the box came during a dinner event for the Software Publishers Association, which had been formed only a few years earlier. They did the standard things industry groups do, like organize speakers and give awards, but their main purpose was fighting software piracy. It would be years before the SPA managed to convince lawmakers it was a serious issue, but in 1986 they would pay $100 to anyone with hard evidence that a dial-up bulletin board was distributing stolen games. They even successfully prosecuted a few cases. MicroProse was one of about 150 companies who attended their regular meetings, along with Sierra, Microsoft, Broderbund, and Robin Williams.

Yes, strange as it may seem, the comedian Robin Williams was connected to the Software Publishers Association. To my knowledge he never dabbled in game design himself, but he felt strongly that all creative jobs should be fairly compensated, and he had such a particular love for videogames that he named his daughter Zelda. According to lore, he and Bill were seated at the same table at an SPA event, and during the course of conversation, Robin pointed out that all the other entertainment industries promoted their stars by name, so why should gaming be any different?

Whether this was a passing comment or a hard sell on my name in particular, I have no idea, but Bill already had plenty of experience with fostering a cult of personality. It wouldn't have taken much to convince the man who styled himself "Fighter Pilot Supreme" that his original instincts had been right after all—that perhaps the only problem with a photo of me and giant bags of money was that it hadn't gone far *enough*. Either way, I can't blame him for wanting to share credit on this one, since "Robin Williams told me to do it" is a pretty good defense for almost anything. All I know is Bill made the executive decision to call the game *Sid Meier's Pirate-Whatever*, and I was too busy thinking about adventure game mechanics to question it.

The good news was there were very few preconceived notions back then about what a game was supposed to be. The bad news was there were no tried-and-true conventions, either. I could put in anything I wanted, but that also meant I was responsible at every turn for what to leave out, and there were exponentially more ways to fail. It was like trying to create a recipe without any knowledge of what ingredients taste good together. With no standard expectations to guide me, I might accidentally end up with the gaming equivalent of breakfast cereal with onions.

All I could do was keep asking myself, "Would I want to play this game?" As long as the answer was yes, the idea stayed in. I knew, for example, that I wanted to avoid the trap of a single narrative path. If the hypothetical log cabin wasn't interesting, I wanted

to be able to walk away from it, without ever needing to find the key hidden under the rug that no one told me about, or spending ten minutes convincing the computer to do normal key things with it. ("Unlock desk?" "Use key?" "Use key with desk?") At the same time, though, too much freedom would leave the player blind. No one prefers fill-in-the-blank over multiple-choice. This was the real problem, I realized, with adventure games that tried to parse free-form commands: they had only one right answer, which was bad, but they also had an infinite number of wrong answers, which was worse.

Recent psychological studies have demonstrated the truth behind this theory of limiting choices. Our brains' executive function, or decision-making capability, tires out over time. Like an overworked muscle, it doesn't matter if you're lifting weights at the gym or stacking sandbags to save your family's home—the importance of the task has no bearing on your exhaustion. Insignificant decisions take just as much brain power as interesting ones, but without any of the satisfaction. One study found that participants scored lower on math tests after being given a large menu of lunch options, while those with fewer choices scored higher. The question of what to eat for lunch was relatively meaningless, but it took a toll. Another found that when giving free jam samples to people passing by, a purchase was more likely if there were only a few jars available, while the full array of flavors caused patrons to become overwhelmed and walk away sooner—even if they reported later that they preferred the table with more options.

There are different theories as to why people instinctively flock toward more choices even when the numbers show we are happier with fewer choices, but I think it has to do with humans' innate curiosity. We want to try everything, which leads to frustration when we can't. We don't ever want to feel like we've missed out on something good. In fact, there is a whole class of so-called "completionist" players in videogames, who make it a point to collect every single item and score every single point possible. Most players are not that extreme, but even among moderate ones, the maxim holds. The more choices players have, the sooner they will tire of the game, and the more dissatisfied they will ultimately be. They might initially feel like they're happier with more choice, but in the end they will walk away, just like the jam-tasters with too many flavors to choose from. It was my job, I thought, to whittle down the options and present only the best ones to the player.

So then: no wrong answers, and more than one right answer, but not too many. I began to jot down ideas. Pirates wooed beautiful young women, so that would be a choice. Pirates pieced together old treasure maps, so that would be a choice. Pirates sometimes had sword fights, so that would be a choice.

Real pirates didn't do any of these things, of course. Real pirates slaughtered innocent people and got scurvy. Not fun. But this was a game, not a simulation, and the romanticized version of pirates was at least as prominent in culture, if not more. The classic film star Errol Flynn made four movies about brave and handsome swashbucklers, and none about greedy sociopaths.

These pre-existing narratives were, in fact, the key to making *Pirates!* as immersive as it was. Players came to the game with a certain backstory in their mind already—good guys wore white shirts and colorful sashes; bad guys wore long black coats and eye-patches. Give the villain a moustache, and he would take on all the characteristics of every moustache-twirling villain since childhood. A single "Arrgh, matey!" could convey the entire feel of the game, complete with setting, characters, and a likely plot. These bits of cultural shorthand allowed the player to fill in the environment without realizing they were doing it, saving us development time and, more importantly, precious computer memory.

Pirates! was an unusual challenge when it came to memory. Ship navigation and sword fighting were in 2D, to keep their calculations to a minimum, but this still left large portions of the game in text form. There wasn't room to animate anything else. True, we were supposed to be skipping all the walking-around stuff anyway, but it was undeniably sparse. So we decided to try using individual illustrations, like a picture book the players were writing for themselves. Graphics cards had come a long way since the days of blocky crocodiles and lumpy monkeys, and Michael Haire's skills had only improved with each title he'd worked on. Between technology and talent, we could manage some pretty impressive works of art on the computer these days—"some" being the operative word. I wanted lots, and it still seemed impossible to fit them all in. Fortunately, a programmer named Randall Masteller came to the rescue, with a new take on an old idea.

Computer operating systems were always optimized to store and display fonts very efficiently, because without text on the screen nothing else could get done. Fonts were the first thing loaded into memory, and the easiest to clear and replace. Thus, programmers had known for years that if you could present information to the computer in the form of a font, it would run faster.

Usually, this technique was applied to small images. In my original ASCII game, for example, I had used an asterisk to represent an asteroid, because standard text characters were my only option. But a font didn't strictly have to be made up of letters and numbers. If by some anachronistic miracle my Nova minicomputer had shipped with Microsoft's playful Wingdings font instead, that asterisk would have appeared as a small envelope. If I had used an uppercase M, it could have been a classic cartoon bomb, or perhaps a cute little rotary phone in place of a number 8. This would have rendered the rest of the computer's functions illegible, of course, but the idea was that you could create a custom font made up of small images, and it would be faster and easier to display one of those "letters" on the screen than to use the graphics chip inside the computer to draw the same picture.

The next step forward had been using fonts for simple animation, which was the trick I'd used in *Floyd of the Jungle*. Each creature had been one letter of a font, with later letters in the alphabet reserved for the slightly different versions of the same creatures. Perhaps the spot normally held by lowercase c would look like the crocodile with its jaws closed, while uppercase C would look like the crocodile with its jaws open. Tell the computer to rapidly switch between c and C on the screen, and the crocodile would look like it was moving. Add two more crocodile letters into the loop, and it could walk and chomp at the same time. Once the font was loaded into memory, you could put one crocodile on the screen, or a hundred, it didn't matter. As long as your new alphabet stayed under the total number of characters in a font, 256, the computer's processor would be able to rotate between them as easily as scrolling down a page of text.

What Randall's tool did was to analyze a large picture, and figure out the most efficient way to make each little eight-by-eight chunk of pixels into a font character. It was like paint by numbers: if the upper left corner was solid blue sky, then the "number 1" character could be a solid block of blue, and all the other big chunks of blue could be number 1s as well. Once we hit a cloud, number 2 would have to represent some angled bit of half-blue–half-white, but then we'd be off to the races again with a long series of all-white number 3s. The simpler the picture, the larger it could be before we ran out of characters to assign. Then after the player selected a menu item on that page, we could clear the font along with everything else on the screen, and load a new font containing the next screen's picture.

The only catch was that we still needed to display real text. The game could contain hundreds of fonts on the disk—and with a different picture on every screen, it did—but it could only load one font into memory at any given time, so the first seventy slots of every font were filled with an identical set of lowercase letters, uppercase letters, numbers, and a few special characters like commas and question marks. The remaining 186 brackets, ampersands, and so on were replaced with a mashup of colored pixels that made no sense unless they were laid out in precisely the right order, at which point they suddenly resolved into a beautiful seaside town, or a governor's buxom daughter.

It wouldn't have been a MicroProse game without a massive manual, so near the end of development, Arnold Hendrick joined our team to begin work on its eighty-eight pages of sepia-toned text. This was without any added bulk for copy protection, because we had graduated to providing players with a separate foldout map of the Caribbean for even greater difficulty in sharing. Physical novelties like this ran double duty as collector's items, and were commonly known as "feelies," a reference to the tactile entertainment featured in Aldous Huxley's dystopian novel *Brave New World*. The first game to include them was Infocom's 1982 murder mystery *Deadline*, which set the bar for years to come with a crime scene photo, police interviews, a coroner's report, a letter from the family's lawyer, and even three pills (made from candy, in reality) that had been "found" at the crime scene. The collection was originally conceived because the designer, Marc Blank, couldn't fit all of the information inside the game, and only after piracy dropped dramatically for that title did everyone realize the potential.

Along with crafting the manual, Arnold also injected a healthy dose of realism into *Pirates!* to counterbalance the cinematic bravado. He pushed for accuracy in the historical campaign mode, and argued against the use of famous pirates who hadn't been alive during the time frame I'd chosen, like Blackbeard and Jean Lafitte. If anything, though, these underpinnings of realism ended up bolstering the larger theme of romanticized adventure. As Arnold explained in the designer's notes, "those men were psychotic remnants of a great age, criminals who wouldn't give up. . . . There was no political intrigue or golden future to their lives, just a bullet or a short rope. We found them unattractive and uninteresting compared to the famous seahawks and buccaneers that preceded them."

That was one tricky thing about seahawks and buccaneers, though: they never died. Errol Flynn couldn't be killed in battle or sentenced to hanging, because that would shatter everything about the universe he hailed from. And yet, a game where you can't lose is not a game; there has to be some form of failure at risk. To make things worse, I had accidentally eliminated any clear moment of victory to end the game on, either. Military games had a set number of missions, with a satisfying explosion to end each one. But a pirate is always ready to set off on another adventure—it's "a pirate's life for me," not "a pirate's singular objective for me." I'd given the player the freedom to choose which adventures to pursue, and in doing so, I'd abdicated the high ground of declaring which one was the best or hardest to complete. You could win a particular battle or quest for treasure, but there was no way to win the game as a whole, and no way to lose at all.

Fortunately, the two problems came together neatly to solve one another.

With regard to losing, it was really just a question of how much punishment a player would tolerate while continuing to believe in the fantasy we had created. Death was out of the question, as was starting over with nothing. Errol Flynn may lose his treasure, his ship, even his crew for a time, but he doesn't lose his reputation. He can always stagger ashore from the shipwreck and rally the men once more. So that was precisely what we did: when your pirate lost a battle at sea, he was left stranded on an island for a time, until being miraculously rescued by his loyal crew, minus any extra ships and gold.

Still, the stranding took only an instant in the real world, which amounted to practically no punishment at all. Time had no real value in the game—unless time was running out. Suddenly, the end point became clear.

This game was not about life and death, I realized. It was about a lifetime. A pirate's career would last about forty years between childhood and old age, and his goal was to accomplish as much as he could in that window—to have an adventurous life with no regrets. Rack up the gold, rack up the victories, rack up the wild stories to tell at the tavern. As in real life, success could only be measured as a combination of your exploits, and how much value you put on those particular exploits yourself.

I decided we would let the player choose when to retire, and instead of a numeric score, we would display a tally of successes, and an appropriate seafaring rank. We even factored in the character's age when it came to fencing skill and ship maneuverability, by slowing the responsiveness of the controls and increasing the probability of a miss. Players could judge for themselves when the risk was too great, and aim to go out on top—or else stubbornly refuse to quit, risking battle after battle as a hunched old seadog until they had handed over their last doubloon. Just like the rest of the game, the decision to end it was theirs alone.

Ironically, our shunning of realism had led to something more realistic than any game had yet attempted. Life is not a steady progression of objectively increasing value, and when you fail, you don't just reload the mission again. You knock the wet sand off your breeches and return to the high seas for new adventures. And if you happen to get marooned on a deserted island a few times, well, that makes for a good tavern story, too.

7

AND THEN BILL BOUGHT AN AIRPLANE

Red Storm Rising (1988)
*
F-19 Stealth Fighter (1988)

THOUGH *PIRATES!* WOULD EVENT-
ually become one of our most popular titles, the flight sims we
were famous for always saw a big burst of sales up front, while
my "action adventure simulation" was a slow, steady burn. It
took a while for feedback to spread, both laterally through word
of mouth and also upstream back to us. When we did hear from
someone who had bought our game, it was usually in the form of
a mailed letter. Sometimes, they would call our corporate phone
number, which Bill often answered himself even though it was no
longer routing straight to his kitchen like in the early days. He
never complained back then when callers forgot to consider time
zones, and he was just as happy to speak to a fan now. It helped
that the comments were usually positive—very few people would
waste a stamp or a phone call just to tell us they didn't like a game.
Sometimes I think we'd be better off going back to a time when
communication took at least a minimal amount of investment.

In any case, once I had sent my genre-Frankenstein out into the world, there was nothing to do except wait for a few months to find out if other people thought it was as fun as I did. In the meantime, I figured I should settle back into more traditional topics for my next game, at least until we had some sales figures and reviews. Bill told me he had just the project: a new submarine simulation, based on Tom Clancy's hit novel *Red Storm Rising*.

I was not entirely comfortable doing a licensed property. On the one hand, a game can hook players more profoundly if someone has already done the work of establishing the shorthand—in pirate-land the baddies have twirlable moustaches, for example, but at Hogwarts moustaches* are okay, because at least it means you have a nose. Players familiar with that universe will come to the game with an emotional framework in place, ready to be manipulated for the sake of drama. On the other hand, as a designer you will be sharing in someone else's creation, and they may not like your interpretation. The nightmare scenario is to realize that for the next year, you'll be contractually obligated to make a game you don't want to make, or that isn't as good as it could be, due to restrictions from the copyright holder.

Bill assured me that we would make sure everyone was on the same page before we agreed to anything. After all, Tom Clancy still had to be convinced that we weren't going to ruin anything, either. And that is how I found myself in the car with Bill in the summer of 1987, driving out to Tom Clancy's house on the western shore of the Chesapeake Bay.

I wasn't sure what to expect, but it turned out Tom was a very down-to-earth guy. *The Hunt for Red October* had been a huge success, but as a debut author he hadn't been able to command the greatest deal with his publisher, and he was still working at his day job selling insurance even as *Red Storm Rising* was flying off the shelves. We sat in Tom's living room chatting, which is to say,

* *Achievement Unlocked:* Sgt. Pepper's Lonely Hearts Club Band— *Gather four moustaches.*

Bill talked and I nodded politely as needed. Despite his business attire, I could practically see the aura of Bill's flight suit on him as he leaned forward on his knees and gesticulated enthusiastically, in the same full-bore conversational style he used at trade shows.

Tom had been in the Army ROTC himself, and he and Bill happily compared military anecdotes well into the afternoon. Eventually it became clear that we'd earned Tom's seal of approval, and the question was tentatively floated: how much control did he hope to exercise over the final product?

"None," he answered cheerfully. "The person you need to talk to is Larry."

Larry Bond had been Tom's coauthor for *Red Storm Rising*, and he was generally reported to be the technical side of the team, the one who kept the details accurate when Tom's plot veered toward the melodramatic. This made him an even more daunting figure, to me, because nothing killed fun faster than a stickler for realism. I'd thought for the briefest of moments that we were in the clear, but if Larry were slated to be our point man instead of Tom, the whole project might be doomed after all.

We had a phone call with Larry, and it seemed to go well, but he insisted that we should come over to his house for a game night with some of his friends. Now, I was more concerned than ever. The only thing worse than an overbearing license-holder would be one who fancied himself an expert on games as well. Bill found a way to get out of it, but the gathering was clearly meant in my honor, and I had no choice but to go.

Larry's wife answered the door as soon as I knocked, but the living room was empty. Not a deck of cards or a pair of dice to be seen anywhere, let alone any guests. I could faintly hear voices coming from somewhere, though. I should have understood immediately what this meant, but it wasn't until she guided me down the basement stairs that my heart lifted.

Strewn across a folding table, in an array too large for any surface upstairs, was a mess of papers, pencils, and plastic figurines.

Larry and his friends greeted me heartily, then went right back to the business of setting up. This was not a dog-and-pony show for my sake. I had been invited to a genuine nerd night, and I felt immediately at home.

I took a seat at one end of the table, eyeing the strategy game laid out before me. It was military-themed and set at sea, just like the project Larry and I would soon be working on together, but it turned out that wasn't the only reason it had been selected for this evening. The game, called Harpoon, was Larry's—not just by possession, but by invention. In addition to writing best-selling military thrillers, Larry Bond had published his own gaming system, which could be adapted to different campaigns and allowed players the freedom to wrap their own story around the numbers.

Larry didn't just fancy himself a game designer. He actually was one.

I think I might have known about Harpoon before arriving, but I hadn't had time to seek it out since talking to him on the phone— perhaps because I'd been afraid of what I'd find. Besides, it's one thing to read a rule booklet, and quite another to see a game in action. The demonstration was so successful that I soon forgot I was being won over at all. Larry was confident and creative with his scenarios, and his gameplay mechanics were finely tuned: ships maneuvered realistically, weapons inflicted accurate levels of damage, and proper naval tactics were rewarded. It occurred to me that in many ways the relationship between Tom and Larry was analogous to Bill and myself, with one effusive advocate to bolster the brand, and one studious craftsman to keep the thing humming. Larry and I would get along just fine.

Still, there were hiccups with our early prototypes, as there almost always are. Much of the inspiration for our last submarine game, *Silent Service*, had come from a book called *Clear the Bridge!* by Richard O'Kane, about the heroic but doomed patrol of the USS *Tang* against the Japanese in World War II. In the introduction, O'Kane noted, "As I wrote this chronicle and replotted the courses, all of the time knowing the actual fate awaiting my crew and ship, it became necessary time and again to saddle up my buckskin and ride into the hills so that, upon my return, I might continue with a clear eye."

Tom Clancy and other authors had successfully portrayed the tension and psychological isolation of submarine warfare, but it was O'Kane's sense of gallantry and valor that had really captured me the first time, and I felt it keenly missing from our early versions of *Red Storm Rising*. Modern submarines were more computer-controlled than ever, and with the book's futuristic World War III setting, we couldn't believably roll back any of those advances for the sake of gameplay. The artists could animate a detailed storyboard for the opening sequence, and an explosive demolition at the end of each mission, but for the most part, a ship's radar was just your dot and the bad guy's dot, and we couldn't pretend otherwise. It felt cold and impersonal, and once again I began to worry about realism's ability to hamstring us.

Fortunately, reality came through for us in a different way. Larry explained that while technology had come far in its ability to detect something out there in the water, it was still very bad at telling you *what* that something was. That job fell, as it always had, to the sonar operator. A good "ping jockey," as they were known by their shipmates, could determine the speed, location, and nationality of a ship just by listening to its propeller noise through millions of gallons of seawater. The enemy was more than a dot. He was a complex and ominous purring in the darkness, and you had to know his song to survive.

Game audio, more properly known as sound design, had once upon a time been considered just another programming task. In the same way that I could paint a portrait of the Ayatollah using a handful of pixels, I could instruct certain notes to play in a relatively melodic fashion, but both were impressive only because a machine was involved. It was like watching a child prodigy do algebra: all signs pointed to an extremely promising future, but the current output, objectively speaking, wasn't actually that special. In my original Atari computer, audio didn't even get a dedicated chip—it had to share space with potentiometer (aka joystick) and keyboard functions, thus christening the hardware in popular terminology as the POKEY chip.

Despite being nicknamed for other processes, you could still do a lot with a POKEY chip. It offered a range of 256 frequencies, which was far more than a standard eighty-eight-key piano provided—though most were just extra steps jammed in between the standard musical notes, and therefore only useful for sound effects. In addition, six types of distortion were available for each frequency, which the programming book *De Re Atari* loosely (and somewhat aspirationally) cross-referenced for its readers into categories like "Geiger counter," "waterfall," and "electric razor." And if, for example, an on-screen character needed to clean up his five-o'clock shadow while simultaneously testing radiation levels at Niagara Falls, the POKEY chip offered four independent eight-bit channels, which could be—or if you prefer, "had to be"—recombined into two sixteen-bit channels in order to prevent pitch problems with more complex background music.

But like everything that was cool precisely because it was so limited, advancing technology meant that sound design couldn't stay in the hands of programmers forever. I had already said a reluctant goodbye to audio during *Pirates!* a year earlier—though my replacement, Ken Lagace, had once again proven that I would be wrong to be offended. Ken was a clarinet player who had taught music for decades, and he had created his own job by simply getting in touch with Bill one day and convincing him that our games needed professional sound design. Third-party sound cards had become common, he argued, with software that could make and reproduce genuine recordings instead of single-tone beeps. I had some musical talent, but not enough to pursue it full-time, and if we didn't keep up, our competitors would. Like its visual counterpart, game audio had officially transformed from a skill into an art, and I sadly but freely relinquished it.

Submarine sonar, however, was in some ways a step back in time from piratical sea shanties. A propeller's asynchronous grinding was more math than emotion, and since we had no real submarines available for recording, those effects would require direct instructions to the Commodore 64's Sound Interface Device, or SID chip. (Clearly it was meant for me.) As Larry explained the ongoing role of sonar operators in modern times, I suddenly realized how we could bring something new to our otherwise bland interface of radar dots. Each submarine in the game could have a unique signature of layered bass tones and filters, and the player could learn to identify them by ear,* just like the professionals. *Red Storm Rising* ended up being one of the first games to use audio as an interactive element—and having smuggled just a bit of it back into my domain, I didn't have to feel quite so jealous of Ken's darkly moving, top-notch soundtrack.

True to his word, that first meeting at Tom's house was pretty much the last time we saw him until after *Red Storm Rising*'s release, when he joined us at the annual Consumer Electronics Show to do some publicity. While he'd had no particular interest in gaming at the outset—if I had to guess, I'd say Larry probably talked him into considering game licenses in the first place—he seemed to be impressed at both the size and the narrative vision on display throughout the show floor.

To be honest, I was too. I'd grown more confident over the last four years, of course, but I never really lost that rush of excitement I felt at our first CES with a single copy of *Solo Flight* in my suitcase. At least these days I could rest easy knowing that our booth design was in the capable hands of our marketing depart-

* **Achievement Unlocked:** Prosthetic Devices—Collect Blackbeard, a peg leg, Van Gogh, and an ear.

ment. The software wing of the conference had continued to shift steadily toward gaming, and by 1988 it was almost starting to feel like we owned the place. Nintendo's booth was rumored to be 20,000 square feet that year, and for the first time ever, Atari had no new computer hardware to show off, only games. The industry as a whole was approaching a billion dollars in annual sales, and some of the resulting investments were a little off the beaten path: one game advertised itself as "a futuristic cross between ice hockey, soccer and utter chaos," while another offered a collection of Italian-themed minigames, including pillow fights on a gondola and greased pole climbing in Verona. But I certainly couldn't argue with their enthusiasm. Based on the crowds, it must have seemed like there was a market for everything.

Before long, Tom began dropping into a more comfortable tone during quieter moments of the convention, speaking for the first time as equals rather than business associates. That night, we sat up late together, expounding on the nature of art, sources of inspiration, and the inevitable connection we develop with our creations. He revealed that the intervening months had been kind to him financially, but not so kind emotionally, as he was forced to adapt to fame and the complications that come along with it. Tom was especially troubled by ongoing contractual issues with his first book, and the fear that he might never again own the rights to his own character. The conversation was eye-opening for me, first in discovering a kindred creative spirit underneath the alpha male persona, and also in the revelation that even someone of his stature could be taken advantage of through poor business arrangements. I'd always had a distaste for business deals in general, simply because it's not the kind of thing I want to spend my day doing, but I was starting to realize that there was potential danger in them as well.

One morning in late 1988, Bill and I sat down to review the state of the company, and look ahead to where we were going next. With the increasingly apparent success of *Pirates!* and our other recent games, we had a little financial breathing room, and it was time to decide what to do with it.

I thought it would be nice to invest in some employee perks, both in gratitude to those who had worked so hard for us, and to lure new talent in the future.

"What about a company condo out in Nags Head?" I suggested. The Outer Banks of North Carolina was a popular vacation destination for many in our area, and Nags Head beach was one of my personal favorites. "We could send teams down there for a change of pace, or a designer who needed to get away and percolate on an idea. Maybe even let folks take their families, if no one else was using it."

Bill nodded thoughtfully, his mouth curling upward in that negotiating smile. "Well . . ." he began.

I knew what he was getting at, because he'd been talking about it for months. I chuckled. "You want an airplane."

"For promotional purposes," he insisted.

"Okay," I said. "You get an airplane, I'll get a condo."

We probably discussed the logistics a little more thoroughly, but that was the gist of the conversation. I hesitate to call it a trade—it just seemed like a good balance of our personal interests, which also happened to coincide with company interests.

The more I thought about it, though, the more I soured on my idea of a company condo. It probably wouldn't get used as much as I was hoping, and the work that did get done there would be in air quotes, at best. We'd have to hire someone to maintain it, and getting into the rental market to recoup our costs was definitely not something we wanted to do. Plus, we already did plenty of team bonding over board games in the break room, and computer programmers were not exactly known for their sunbathing habits anyway.

I shared my doubts with Bill.

"You're right, it probably doesn't make a lot of sense," he said.

Then he shrugged to indicate that my half of the deal had no bearing on his. "I still want an airplane."

So, Bill got an airplane.

The model he chose was a retired North American T-28B Trojan. It was a design that had been used in counterinsurgency during the Vietnam War, as Bill liked to mention, though it was more frequently employed as a training vehicle, which didn't get mentioned as often. Whether or not our particular plane had flown overseas, though, it was a true military aircraft, and Bill made sure our custom paint job left the large Air Force symbol intact. A wide, sky-blue stripe down the middle separated a royal-blue top and a cream-colored underbelly, with our company insignia and slogan carefully stenciled on the side just beneath the cockpit. He named it the *Miss MicroProse*, and kept it hangared at Martin State Airport, the same place he and I had taken our first flight together.

Bill made sure it lived up to its promotional—and tax write-off-able—value right away. He offered to take up any games journalist brave enough to fly with him, and many agreed, writing glowing articles about the experience as he'd hoped. Of course, there was a product tie-in, too: just a few months after *Red Storm Rising* hit shelves, I took the opportunity to return to the flight simulator genre with a game called *F-19 Stealth Fighter*. It was a half upgrade, half sequel to an existing game called *Project Stealth Fighter*, with the major distinction being that this version would be developed on the IBM personal computer. A few older games had been directly ported up to the new system, but they didn't take advantage of the new technology; they just looked like C64 games running on a bigger machine. *F-19 Stealth Fighter* would be MicroProse's first chance to demonstrate what we could accomplish with the latest and greatest tech. I was intrigued by the chance to explore this topic with an entirely new code base; plus, the F-19 relied on stealth rather than maneuverability, so there were interesting new gameplay aspects to fiddle around with as well.

Ironically, there was no such thing as an F-19 fighter jet in real life. The Air Force had numbered its jet models sequentially since the 1960s, although they skipped the F-13 due to superstition. But after the release of the F/A-18 in 1978, the next plane announced had been the F-20 Tigershark in 1982. There was no explanation for the missing number, and the popular assumption was that the F-19 was a top-secret stealth fighter that already existed, but couldn't be admitted to. Authors wrote military thrillers about it, toy companies sold hypothetical plastic models, and soon the fiction became so well-known that when we announced our upcoming game, some fans assumed that we had access to classified information through Bill.

Then, by complete coincidence, the Pentagon *did* announce the existence of a secret stealth fighter jet, on the exact day our game was released—but instead of the name that everyone in the aeronautics community had taken for granted, they called it the F-117A. Some believed the F-19 was still out there, while others speculated that this seemingly random number had been swapped in only to disconnect it from the widespread assumptions. In the years since, new Air Force jets have stayed faithful to the original numbering scheme, and no other plane has ever been acknowledged in the 100-plus range. Then again, it was probably fair to put the stealth bomber in a numbering category all by itself, since it looked nothing like anyone had imagined the F-19 ought to, ourselves included.

Bill was overjoyed. For one thing, it was a marketing coup that we couldn't have planned better if we'd tried. But for another, it seemed to everyone involved that our plane was actually better than the real one. Maybe not when it came to staying off enemy radar, but definitely in the traditional "it's cool to blow stuff up" kind of way. I felt I had something new to contribute to the flight sim genre because stealth had finally become a factor, but the real plane was so stealthy that there was almost nothing to do. The F-117A only ran missions at night, and the lack of curved surfaces meant that adjusting rudders and flaps was mechanically difficult, to the point that real pilots had to rely almost entirely on the plane's computer to fly for them. Target locations were calculated in advance, and the payload was fired blindly according to the math. Then the pilot simply turned around and came home. It was like sneaking around with an invisibility cheat turned on; there was no thrill.

The Air Force had been so sure of the plane's ability to avoid enemy encounters, they hadn't even put any guns on it. As the company that had gone out of its way to add a gun to a submarine, it was no surprise that our version of the stealth fighter did, in fact, come with lots of guns. Even better, our missiles had cameras on them, so that you could ride one all the way in and watch your target explode at close range. None of us were under the impression this would be a real military feature any time soon, but in this case, Bill was happy to throw realism out the window. It gave him great pride to know that for once, the military had gotten it wrong, and we had gotten it right.

Apparently, others felt the same way. In addition to its commercial success, the Smithsonian Institution decided to put a playable version of *F-19 Stealth Fighter* in the National Air and Space Museum, as part of a new gallery called "Beyond the Limits: Flight Enters the Computer Age." Most museum visitors had never seen anything like it. "Personal computer" had only recently become a pair of words you could string together without sounding like a lunatic, and those who worked with them were often limited to corporate tasks. *F-19* brought the concept of computer gaming into the mainstream for a large portion of the population.

Having taken every willing journalist up in the air with him, Bill then devised a contest called "I Cheated Death with Major Bill," asking fans to submit a 200-word essay on their favorite Micro-Prose game. Three grand prize winners would take a stunt-filled flight lesson in the *Miss MicroProse*, while another hundred or so would receive an assortment of model airplane kits and company

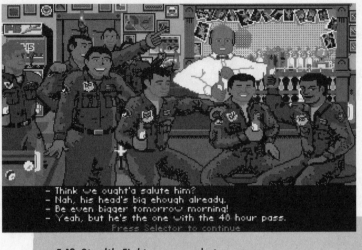

F-19 Stealth Fighter screenshot.
© 1988 MICROPROSE, WWW.MICROPROSE.COM.

T-shirts. Along with all the popular computer publications, the contest was advertised in *Boy's Life* magazine, though for liability reasons I'm sure—okay, I'm pretty sure—I *hope* that Bill never would have let a child win the grand prize.

Fortunately, we had plenty of adult submissions to choose from. One was a defense contractor in his forties, who came all the way from California for the opportunity. Another was a captain for the Philadelphia Police Department. But the essayist closest to Bill's heart was a twenty-eight-year-old engineering student from Staten Island named Joe. He wrote that his dream of becoming a real fighter pilot had been cut short by nearsightedness, but *F-19 Stealth Fighter* had given him a chance at the next closest thing. As someone who had barely fought past the Air Force vision regulations himself, I'm sure Bill had that kid in the winner pile from the moment he opened the envelope.

Ironically, I never flew in the *Miss MicroProse* myself. Over the years Bill took many other employees through high yo-yos, double barrel rolls, Immelmann turns, and all the other maneuvers we'd so carefully articulated in our early games, but I'd been uneasy enough just flying with Bill upright at normal speeds, and I knew the death-defying aerobatics weren't for me. Eventually, the novelty wore off and we sold it again, but it was a tough little plane, and the federal aircraft registry shows that it's still in service today at a flight school in Cincinnati. So if I really wanted to, I could still go cheat death in the *Miss MicroProse*. But I think I'm good.

Sometime after that, I was called into a company meeting in the break room. With our steadily growing staff, it was the only place everybody could fit all at once, and we often gathered there for birthday celebrations and other announcements. So, nothing about it struck me as unusual, until I saw the five-foot-tall rectangle draped in fabric.

Somebody gave a little speech, and then the cover was whipped off to reveal the *Red Baron* arcade cabinet that Bill and I had bonded over in 1982. Apparently one of our office managers had gotten in touch with the MGM Grand hotel in Las Vegas, and the staff there had managed to locate the original machine in the casino's basement storage. Or at least that was their story; it's not like we carved our names into it or anything. But the model was close enough to identical, anyway.

Bill beamed with pride as the two of us posed inside for several photos. It was an undoubtedly cool piece of memorabilia, with a lot of great memories attached. At the same time, though, it was a poignant reminder for me that he and I were gazing into increasingly disparate futures. Bill saw this old airplane game as a bulwark of who we were as a company, a touchstone that we would always come back to. *F-19* was not a fun little throwback for him, or even a final capstone on a successful run in an outdated genre. To Bill, it was the beginning of something even greater. He would never lose his passion for flight simulators.

But as I sat in that plastic pilot's seat, smiling this way and that for the various camera angles, it was clear to me that these memories, wonderful as they were, belonged in the past. I'd never be making another flight simulator again.

8

OVERT PROTRACTION

Sid Meier's
Covert Action (1990)

NINETEEN EIGHTY-NINE WAS a complicated year. For the first time in a decade, I wouldn't release a single game, and for the first time ever, I would prepare to be a father. Not that the two had anything to do with each other, except maybe that both were indications of my growing job security.

As a company, we were now releasing three or four games a year and generating around $15 million in revenue. We'd recently opened a London office with an additional thirty staff members, and the executive team was busy looking for more ways to expand without bogging down our existing development teams. Officially, Bill's title was President and mine was Senior Vice President, but in practice we were equals over separate domains. Sometimes I compromised and worked on a military title I felt lukewarm about, and sometimes he compromised and sold a pirate game he couldn't see the point of, but in general I left all corporate policy-making up to him, including issues of expansion. Bill and the other directors decided to create an internal label called Microplay, and use it to publish titles from third-party studios. It was a reasonable idea from a growth standpoint, and took some of the pressure off the in-house teams to churn out one hit after another. It also removed whatever pressure was left on me personally to create more military content, and allowed me to set up camp permanently in the action-adventure-simulation genre, wherever that was. Maybe it was just the Sid genre.

Unfortunately, the rapid third-party expansion wasn't necessarily great for quality. Before the year was out, the Microplay division would publish ten new games across multiple platforms each. Many of us on the development side felt their standards could perhaps have been a little higher, and we rebelled by referring to our core team as MPS Labs. The term "labs" was being thrown around a lot in those days as computers became more associated with scientific progress, and Bell Labs in particular had recently won several Nobel Prizes for their research, so at the time it felt like a hip way to elevate ourselves a little from the Microplay name. We designed a new logo to be displayed at the beginning of our games, and someone went so far as to take a picture of me in a lab coat and tape it to the main development door, with the stern safety warning that "You Are Now Entering MPS Labs." We had no shortage of self-esteem.

Not all the third-party games were iffy, though. As in many industries, there were two types of independent outfits: those who were still knocking on publishers' doors trying to establish themselves, and those who had proven their talent so thoroughly that they could wait for publishers to knock on theirs. Dan Bunten was one of the latter.

I had met Dan at my first Computer Game Developer's Conference a year earlier, but I'd known his name much longer than that. He had been making games since 1978, and by 1983 had already created *M.U.L.E.*, which many consider to be one of the best computer games of all time. Loosely inspired by the Robert Heinlein book *Time Enough for Love*, the box described it as "a game in which up to four players attempt to settle a distant planet with the so-called help of a mule-like machine they all learn to hate."

I'd like to say that at least I beat Dan to the punch on the four-player thing, since *Floyd of the Jungle* had been released one year before *M.U.L.E.* in 1982. But in fact Dan's very first game, *Wheeler Dealers*, had shipped with a custom four-player controller that he had designed himself. He'd wanted to play a particular type of game, and the fact that it didn't exist yet was no deterrent—hardware included. It was a feeling I could relate to.

Meanwhile, the game he signed on to make for us, *Command HQ*, was one of the first to include head-to-head online play over a modem. Dan was absolutely evangelical about multiplayer, and many of his games shipped without a single-player option at all, even when his publishers begged for one. He felt that the most important thing computers could offer us was a connection with each other, and without it, they were essentially worthless.

Another thing Dan was well ahead of his time on was gender issues. He felt that more designers should be women, and failing that, more designers should be seeking the input of women—and failing *that*, more designers should at least have a woman's influence somewhere in their lives. At one early CGDC, he gave a speech in which he urged designers to get married, have kids, and "stop spending all their time alone in front of computers." In 1992, he underwent a sex change operation, and became Danielle Bunten Berry. I'm proud to say my fellow designers had a very progressive attitude about it, especially for the era. It was a little awkward at first, but only in the way that a room full of nerds would have been awkward around any woman, and she never suffered any outright rejection that I'm aware of, at least not from us. We were a community of people who, on average, had experienced a fair amount of social rejection ourselves, so perhaps we were more sensitive to the hurt it could cause.

Pronouns are a big deal these days, to the point that it would be almost impossible to talk about my friend without angering someone. But Dani, as she went by after the surgery, always envisioned herself as a different person in the second phase of her life, and never wanted to erase who she used to be. She often specifically referred to her transition as her "pronoun change," joked about how she only did it to increase the number of female designers in the industry, and once said of her former self, "I'm not as good a programmer as he was. I'm also not as willing to sit for hours in front of a computer. . . . I tend to need to socialize far more often than he did." I honor both Dan's and Dani's memories by speaking about them the way she preferred.

In any case, Dan was already a strong voice for equality in gaming before his transition, and by 1989, the American industry was just barely starting to listen—the Japanese and European markets being ahead of us on this one by many years. American gamers tend to mark our own Lara Croft as a critical turning point for female heroines, and her contributions are not to be dismissed, but *Tomb Raider* wasn't released until 1992. Nintendo had already cast Samus Aran as a woman six years earlier in *Metroid*, which itself was notable only because it infiltrated the American market. Plenty of earlier Japanese games had lead characters who openly admitted to being women on the title screen, rather than in the final seconds of the game as *Metroid* had.

But just as Dani would have quipped in her soft Arkansas twang, slow progress was better than no progress. Text-based games had been accidentally inclusive for years by asking players to enter their own name, and the adventure game genre inched ahead of its peers again when some began offering a choice between a male-ish or female-ish clump of pixels. Electronic Arts released *Murder on the Zinderneuf* in 1983 with a selection of six male and two female sleuths, and Atari's well-known *Gauntlet* series offered one female action-adventurer out of four. It was something, anyway.

We had actually discussed the possibility of a female option in *Pirates!*, but it would have required an alternate set of art for the entire "wooing the Governor's daughter" portion of the game. There was only so much we could hope to get away with in 1987, even as our own publisher, and a female pirate making the moves on a female aristocrat was definitely not on the list. It would have been fun to animate a fastidious governor's son getting swept off his feet by a tough and capable piratess, but doubling the romantic content would have meant cutting an equal amount of something else, and we simply couldn't afford the memory. Someone pointed out that there were female pirates who had lived and dressed as men, so why not offer the choice and then keep the game exactly the same, masculine player and all, but that just seemed like inviting trouble from both sides. So, *Pirates!* shipped as it was.

But now we were nearly in the nineties, for Pete's sake. I was already a couple of months into development on a new title called *Covert Action*, which we'd pitched to Bill as "like *Pirates!*, but with spies," and from the outset I knew that the game was going to be gender-neutral. We fit the extra data into the game by always addressing the character as "Max" Remington, and asking the player at the beginning whether that was to be short for Maxine, or Maximillian. In reality, it was short for nothing: Max Remington III was our lead artist on the project, and he agreed to let us steal his very espionage-suitable name.

Spies fit the *Pirates!* framework in the sense that they did a lot of different activities, such as code breaking, clue chasing, and the occasional hostage taking. Even better, it was possible for a spy to identify the bad guy by focusing on the skill he or she happened to enjoy most. Wiretap enough phones, and you'd eventually get the incriminating evidence without sneaking into the building—or you could just strap on a gas grenade and walk through the front door, if that was your preferred method. Either way, the henchmen would still be going home to their families, because all of your weapons were nonlethal, up to and including the rubber bullets in your top-of-the-line spy pistol. *Covert Action* was the closest I had ever come to making a violent game in the immediate, bodily sense, and I was determined not to cross the line.

This is not to say that I'm in favor of any form of censorship. Videogames are an art form, and it's never a good idea to stifle creativity. I can say with personal certainty that gamers are mature and intelligent people, and we have the ability to distinguish between fantasy and reality. But when it comes to the creations that happen to inspire me, I don't think violence is necessary. The world is often a very negative place, and I'd rather push it in the opposite direction whenever I can. There's an argument to be made that by exposing the unpleasant reality of violence, you can inspire others to push against it, too, but this generally requires a removed perspective, rather than the inherent first-person nature of games. It's hard to claim that our products are immersive, but somehow insist that the experience has no impact. A game with no impact is simply a bad game, and the hand-waving dismissal that anything we make is "just a game" is even worse when it's coming from a designer's own mouth. Excessive gore is, at best, a cheap and short-lived path to player engagement. There is a line to walk, an audience to tailor to, and a purpose to consider in everything we do.

My partner on *Covert Action* was a designer named Bruce Shelley, who had previously worked at the board gaming company Avalon Hill. It wasn't unusual for us to hire someone with no background in computer games, since the industry hadn't been around long enough for anyone to build a worthwhile résumé. Most of our employees began with a particular nondigital expertise, and learned on the job how to integrate it within the structure of computer games. But even with specialized artists, sound engineers, and playtesters, design at that time was still mostly synonymous with programming. For us to bring a designer on board without a coding background meant he had to be pretty darn good.

Fortunately, Bruce's talent was obvious to whoever interviewed him. I wasn't usually involved in hiring—pretty much everyone got a "sure, they seem nice!" appraisal from me, so my input wasn't very helpful—and I don't know that I would have been able to pick Bruce out as someone special, in the beginning. He was quiet, and humble. But as he had studiously chipped away at various tasks within our large *F-19 Stealth Fighter* team, I had begun to notice a core of determination and insight. He was the type to stick with a problem until it was solved. He liked for things to be done right, and no matter what you showed him, he always had an idea for at least one detail that could be improved.

Like many introverts, we bonded over the things we liked at first, rather than a particular affinity for each other. We talked about television shows, and historical fiction. We played board games in the break room, including several he'd designed himself back at Avalon Hill. After *F-19* shipped, Bruce was officially assigned to work on another flight sim, but unofficially, he became my trusted assistant and sounding board, helping me clear away the debris and figure out what exactly this spy game was supposed to be.

One way that spies did not fit into the *Pirates!* framework was the inherently linear nature of their story. A pirate could choose to sword fight indefinitely, but a spy can't just travel the world wiretapping every building he comes across for no good reason. Clues lead from one to the next. You might have a few different ways of gathering those clues, but eventually they were all going to lead to the same evil mastermind. Once the mystery was solved, why would anyone play our game a second time?

No problem, I thought. We'll just have the computer write new mysteries!

It was only a little bit impossible, which is not the same as completely impossible. One early proponent of computational creativity was Christopher Strachey, who had been a college classmate of Alan Turing's in the 1930s. Their paths diverged for a bit after graduation, but Strachey eventually reconnected with Turing in 1951, after hearing about his new Manchester Mark 1 computer. Strachey later reported to the national conference of the Association for Computing Machinery that his work on Turing's machine had been a success: the Manchester Mark 1, he declared, "will in fact play a complete game of Draughts at a reasonable speed." In other words, he'd programmed it to play checkers.

Shortly after that, the improved Ferranti Mark 1 model was released, and Strachey again pushed it toward artistic, rather than mathematical, purposes. First, he devised a way to alter the pitch of the computer's usual clicks and grinding, and arranged them into renditions of "God Save the Queen" and "Baa, Baa, Black Sheep." Then his focus shifted once again in 1952, when he decided that what the Ferranti Mark 1 really needed to do was write love letters.

Strachey programmed a template that randomly combined a few different sentence structures and word choices within a basic letter format. The results were stilted, but comprehensible. Occasionally the computer even created something approaching poetry, like "You are my covetous burning, my affectionate yearning," or "My adoration keenly sighs for your infatuation." Though most of it is not especially romantic by today's standards, the word list still serves as a fascinating reminder of what passed for terms of endearment in 1950s Britain. "Little liking" and "fellow feeling" are considered synonyms for love, and the list of salutations includes now-bewildering items like "duck" and "moppet" alongside classics like "honey" and "dearest."

The industry term for this type of randomized template—or more specifically, the ideal of perfecting randomized templates into actual creativity—is known as procedural generation. Start with Shakespeare's *Hamlet*, for example. But instead of Denmark, set it in Africa, and instead of people, make them lions. All of a sudden you've got *The Lion King*, complete with a murderous, usurping uncle and an angsty protagonist who disappears for a while then returns to claim the throne. Or start with *Romeo and Juliet*, except swap fair Verona for urban New York, turn the feuding families into rival street gangs, and make everyone a little older for decency's sake. Now it's *West Side Story*. The more individual elements you change, the closer you are to a brand-new story that no one recognizes anymore. Give a computer a starting point, tell it what pieces are allowed to change and in what kinds of ways—you can't swap Denmark with bees, for example, only other locations—and that's procedural generation.

Interestingly, the popular children's game Mad Libs was being invented elsewhere at almost exactly the same time as Strachey's first attempts at formulaic love letters. Chris Crawford, the founder of CGDC who had once thrust a sword in the air for art, became particularly obsessed with the idea of a computer that could make up new stories, and eventually left the games industry to develop his "Storytron" invention full-time. I was not prepared to go that far, but I did know that without some level of procedurally generated plot, *Covert Action* would be dead in the water.

After several months of work, the prototype I had was not dead, exactly, but kind of treading water with its boots on. Bruce and I had come up with about twenty or thirty crime story templates that could feature different bad guys, cities, and shadow organizations each time. It was enough variety to keep the casual player happy, but wasn't the breakthrough I'd been hoping for. The patterns were recognizable after a while, the templates too predictable. The very nature of a fill-in-the-blank story meant that everything outside the blanks was set in stone, and no randomized piece of information could have any effect on the ones that came after it. Usually the answer to this sort of problem is just more data—more templates, more swappable elements, longer lists to choose from. But even if we'd had the computer memory to spare, which we didn't, the result still wouldn't have satisfied me. I wanted a story that was laid out from the beginning, but not apparent until the end, like a Sherlock Holmes mystery.

To be honest, I'd imagined this whole project as a technical warm-up to a better game along those exact lines, and I've never stopped dreaming about it to this day. How cool would it be to have a game that could sneak in that one crucial piece of evidence in the beginning, just waiting for you to deduce its meaning? Not from a preplanned list of clues, like a worn keyhole or a dirty shoeprint, but from a more general understanding of what is normal, and what would therefore not be normal. You'd have to set down rules for the real world, establish all the cause-and-effect we take for granted, and then follow up with a nearly infinite ruleset, laying out the consequences of a break anywhere in the chain, and how those breaks would affect each other . . . anyway. Still dreaming, like I said. The point is, *Covert Action* wasn't it.

Bruce could sense my energy for the project flagging, and I think he felt the same. We both knew it was an okay game, but not a great game, and it probably never would be. At the same time, my wife Gigi had just become pregnant with our first child, and I was experiencing the usual priority shifts and personal reevaluation that all new parents go through. I was contending with The Future, and it was making The Past look sort of universally rusty.

But it was hard to admit defeat when I still believed wholeheartedly in the idea's potential, if not its current execution. I had walked away from failed prototypes before, but never after spending this much time and energy on one. Plus, it wasn't just my own time we were talking about anymore. When I created games alone, I had only myself to apologize to if something fizzled out, but Bruce had been working alongside me from the beginning, and I didn't want to feel like I had dragged him into anything unfairly.

I wanted to drop it. I didn't see how I could drop it.

I needed a vacation.

HANG ON
A SECOND

F-15 Strike Eagle II (1989)

THAT WASN'T ENTIRELY TRUE,
what I said a little while ago. Technically, a flight simulator with
my name on it—not in an on-the-box sense, just in the normal
place on the credits page—was released in 1989, called *F-15 Strike
Eagle II*. But I don't think I really worked on it. And if I did, I don't
remember anything about it.

The game was basically just a repurposing of the *F-19 Stealth
Fighter* code, nothing new to see. Maybe what happened was I was
supposed to be working on it, but I chose to stay in my office making the *Covert Action* prototype instead. Or maybe I really did
tweak the programming a little bit, and flight simulators were so
uninspiring to me at that point that I blocked the entire experience.
I don't know. But I'm not comfortable taking credit for a game that
I truly don't recall contributing to in any way. Six flight simulators
on my résumé is plenty; I don't need to claim a seventh.*

✶ *Achievement Unlocked:* Life Is Short—*Finish a chapter in less than
one page.*

10

ALL ABOARD

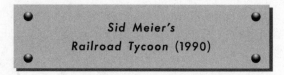

*Sid Meier's
Railroad Tycoon* (1990)

TWO WEEKS AT THE BEACH TURNED
out to be just the thing I needed. I returned to the office that August
with a tan on my face, a disk in my hand, and all of my worries
about *Covert Action* a distant memory.

"What's this?" Bruce asked, a little surprised—or maybe not—
to see that I'd been working while I was out. He turned the unla-
beled disk over in his hands. "Another spy prototype?"

"Nah," I said. "This is new."

I hadn't intended to come back with something dramatically
different, but over the next several years it would become a fairly
reliable pattern. Apparently, I do a lot of my most inspired work
while on vacation. I'm not incapable of taking a break—my computer and I have a strong, but healthy, relationship. I never saturate
myself in it, and I don't neglect the outdoors or family members.
Most days, I have about two or three hours' worth of ideas to play
around with, and after that I have to go recharge elsewhere. But to
me, my computer is the very definition of a leisure activity, and it
wouldn't make sense to go without it. These days everyone travels
with their laptops; I just happened to live in a time when computers were slightly more cumbersome. Bringing a computer to the
beach admittedly turned some heads back in 1990, but loading a

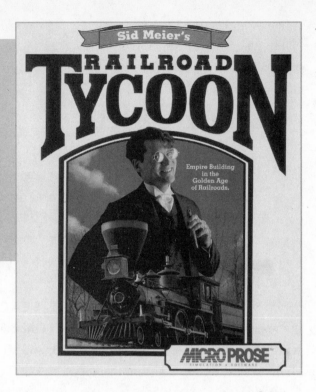

big metal box and a monitor into the back of the car wasn't nearly as hard as people made it out to be.

The important distinction was that I could do what I wanted on vacation, without any expectation of progress or success. It was the perfect time to experiment with something wild, or just mess around with whatever struck my fancy. Often it was game-related, but sometimes I'd doodle in an art program, or compose digital music. On this particular trip, I'd been willing to consider any diversion that wasn't spies.

"Model railroads?" Bruce asked. As usual, his tone wasn't overly excited or skeptical, just thoughtful. "Interesting."

My father and I had once built a model railroad together when I was a kid—or at least, we started building one. It never really got finished, although I think that might be an intended feature of model railroading in general. It did, however, manage to take over the whole dining room. First we had to construct a large wooden frame for our future track to sit on, and then my father brought in rolls of chicken wire to sculpt a papier-mâché landscape over it. It was clear he enjoyed the painting and crafting more than the trains themselves, but they had recently become an obsession of mine, so he was willing to compromise for the sake of father-son bonding.

Unfortunately, it was not 1:87 scale trains that had caught my eye. I had gone to Switzerland a few summers earlier to visit my paternal grandparents, and discovered to my delight that their large family property was flanked on one side by railroad tracks, with the station itself only half a mile away. The train platform served double duty as the town's central plaza, and included a smattering of shops where one relative or another would occasionally buy me a treat. But even without the promise of ice cream, I soon found myself hiking there alone each day to watch the trains. I could have basked in their thrilling size and complexity from the comfort of my grandparents' porch, but what I really wanted to see was the large clock on the station wall. The trains always came in *exactly* on time, one after the other. I waited for one to be a minute early, or two minutes late, but they never were. Somehow, the trains just knew.

My grandfather got me a copy of the train schedule, a thick book that held the times for every train in every station across Switzerland. I began to learn which engines made which routes, and mentally follow a particular train's path in the book for days until it returned once again to our little township of Bülach. The efficiency of the whole thing was both awe-inspiring and deeply satisfying, and I tried to imagine the person who ran the system, planning and coordinating and never being off by even a single minute.

I had been unhappy when I first arrived in Switzerland, and for several days I wrote entries in my diary begging the universe to let me go home. When the universe did not comply, I registered a formal letter of complaint with my parents back in Detroit, but they remained unmoved. If anything, my protests were seen as further evidence, to my father at least, that I needed this grounding in European family tradition. On the one hand, he had been the black sheep of his family, first marrying a foreign woman and then striking out for America with dreams of owning land, which was extremely uncommon in Switzerland. But on the other, I think part of him wanted to prove that his son was just as Swiss as any of my homesteaded cousins.

Whether he was right was up for debate. By lineage I was also half Dutch, by birthplace I was technically Canadian, and culturally, I considered myself totally American. Like many first-generation children, I often served as my parents' guide and ambassador, and one of my favorite arguments against my mother's rules was, "That's how they do it in America!" I successfully applied this social blackmail to missed bedtimes, scattered toys, uneaten vegetables, and pretty much anything else I wanted to get away with. I wasn't being disobedient, I assured her. I was being *American*.

But between the trains and the many young cousins living on the property, I soon discovered that I loved it in Bülach. My parents had emigrated from Europe before I was born, and prior to this trip, I had been only nominally aware of our extended family overseas. There were at least ten relatives living in the homestead where my father grew up, plus another twenty or so within walking distance in town, and it wasn't unusual for most or all of them to gather for a meal or weekend celebration. In Michigan, I was an only child with no aunts and uncles, but in Switzerland, I belonged to a classroom's worth of children—and unlike school, where my shyness occasionally got in the way, I was accepted immediately because I was family. I could also appreciate the organization and routine that went into running a household of this size. With so many people coming and going on their own schedules, we were practically a miniature train station ourselves.

Toward the end of the summer I wrote a new letter to my parents, explaining that I had changed my mind and asking if I could stay for longer. There was a local school I could attend, and my

Swiss was fluent enough to manage. (Most people in Switzerland write in German, but the spoken language has evolved into a unique dialect, in the same way that Chinese diverged into Mandarin and Cantonese.) I'm sure there was plenty of discussion between adults that I wasn't privy to, but ultimately, my parents agreed to let me stay through the end of the first semester.

Four months later, I wrote them again, to ask if I could stay indefinitely.

"No," was my mother's emphatic answer. "We're coming to get you."

I had originally flown to Zurich by myself, but she didn't trust me to willingly board the plane back home, so she and my father flew out in person to guarantee it. In retrospect, I think she probably never wanted me to go in the first place, but my father had insisted that it would be good for me. And it was, overall—though I think back to when my own son, Ryan, was eight, and there's no way I'd have let him live overseas for most of a year. So, I can certainly understand my mother's position. Especially after she ran to embrace me, and we discovered that I'd forgotten how to speak English.

It only took about a week for the words to start to come back to me, and during that time I was still able to communicate with my father in Swiss. But I can imagine the dirty looks my mother must have been giving him behind my back, thinking that he had allowed her son to forget his home entirely. Eventually words like "train," and "station," and "totally cool 200-page schedule" emerged, and she began to get a glimpse into my new obsession. I don't know how long it was before my father decided we should make a model train, but her tolerance for our sprawling project may have been bolstered by the hope that, on some level, it might help Detroit compete with Switzerland.

Like I said, though, it didn't really work. The problem was that model trains are less about the running, and more about the building. One of my recurring tasks was to push in these tiny black railroad spikes, with the traditionally hyper-accurate kit demanding around ten spikes for every one inch of track. I don't know what my father was working on, but the spikes were all mine, and I spent hours and hours pushing in each tiny connector. This was not the part of trains that I was interested in, and it clearly wasn't his idea of fun, either, so it's not surprising that we never managed to finish the thing. At some point, my mother's patience waned, and the whole setup quietly disappeared. She got her dining room back, but I never lost that childhood fascination with schedules and routing, which is how I ended up with the model train simulator that Bruce was now holding in his hands.

It wasn't a game, really, just a way to lay out tracks without making your fingertips sore. But Bruce was more of a typical train enthusiast, with a stockpile of knowledge about different engines and historical nuances that I'd never delved into, and he saw the potential. Back at Avalon Hill, he had even designed a railroad board game called 1830, though it focused on general land control instead of hands-on routing. Bruce immediately began suggesting details that could be added to the prototype, and I was happy to oblige, as long as it meant I didn't have to think about *Covert Action*.

Then, something revolutionary happened. Fellow designer Will Wright released his magnum opus, *SimCity*, and the phrase "god game" entered the lexicon. The idea had come to him while working on a different title, *Raid on Bungeling Bay*, after he realized that he enjoyed designing the levels more than bombing them. Not entirely surprising for a game designer to feel that way, but he came to the radical conclusion that others might agree with him. Will had spent years trying to convince publishers that his city-building simulator was a game at all, until finally he and a partner formed their own company to release it themselves in February 1989. The first version was for the Macintosh, but with success came ports to other machines, and sometime later that year—just as *Covert Action* was floundering, and my model train prototype was emerging—I got the chance to play *SimCity* on the PC.

It was a game. It was about creating, rather than destroying . . . and it was a game. The objective was dominance over one's own limitations, rather than a morally inferior antagonist . . . and it was a game.

My railroad simulator was a game, too.

In hindsight, it's a little odd that I hadn't yet drawn the parallel between planes and trains. Of course a simulator could be a game! My career had been built on blending game fiction with aeronautic fact, and it would have made sense to forge the same alloy with other vehicles. True, trains never shot each other down, but there had been no weapons in *Solo Flight*, either, just a friendly mail bag waiting to be delivered.

Possibly I'd missed the connection because train simulators were already uncharted territory. The flight simulator genre was established and even somewhat crowded, so it had been necessary to put my own twist on things—combining gameplay with technical realism—in order to stand out. But with trains we were alone, making it up as we went along with no challengers to urge us forward. It's hard to think outside the box when there is no box. At any rate, *SimCity* was either the kick I needed to see what was right in front of me, or else maybe the reassurance that my intuition was feasible after all, and from then on, I knew this wasn't a distracting little side project. We were making a railroad game.

I began prototyping in earnest, delivering copies to Bruce for feedback on an almost daily basis. Before long we had added an economic system to carry commodities from one city to another, and terrain challenges like mountains and rivers. There was even a postal delivery option, just like in *Solo Flight*.

1989 came to a close with no completed projects from me, but Bruce and I narrowly managed to convince the executive team that

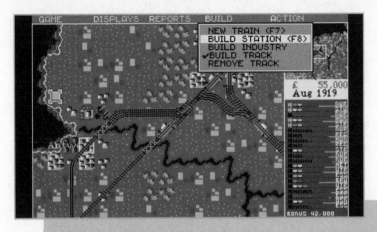

Sid Meier's Railroad Tycoon screenshot.
© 1990 MICROPROSE, WWW.MICROPROSE.COM.

the railroad prototype was worth finishing. *SimCity*'s proven success in the marketplace probably helped a little, but I think they mostly agreed because I was only using a bare minimum of staff. Sure, I could have forced a confrontation, and they would have thrown up their hands and said, "Well, Sid's going to work on what he's going to work on," but the assignment of paid employees was pretty clearly in their domain, and I wasn't prepared to go back to doing everything by myself. So we made our case, and they agreed to let me keep Bruce, plus one artist and a handful of support staff toward the end of production. But most of the in-game graphics would have to be mine, and we were to wrap it up quickly.

Soon after that, Bruce's feedback took an unexpected turn. It was unfair, he noted, that his bridges kept washing out in floods. I countered that *SimCity* had included a robust variety of natural disasters, including tornadoes, earthquakes, and non-copyrighted Godzilla-ish monsters who stomped through buildings with abandon. Compared to all that destruction, the occasional bridge washout didn't seem so ruthless. Besides, flooding was a legitimate concern for rail companies, certainly more so than sea monsters were for city planners.

But Bruce reminded me of one of my own axioms of game design: make sure the player is the one having the fun. "When my bridge is knocked down for no reason," he said with a placid shrug, "I'm not having fun."

He was right, of course. It seems like players ought to appreciate the hardships we throw at them—that the whole reason they play is to prove their worth. But it's not. People play games to feel good about themselves, and random destruction only leads to paranoia and helplessness. Thwarting an enemy's attack feels worthy, but recovering from an ambush is a relief at best. Unfortunately, the flip side of that imbalance is that the designer feels powerful and clever, which is what makes these unexpected setbacks so tempting to implement. As major plot points, they're practically universal: your trusted partner steals the treasure; the damsel who begged for help is a double agent; the noble scientist has a secret weapon to wipe out mankind; the princess is in another castle. Or in other words, the player did everything the designer asked of them, and then the rules changed for no reason. A sudden reversal of fortune is only exciting or dramatic when it happens to someone else. When it happens to you, it's just a bummer. The player may soldier on out of defiance, or irritation, or just a basic acceptance that this is how games are supposed to be, but their experience has been diminished nonetheless. I had recognized these pitfalls when they were part of a linear storyline, but Bruce's comment helped me see that the same principle applied to even the tiniest plot points in open-world games. All random obstacles are, on some level, crafted with an "imagine the look on their faces when" mentality, which can also be loosely translated as, "Hey! Hey! I designed this! Look at the big brain on me!" The game isn't supposed to be about us. The player must be the star, and the designer as close to invisible as possible.

The key difference between a gameplay challenge and a betrayal, I realized, was whether the player had a fighting chance to avoid it. So rather than eliminate the flooding, I introduced different kinds

Sid Meier's Railroad Tycoon screenshot.
© 1990 MicroProse, www.microprose.com.

of bridges. A wooden bridge was cheap, and would get the railway up and running right away. A fancy stone bridge was more expensive, and took longer to build, but would be impervious to flooding. By giving the player control over how much risk they would tolerate, the floods not only stopped feeling unfair, they became a source of genuine reward. To imagine their bridge emerging whole from the receding water line felt better than if it had never flooded at all.

There was one other detail that was bugging me about the bridges. My aversion to violence was well-known around the office by then, and it had become a sort of joking mantra that "no one dies in a Sid Meier game." I'd glossed over a few theoretical characters in the early military titles—we didn't have the resources to animate pilots parachuting out of their planes, or submarine captains diving through an escape hatch—but you also couldn't prove they *didn't* survive the wreckage. In *Pirates!*, the enemy's men never drowned; they were always captured and put to work. And up until I'd abandoned it, the *Covert Action* prototype had made it clear that your weapons were nonlethal. Yet now, in my least aggressive game ever, trains full of innocent crew members regularly plunged to their death over a washed-out bridge.

The loss of the train was necessary, otherwise there would be no incentive to pay for a sturdier bridge. But the wholesale slaughter of loyal employees made me uncomfortable. So I asked our artist, Max Remington, to draw the engineer and other crew members clearly jumping out to safety just before the train went over the edge. It was a tiny detail, but it kept the game's universe consistent.

Enforcing my "no one dies" rule was especially important to me in this case, because like *Pirates!*, management had declared that this weird little railroad game would need my name on the box to help it sell. It would turn out to be the tipping point for all future name-branding, but the ramifications hadn't yet become apparent to me. I had released several games in the interim without my name, and frankly, the executives seemed to be using it as a mark of low confidence rather than any kind of personal exaltation. But I couldn't allow my name to go on something I wasn't completely proud of, so there had to be no ambiguity. The conductor lived.

A few weeks after *Sid Meier's Railroad Tycoon* was released, Bruce and I sat together on an Amtrak train headed up to New York. (If only I could have given their schedulers a copy of the game.) We were on our way to some kind of promotional event, but our minds were not focused on the interviews awaiting us. As always, we dreamed about what came next.

"This game was pretty fun to make," Bruce said.

"It was," I agreed. "We should do another one."

I had never committed to collaborating with a particular team member without at least a working prototype before, but I had liked working with Bruce very much, and didn't want to lose him to another project. Aside from our similar demeanor and work ethic, Bruce had proven during *Railroad Tycoon* that he could fill in the gaps.

The best working relationships are between people with complementary skills. Bill Stealey filled in my gaps on the business side, so he and I worked well in that regard, and obviously the sound and art guys were better at doing their jobs than I was. But when it came to design, I had been predominantly alone, or else collaborating with people who were skilled in all the same ways I was. I'm very good, for example, at ruthless self-evaluation. Even talented people have mostly bad ideas, and it's critical in creative fields to let go of your ego and immediately bag anything that isn't pulling its weight. But sometimes the wheat gets in with the chaff, and Bruce often saw a glimmer of value in an idea that I was ready to scrap. At the same time, he never got distracted by the parts of the game that weren't finished yet. I could hand him a broken prototype with terrible graphics, overpowered enemies, and a crash bug three turns in, and he could look right past these immaterial complaints into the heart of what the game was really about. Where there was potential, he saw potential, and he could isolate areas for subtle improvement without getting distracted by what we both knew was easily fixable.

Fortunately, he was on board.

"Something bigger."

"What's bigger than the history of railroads?"

"The entire history of human civilization!"

We laughed at the absurd truth of the statement, but as soon as it was said out loud, I don't think either of us could have settled for anything less. We were not the type to turn down an interesting challenge. At the age of twenty-eight, I had declared in my very first instruction manual that I would one day "write the ultimate strategy game." Now, at thirty-six, I figured I was ready. Age and experience may bring wisdom, but sometimes it's useful to be a young person who hasn't learned how to doubt himself yet.

11

HISTORY OF CIVILIZATION, PART I

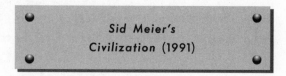

Sid Meier's Civilization (1991)

A WEEK OR TWO LATER I SAT in the hospital, proud husband and new father. People try to tell you what to expect when your first child is born, but it never does justice to the real thing, so I won't attempt to here. In a nutshell, it was amazing—and despite being objectively very similar to every other wrinkly little kid in the world, this particular kid in front of me was actually the best one.

But once the action is over, hospitals are pretty boring. Someday it would be socially acceptable to bring digital entertainment with me, but I had known better than to try it this time. Gigi and our son Ryan were both resting, so I decided to take a walk and maybe find something to eat.

The Indianapolis 500 was playing on a television out in the hallway, and I studiously assigned some of my attention to it so that the time might pass quicker. It was an interesting race, as far as those things went. There had been a big upset after the front-runner, Emerson Fittipaldi, had to make an early pit stop for failing tires, and now it looked like Arie Luyendyk, "the Flying Dutchman," would take the crown. It's possible I felt a bit of patriotic pride for Holland as I watched him zooming around the track.

Car racing requires deft maneuvering, of course, but strategy is at its core, as Fittipaldi had been so recently reminded. A professional driver must take a holistic approach to winning, with particular focus on the resource management of tires, fuel, and mechanical parts. A few racing games had begun to pay lip service to the player's overall career, as we first had in *Gunship*, and some even offered a system of vehicle upgrades between races, but none had yet captured the mental side of the experience. What if you could find a way for those equipment decisions to be weighed mid-race, just like the drivers did? It wouldn't be easy to keep track of so many elements while swerving around the track, but maybe you could let go of some of the speed in favor of the strategy. Taken to its logical conclusion, you could even have a turn-based racing game.

This was the eternal divide in the strategy genre: real-time versus turn-based. When the clock keeps running and everyone can play at once, there is an immediate increase in excitement. Quick thinking is rewarded over precision, and those with short attention spans finally get their day in the sun. But while the payoff is instant and ongoing, the ratcheting intensity can easily overflow into confusion and frustration. Turn-based gaming, on the other hand, is slow and methodical, and any excitement felt in the beginning is anticipatory at best. The comparative lack of intensity can risk sinking into boredom, but by the end, the payoff is usually bigger, because you've invested more time and personal choice into the outcome.

Both styles can be a disaster in the wrong setting, but sometimes the most interesting games come from a deliberately nontraditional choice. Consider, for example, a real-time chess match: all the same rules as regular chess, but with no requirement to wait for your opponent to take their turn. If you were quick enough, you could slide a bishop diagonally across the board, capture a piece, and slide back out of range before your opponent could retaliate. Then again, they might have snuck in and captured your knight while you were busy with the bishop. You'd probably have to institute some new rules like "one hand at a time" and "no shoving" just to keep things sane, and I don't know if it would work in the end—but it's easy to see how changing that one factor creates a radically different game.

Now if only parenting could be modified into a turn-based campaign, instead of the white-knuckled real-time melee I knew I was in for. But like I said, when you play in real time the payoff is instant.

Paternity leave wasn't really a thing back then, but I did take some vacation days after Ryan was born, which in theory meant I could work on whatever I wanted—at least when he was sleeping. But the timing was such that I was still enthralled with my latest project. Just two weeks earlier, I had handed Bruce the first playable prototype of *Civilization*.

It was not good. It wasn't horrible, necessarily, but no fan of the series would recognize it today. The clock ran in real time, as it had in *Railroad Tycoon*, but really it was more like *SimCity* on a global scale: zone some areas for agriculture, zone some others for mining, then sit back and watch your empire grow.

Unfortunately, neither "sit back" or "watch" are features to be proud of in a game. That's what movies are for. Making players stop to ponder their next move is fine, but taking over the story is not our job—nor are we very good at it, despite the perpetual instinct among designers to try. We simply can't compete with the panorama of a movie, or the length of a novel, or the acoustics of an album, and prioritizing these features over gameplay will always lead to disappointment. As Chris Crawford once wrote, "The time has come for us to outgrow Hollywood envy. . . . Sid Meier makes a pathetic Arnold Schwarzenegger, but he makes a magnificent Sid Meier." Other works of art are successful when the performer is interesting, but a game is successful only when the player is interesting. Our job is to impress you with yourself, and on that, we have a monopoly.

I had run into a similar issue a few years earlier, with my wargames that could play against themselves to a completely predictable outcome. This time around, at least, I sensed there was a problem right away. But before I could identify what it was or how to solve it, my lack of published titles finally became too much for executives to put up with.

"I need you to finish *Covert Action*," Bill told me. "We have to sell some games."

Though I didn't like being derailed, *Civilization* was admittedly stalled for the moment, and *Covert Action* was close to being done, if you were willing to tolerate the repetitive story lines. So, Bruce and I set *Civ* aside, and dug in to finish our old spy prototype as quickly as we could. I wasn't embarrassed by it, but I wasn't especially passionate about it, either. Only after the game was on shelves did it strike me how I might have fixed it.

Just like in *Pirates!*, the primary gameplay feature of *Covert Action* was jumping back and forth between the overarching story and the various minigames—lock picking, code breaking, and so on. What had made *Pirates!* successful, however, was the fact that the main story line was relatively simple. With *Covert Action*, I had tried to increase the narrative complexity without sacrificing any details in the minigames. It was like two games in one, which sounds great in theory, but in practice was as distracting as switching back and forth between two different movies. After spending fifteen minutes breaking into a building, the players would emerge with only a vague memory of which clues had sent them inside to begin with. I should have simplified the minigames, or even better, cut way back on the procedurally generated stories that I was never happy with in the first place. Each half was strong on its own, but forcing them to compete dragged them both down. Combining two great games had somehow left me with zero good ones.

The notion that "one good game is better than two great games" was such a revelation that it became known in my mind as "The *Covert Action* Rule." Many of the designers I mentor now weren't even born when that game came out, so we're more likely to talk about the issue in terms of where a game's "center of gravity" is. But the lesson holds, and I've never stopped citing the truth of it to myself or others. If anything, it's grown in relevance, since back then we at least had limited computing resources to restrain us. These days, the easiest thing in the world to do is *more*, and if we're not careful we can end up with three or four games all jammed into one. Deciding what doesn't go into the game is sometimes more important than deciding what does.

Despite being an involuntary assignment, the break to work on *Covert Action* was good in the long run, because it allowed me to spend some time mulling over just what was going wrong in *Civilization*. Finally, it occurred to me to try it as a turn-based game, and just like it would have in chess or racing, that one decision changed everything. Suddenly, the player was *doing* instead of watching, anticipating instead of scrambling to figure out what had just happened. Their whole brain was engaged, rather than just the tips of their fingers.

Other changes quickly followed. There was something magical, I realized, about starting from nothing. Even an empty map is still a map, full of mountains, rivers, and predetermined expectations of what the player can or can't do. But a hidden map—a single settler dropped into the wilderness, able to see nothing but the nine squares surrounding them—was quietly grand. It allowed the player to imagine a seemingly infinite set of possibilities in the blackness beyond. There might be treasure just one square over, or an enemy lurking perilously nearby, and that uncertainty made the urge to start exploring both intense and immediate.

What's more, if this was (as I now understood) a game about personal decision-making rather than the uncontrollable march of time, then the first step shouldn't be zoning a theoretical city.

It should be *establishing* one: declaring your place in the world and your intent to rule it. Symbolically, it felt like the difference between signing a deed for a distant frontier versus driving a flag into the dirt with your own callused, sweaty hands. The player should plant their first city right where they stood, I decided, or close enough to it, and it should trigger a suitably commemorative, full-screen animation. *Rome founded: 4000 BC.* Never mind the covered wagons and simple yurts—this is Rome, capital city of a mighty civilization, and it will be glorious. To this day, when I play *Civilization*, I almost always choose the Romans.

The question of who else to include, however, was a tricky one. From a practical standpoint, I could store data for only about fourteen civilizations. (I really would have preferred sixteen, because the nature of binary code makes 2^4 much more satisfying than $[2^3 + 6]$, but computers are notoriously indifferent to such feelings.) The geopolitical landscape in 1990 encompassed nearly two hundred countries, and that wasn't even counting all the great historical civilizations that didn't exist anymore. Obviously it made sense to skip the most obscure ones, but that still left a lot of mid-tier rivals: who was to say whether samurai or Vikings would be more compelling for the player?

Meanwhile, there was at least one major entity on the world stage that should have been a given, but I hesitated to commit due to historical baggage—namely, our sometime nemesis Germany, which had finally allowed the last of my banned games, *F-15 Strike Eagle,* back onto its shelves barely one year earlier. I knew I wanted each civilization to have its most iconic ruler at the helm, but German law prohibited any media that mentioned Hitler by name, regardless of context, and it felt wrong in any case to create a game where he could potentially come off as the good guy. On the other hand, leaving the Germans out felt like a blend of cowardice and censorship—and for all I knew, the BPjM would still ban *Civiliza-*

tion even without the presence of their former Führer. But again, this was Hitler. I didn't want anyone using my game to celebrate him. (It's worth noting that Chairman Mao and Stalin both went into the game without any doubt on my part or comment from others. The rules about what was acceptable didn't always make a lot of sense.)

I struggled over the inclusion of the Germans right up until the end of development, before finally putting them back in under the leadership of Frederick the Great. We'd probably all know a lot more about poor Frederick if Germany didn't dominate the history books in other ways: he had one of the longest reigns of his era, and won several wars despite tactical disadvantages. He was a generous patron of the arts, instituted freedom of the press, and encouraged the lower classes to become judges and government officials. It's not his fault someone else stole the spotlight through notoriety instead of the traditional qualities of leadership. At any rate, the Germans' reinstatement came so late in the process that our first run of manuals still referred to their former placeholder, the Turks, and we had to include a note in each box explaining the discrepancy.

In the meantime, however, there were plenty of non-controversial game elements that needed my attention. Some strategy games focused on military battles and maneuvering, while others prioritized resource gathering and economic strength—but I wanted both. Players should be able to engage their troops over a piece of land precisely because it contained valuable resources, I thought, while simultaneously developing technologies to use those resources in increasingly advanced ways. This was supposed to be a game about the entire history of civilization, and I wanted the player to control everything a real world leader did.

Likewise, it was common for games to set rules for governing cities, but in reality there were a number of political systems to choose from—or even switch between. History revealed a reasonably clear progression through anarchy, despotism, monarchy, communism, republic, and finally democracy, but that path was rarely stable. War or mismanagement could easily knock a population back a few steps, and even forward progress often brought a period of transitional chaos.

All of these factors went into the game. To advance from despotism to monarchy, for example, the player had to first develop the concept, or "technology" of monarchy (which itself could lead to feudalism, and then chivalry, which enabled the player's military units to upgrade to knights). Then they had to stage a revolution, and suffer through a turn of anarchy before officially ascending the throne. As governments modernized, however, so did their constraints. Things like martial law—i.e., calming a discontent citizenry by stationing military units inside your own cities—shouldn't be available, I decided, to rulers who had advanced beyond communism. Keep the people happy, or you'll find yourself forced to regress your society in order to retain control at all.

It was an admittedly simplified understanding of political history, but that was intentional. Unlike our military games, which relied on technical manuals like the *Jane's Fighting Aircraft* series, research for *Civilization* tended to come from more generalized history books, some even aimed at children. I wanted to simulate the overall experience of building an empire without getting bogged down in the specifics of how existing empires had done it. It didn't matter, for example, that gunpowder was originally developed for medicinal purposes in China—what mattered is that you, as a civilization, *could have* discovered it any time after the perfection of iron smelting. You were rewriting history, not reliving it.

Besides, "simplified" was already proving to be complicated enough. The more elements I added, the more I had to acknowledge the overlapping nature of their prerequisites. Astronomy (for improved navigation) grew out of mysticism (increased content-ment for your populace), but it also required mathematics, which could separately provide catapults to the military without any help from mysticism. I began laying out the various cultural advance-ments into a complicated flowchart I dubbed the "tech tree." No branch of it could be neglected forever, but players should be able to decide whether mapmaking or ironworking was a higher prior-ity for them, perhaps based on whether their first city was estab-lished closer to a coastline or a mineral deposit. More choices meant more personal investment in the outcome, and more rea-sons to try again for a successful one.

In fact, I realized, the definition of success itself should be per-sonal. Just like in *Pirates!*, where the player could choose to ter-rorize the seas, hone their fencing skills, or win the heart of every governor's daughter in the New World, the ruler of a great civi-lization didn't necessarily have to dominate through brute mili-tary strength. A rich nation could outspend its enemies; a scientific one could defeat them with superior technology; a highly artistic one could siphon immigrants their way through desirable lifestyle alone. Victory conditions in *Civ* would require a complicated algo-rithm that weighed all of these factors and more, and I couldn't wait to program it.

Right as I was gaining momentum, however, the executive team began pushing in a completely new direction. Bill, especially, was taken with the idea of expanding into coin-operated arcade games. I had a fair amount of nostalgia for the genre myself—he and I had started our business over an arcade experience, after all. But for me, it didn't extend past nostalgia. Arcades had been falling in popularity for years, and the cost to manufacture the entire cabi-net would be significant. In the home computer market, we let the players buy their own hardware.

Besides, I pointed out, even if we could afford to jump into a new format, the games I wanted to make weren't suited to quick head-to-head challenges. Bill assured me that the new venture wouldn't replace our existing goals, but I knew that many of the executives still saw the success of *Railroad Tycoon* and *Pirates!* as an anomaly. They had even canceled a sequel to *Railroad Tycoon* that Bruce and I had been outlining while I pondered *Civ* in the back of my mind. To them, strategy titles were something they indulgently let me get away with, not a viable business model.

Bill was adamant that the arcade market was poised to make a comeback, and I felt that it was a mistake. Over the course of several conversations, it became clear that neither one of us was going to convince the other, and it wasn't the sort of thing that could be compromised on. We couldn't make half an arcade game.

I didn't like this new direction for the company, but I also recognized that business decisions can't be made by committee. One person needed to be at the helm, and I still didn't want it to be me. Bill and I agreed that the best option was for him to buy out my half of the company, giving him the freedom to steer while protecting me from risky maneuvers. Outwardly nothing would change, and no one beyond the executive team would know about the arrangement for years to come. I still sat in the same chair, attended the same meetings, collaborated with the same folks. But on paper, I became an independent contractor, receiving payment and royalties only for the games I personally created.

It was the right time for everyone involved, because while I no longer had a vote in company projects, no one else had a vote in what I worked on, either. I had been afraid—rightly so, as it would turn out—that the executives would not recognize the potential in *Civilization*, and now I, too, had the freedom to steer without fear of getting canceled. It was a little sad to see the end of the partnership that had built MicroProse, but neither one of us wanted me to leave, and this seemed like the best way to address both of our needs. Bill and I had always worked well together precisely because we were opposites, and it was probably inevitable that we would end up pursuing different paths in the long run. Creatively we'd been drifting apart ever since *Pirates!*, and this new arrangement was not so much a dramatic change as it was an overdue acknowledgement of reality. But from my perspective, there was no bitterness; it was just the natural progression of our careers.

Unlike me, Bruce still had official assignments within the company, so he and I settled into a routine of concentrated feedback. Before I went home each night, I would leave a disk on his office chair with the latest version of the game. When he came in early the next morning, he would spend some time testing out new features, then sit down and share his thoughts with me when I arrived. I would go work on the game all day while he kept up with his own responsibilities, and that evening, the process would begin again.

Eventually, Bruce migrated to *Civ* full-time, and word got out that this new project was something serious. Folks began dropping by Bruce's office to check it out, which I didn't mind, but for a long time he was the only one allowed to play it. Aside from his skill in looking past broken and nonexistent parts of the game, Bruce also didn't suffer from excessive deference. With the release of *Covert Action*, MicroProse had now put my name on the box three times, and people were starting to treat me differently around the office in subtle but definite ways. It made me uncomfortable, but worse than that, it was detrimental to the final product. I didn't want to spend my day convincing people that they were allowed to tell me what they hated about the game. Bruce was always polite, of course, but if something felt wrong to him, he wouldn't hesitate to tell me.

I've never been able to decide if it was a mistake to keep *Civ* isolated as long as I did. On the one hand, I do think it's better to have as many eyes as possible on a product while it's in development. You want to make a game that appeals to everyone, not just your favorite kind of player. But on the other hand, Bruce and

Sid Meier's Covert Action advertisement. © 1991 MICRO-PROSE, WWW.MICRO PROSE.COM.

I spoke each other's language so well that the process might have taken longer with others on board. He was both playtester and designer, which meant his feedback was rooted in real solutions, while I was both designer and programmer, which meant I didn't have to waste my time on a bunch of meetings with myself.

The idea of not wasting time is perhaps the most important factor in my whole career. Each new version of a game—or anything else it suits you to make—is another opportunity to take a step forward. The more iterations you can rapidly cycle through, the more precise your final product will be.

There is a well-known story about Michelangelo, who supposedly said of his famous David statue that he "simply chipped away anything that didn't look like David." There's no evidence he actually said it, and versions of the quote have been attributed to a number of other artists as well. But I think the popularity of the story reveals what most people *imagine* the creative process to be, versus what it actually is. Of course, I can't speak for every other creative person out there, but for me personally, I can't chip away at marble. I only know how to sculpt with clay.

Start with a lump. Add a bit here. Does that make it look more or less interesting? Add another bit—no, that went too far. Scrape it off.

Mistakes are a given, and the important thing is to catch as many as you can, as fast as you can. Ideally, you'll reevaluate your creation every single day, perhaps even multiple times a day, and each iteration is an opportunity not to pat yourself on the back, but to figure out where you've already gone wrong.

This is not to say that every step needs to be tiny. Efficiency is the goal, which means many iterations, but also getting as much information as possible out of each iteration. One of my big rules has always been, "double it, or cut it in half." Don't waste your time adjusting something by 5 percent, then another 5 percent, then another . . . just double it, and see if it even had the effect you thought it was going to have at all. If it went too far, now you know you're on the right track, and can drop back down accordingly. But maybe it still didn't go far enough, and you've just saved yourself a dozen iterations inching upward 5 percent at a time. Less than a month before *Civilization* was published, I cut the size of the map in half. Of course a game about the entire history of civilization has to have a large map, but it turned out that the size wasn't as important as the sense of relentless progress. With a smaller map, the game moved faster, and that in turn made the map feel more epic than it had when it was twice as big—and if I'd been afraid to deviate too severely from what we already had, I never would have gotten to the right size in time before the game shipped.

This is also why I never write design documents. Some managers are irrationally devoted to them, expecting to see the entire game laid out in descriptive text and PowerPoint slides before a single line of code is ever written. But to me, that's like drawing a map before you've visited the terrain: "I've decided there will be a mountain here." Lewis and Clark would have been laughed out of the room if they showed up with a design document. Instead, they just said, "We'll get back to you," and started walking. The mountain is where the mountain is, and your job is to find it, not insist where it should have been.

Here are some bits of clay that I thought belonged in *Civ*, but later scraped off:

First, the real-time clock. That was really more like tossing the clay in the trash and getting a new lump.

Then, I toyed briefly with the cyclical rise and fall of nations. Though historically accurate, this was like flooding the railroad bridge on a grand scale. The moment the Krakatoa volcano blew up, or the bubonic plague came marching through, all anybody wanted to do was reload from a saved game.

The branching tech tree of advancements was a pretty good idea from the start, but the actual elements of it flip-flopped all over the place for months until it felt right. For a while, there was a whole secondary tech tree of minor skills like beer brewing (obviously a source of happiness points for your population,) but we had to ditch it for being too unwieldy.

For a while, I tried to include land mines as a weapon, but I couldn't get the game's AI to place them intelligently, or to stop walking over their own mines, without dragging the processing speed to a crawl. Out they went.

There were religious leaders, and then there weren't.

There were Germans, and then there weren't—and then there were again.

The point is, there are bad things in my games, at least until I manage to pin them down, but I don't let the possibility of mistakes hold me back. I won't ponder for hours whether a feature would be a good idea, I just throw it in the game and find out for sure. If it's clunky, I cut it back out again. There is no map before you've explored the wilderness, and no overriding artistic vision on Day One. There's just the hard, consistent work of making something a little better each day, and being as efficient as possible in your discovery of what it's going to turn out to be.

12

TURNING
POINTS

Pirates! Gold (1993)

*

Sid Meier's
Railroad Tycoon Deluxe (1993)

THAT CHRISTMAS, WE TOOK A
trip with my parents and siblings to a ski resort in Massanutten,
Virginia. Ryan was seven months old, so his snow activities were
limited, but he got to experience the baby version of a ski lift as
he was passed joyfully from family member to family member. It
was interesting to see how my two younger siblings interacted with
him, since they were now roughly the same age as I'd been when
they were born.

My sister, Vicky, had arrived during my sophomore year of high
school, after my parents evidently got a second wind. Then my
brother, Bruce, came along a year before I graduated. (Though
relatively rare today, the name peaked in popularity just as my
coworker Bruce Shelley was born in the late forties, and remained
in the top 100 until several years after my brother was born in the
early seventies, resulting in the odd bit of trivia that the first two
people ever to play *Civilization* were both named Bruce.)

Like most teenagers, I was very wrapped up in my own interests, which, while diverse, did not include babies. They were too young to be siblings in the traditional sense, but I wasn't comfortable with any kind of paternalistic role. No one who looked at fifteen-year-old Sid Meier would peg him as the "cool uncle" type. We grew closer once they matured into real people with personalities, of course, but in the beginning, it felt more like my parents had taken up some weird new hobby. I'd help my mother with the little ones if she asked, but in general, I looked at it as something she had signed up for, not me.

I did find my tiny roommates intriguing to examine from a distance, though, and even signed up for a child psychology course my freshman year of college. All things being equal, I would have preferred another math class, but there were token liberal arts requirements to satisfy, and I figured that Bruce and Vicky might give me an advantage over the other students. Not only was my exposure to young children probably more recent than everyone else's, but if any research needed to be done, I had a captive pair of test subjects.

Sure enough, our final term paper was open topic, and I was ready with a slam dunk. Somewhere in the assigned reading there had been a section on the made-up languages between preverbal siblings, and I thought it would be noteworthy to document one of these unique communication patterns in the real world. With my superior grasp of data analysis, and the only real-life guinea pigs in the class, I was pretty sure I was about to do the Developmental Studies equivalent of a mic drop.

So I went home one weekend, and slipped a tape recorder into the room my brother and sister shared, ready to capture whatever mysterious words they babbled to each other before falling asleep each night. It was a low-stress and low-priority project for me, as far as college assignments went, so it wasn't until a few days later that I finally got around to listening to my tape.

It was, effectively, silent. Turns out my siblings did not have a secret made-up language, or any language at all, save for a few grunts and snores. And it was far too late to change topics now. So instead, the paper became an exercise in creative writing, forcing me to pull a compelling, fact-based narrative out of thin air—which, in the long run, was probably more useful to my career than anything else the class could have taught me anyway.

Besides Vicky, I did have one sister my own age, but she passed away when I was young. We were fairly close, and I have many memories from before she got sick, but the years surrounding Dorothy's death are, sadly, a bit of a blur.

I can remember my mother leaving me home alone in the evenings while she visited my sister in the hospital. I remember the quarter she'd give me each night to buy a bag of chips across the street, and watching the old sitcom *My Mother the Car* while I waited for her return. I remember getting only vague answers, but understanding enough to know that Dorothy wouldn't be coming home with her any time soon.

I don't remember how many years her illness dragged on, but I do remember that when my parents flew to Switzerland to retrieve me from my grandparents' house, part of the trip involved a detour to Germany, where they visited a clinic that promised some kind of last-resort treatment that American doctors wouldn't or couldn't provide.

I remember the large swelling on the side of her neck. I remember learning later that her disease was called Hodgkin's lymphoma, and that it is now mostly curable.

I remember walking to school alone.

I remember visiting her gravesite with my father, flowers in hand. And I remember considering for the first time, many decades later, that my trip to Switzerland may have served at least partially to shield me from what was going on at home, and that lengthening the stay might not have been entirely, 100 percent my idea.

It seems impossible to think that the experience had no lasting effects on me, but I've successfully blocked most of it from memory. Certainly everything must have been harder on my parents. As a parent now myself, I had a new understanding of their emotional reality—and yet somehow, I never worried about losing Ryan.

The day after he was born, something large and metal had fallen outside our hospital room with a horrendous crash. I jumped in surprise, as did Gigi and her parents. Babies up and down the hall began crying, but not Ryan. He glanced up curiously, then kept right on with whatever important baby thing he had been doing before the interruption. I'm not sure why, but at the time it seemed significant: an indicator of the boy, and eventually the man, to come. Ryan was calm and sensible, a rock that could withstand any storm. From that moment on, I just kind of decided he was indestructible.

So far, he was living up to the hype. Some babies would have fussed at all the disruption and over-stimulation of a big family holiday, but little seven-month-old Ryan was still at peace with whatever came his way.

As usual, I had brought my computer with me to Massanutten, as well as the latest version of *Civilization*. I casually showed the prototype to my family, knowing that Bruce especially would be interested in trying it out. He had worked as a playtester at Micro-Prose during his last three summers in high school, living in our spare bedroom in Baltimore while he earned his place in the *Crusade in Europe*, *Gunship*, and *Pirates!* credits. But since going off to college, he'd been too busy to spend summers in Maryland, and possibly even too busy to play games at all. He was overdue for some fun.

Bruce started playing, commenting helpfully on this or that feature, until at some point I got called away to the living room. Eventually, someone asked where he was.

"Oh," I said, looking around. "I think he's still in the back, playing *Civilization*."

I glanced at my watch. Six hours had gone by.

Up to that point, I knew the game was special only in the same way that I knew all my games were special—including the ones that had been disappointing in certain ways. No child is perfect, and you love them all anyway. Even now, with some games labeled as my legacy and others all but forgotten, each one holds an equal place in my own heart. You don't stop inviting half your kids to Thanksgiving just because the other half become celebrities.

But when my brother disappeared for most of a day into a barely playable prototype, that got my attention. What made him stick with it? Where did the momentum come from? The game wasn't terribly complex yet, just a few simple systems tossed together into one space, yet he'd apparently been conquering and surrendering the terrain over and over, just rearranging and exploring those same basic parameters.

My brother's interaction with the game would end up illustrating one of the most important features of *Civ*, that "simple plus simple equals complex." Agriculture generated food at a predictable pace. Military units fought for just one turn, and instantly one side or the other was declared the victor. Most of the game didn't even use numbers, it was all barter and equivalence—fill up your "shield" bucket, and you got another spearman; spend enough turns learning the skill of pottery, and you could exchange it with a neighbor for bronze working. Like chess, each piece's function was easily understood, and only after you began looking at moves in combination did the really interesting paths emerge.

This sense of aggregated simplicity had clear roots in the expansion and economic systems in *Railroad Tycoon*. Meanwhile, *Pirates!* had informed the need for balance. Which was the stronger chess piece, the rook or the bishop? Well, it depended on the layout of the board. Maybe in this round diplomacy was best, but under other circumstances the only way out was war. As always, I refused to declare one choice superior, because it was the player's story, not mine. Considered in this light, *Civilization* seemed less like a stroke of genius and more like a logical progression that I'd been building up to for years. Without its older siblings to lay the

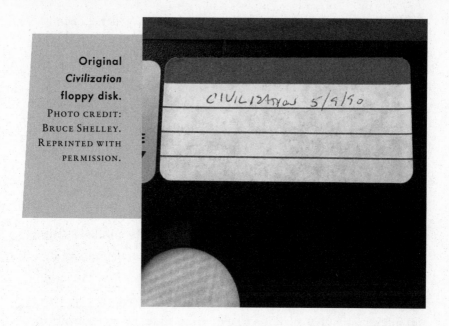

CIVILIZATION 5/9/90

groundwork, I'd venture to say the game never could have been made at all.

Bruce Shelley, on the other hand, did not feel the same loving equivocation that I did about our various projects. He says he always knew *Civ* was unique, from the moment he played the first prototype. He even saved the original disc, partly because he regretted having no mementos from *Railroad Tycoon*, but also because he was sure it was destined to be "another Sid masterpiece," as he puts it. I guess that's one more reason Bruce's input was so valuable: he was always better at predicting a game's popularity than I was. To me, public reaction is something I have limited control over, so it would be foolish to bend over backwards for it, let alone stake my self-worth on it. Consequently, I'm not as impressed with myself as others sometimes insist I should be—but I also don't feel too badly if a game doesn't sell well. As long as I'm proud of my work, then it's a success.

In any case, my intrepid codesigner turned out to be right. Once I finally allowed the game to spread beyond people named Bruce, the excitement among the other developers was fierce. Many would stay after-hours playing the prototype for fun, and random coworkers began coming into my office with feedback. What if you could establish caravans to improve your trade routes? What if pollution was a factor you had to deal with as your cities grew? What if certain settlers could be assigned jobs like taxman, scientist, or entertainer? What if building one of the Seven Wonders of the World gave you special abilities? What if there were more than seven of them? What if aqueducts prevented fires, granaries prevented famine, city walls prevented floods? What if lighthouses increased your navy's speed, but suddenly became obsolete after the development of magnetism? It seemed almost compulsive, for both them and me. The more they played *Civilization*, the more ideas they all had, and every idea brought with it dozens of potential interactions that I couldn't help but include. Every element of the game was connected, and every cool new suggestion spider-webbed out into days (and nights, and weekends) of code changes. Eventually, I had to close my door and enlist Bruce as my gatekeeper, just so I could get any work done at all.

Even then, however, I wasn't convinced the world at large would share our enthusiasm. My projects had been straying farther off the beaten path each time, and I was occasionally referred to in the press as a "designer's designer," implying that my games possessed a deeper brilliance that could only be appreciated by the connoisseur. I wasn't sure it was an accurate characterization, but it did hold up in the sense that (1) I was a designer, and (2) I made games that I personally wanted to play. It didn't bother me that strategy remained a dirty word in the industry—casual, non-threatening things like "adventures" and "action" were okay, but everyone knew only nerds were into strategy. Conventional wisdom said you could make a specialized product for the hardcore audience, and it might turn a profit if you kept development costs down, but a strategy title would never make the big money. I loved

Civilization, and my coworkers loved *Civilization*, but if the game had been a massive flop with everyone else, I wouldn't have been shocked in the slightest.

Of course, it wasn't.

MicroProse hadn't put a big marketing push behind it, so like most of my recent games, it started as a slow burn. Ironically, the game still seemed to appeal mostly to game designers, it was just that *Civilization* brought out the inner game designer in everyone. When the first fan letters trickled in a few weeks after the game's release, they had a decidedly different tone than we were used to.

"Dear Sid," an old letter used to begin. "I played your game *Sid Meier's Pirates!,* and I thought it was really good. The land battles were dumb, though. Sincerely, Your #1 Fan."

No hard feelings; everyone has an opinion. We rarely got a letter that didn't include some kind of criticism buried in the praise, and usually they ripped the Band-Aid off pretty quickly. But not with *Civ.*

"Dear Sid," the fans would write. "I played your game *Sid Meier's Civilization,* and I thought it was really good. I'm curious why you chose to start the Aztec civilization with bronze working when they're obviously more well known for their pottery. Also, it would make sense for the trade caravans to move a little faster as your cities grew, and if you could set them up to run automatically, that would be even better. By the way, I've figured out a strategy that's guaranteed to beat the game every time, using only chariots. Here's how it works . . ."

In short, we had stamped our game with the tagline "It's good to be King," and they had agreed.

Some of the letters were several pages long, and included phone numbers in the hopes that we could discuss things in greater depth. Many asked for a job at MicroProse so they could personally implement their improvements. Rather than being discouraged, I saw the critiques as a net positive, because it meant we had gotten players thinking on a deeper level. They were interacting with the game as a tool, rather than an experience. Other games offered entertainment, but somehow—and I wasn't quite sure what all the magic ingredients were yet—*Civilization* offered empowerment. Fans had enough control over the outcome that they no longer saw a boundary between the fantasy and the game itself. All of it belonged to them.

The next several months were both surreal and anticlimactic. The game went viral, or "became really, really popular," as we would have said in those days. Bill called me in jubilation on the night we won our first major award for the game, but soon we had so many that he was letting news of the latest accolades wait until the following Monday, or maybe Tuesday if there were too many meetings. Meanwhile, I started to get a kind of publicity I'd never had to deal with before. Interviewers asked the same questions over and over, most of which I had no concise answers for. I couldn't explain in a single sentence where I'd gotten the idea for the game, or what made the mechanics so addicting. I was grateful, I was honored, and I would never complain about being so fortunate—but I wasn't very used to it yet. Just four years earlier, Tom Clancy had warned me of the pitfalls that can come with fame, and I tried very hard to keep his advice in mind as I blindly navigated the terrain myself.

I think I did okay. As time went on, I got better at knowing what to say, but also further removed from the experiences I was supposed to be talking about. New fans were discovering the game every day, but for me it was slipping into the past, becoming that game I made six months ago, a year ago, two years ago. I had poured everything I had into *Civilization*, and I was honestly ready to think about something else for a while.

I lent a helping hand on a few projects around the office, talking other programmers through the kinks in their code or giving advice on the latest flight simulator when asked. I put my stamp of approval on the re-releases of *Pirates! Gold* and *Railroad Tycoon Deluxe*. I fiddled around with my ongoing collection of half-working prototypes. I took some time off.

But mostly, I just struggled to find a path forward, and quietly worried about how long a state of burnout could persist before it became permanent.*

* **Achievement Unlocked:** Midlife Crisis—Whoa, we're halfway there.

13

IF IT AIN'T
BAROQUE

"WHAT'S SID GOING TO DO NEXT?"

For the first time, this question wasn't just being asked by my bosses and occasional coworkers. Fans and journalists—even those who didn't generally cover games, and had never heard of me before that year—were clamoring for news, and speculating wildly in the absence of any. There were rumors of a sequel set in outer space, and a Civil War prototype, and a phone book's worth of industries with the word "tycoon" tacked onto the end. Some of the letters about *Civ* took time to offer tips for these fictional titles as well, while others simply begged to be let in on the secret.

None of them wanted to know as much as I did.

How do you top the thing that critics were calling "more addictive than crack," and "as perfectly executed as any simulation we've seen?" How many Game of the Year awards can you receive before you start to worry that you'll never be this good again?

It wasn't hard to see that madness lay in that direction. I couldn't let myself get caught in a cycle of always trying to outdo my last game, or I would lose whatever sliver of sanity I still retained after such an exhausting, complicated endeavor. It wouldn't even be enough for me to step outside the strategy genre, I realized. I had to do something that no one could possibly compare to *Civ*, including myself.

Normally I would have looked to my own interests for inspiration, but *Railroad Tycoon* had taught me that even a casual diversion might turn into a serious title when I wasn't looking. When all you have is a joystick, the whole world looks like a game. Every potential project had this dangerous mental tug-of-war looming over it, and in the end, I could only come up with one topic that I was sure I could never turn into a strategy game.

I'd been interested in music since I was very young, which is probably no surprise given my love for mathematics. The neurological connection is well-documented, and many math geniuses throughout history have also been virtuosos on at least one instrument. I don't claim to be either of those things, but perhaps it's fair to say that "math genius" is to "virtuoso" as "math enthusiast" is to "basement band keyboardist." The piano entered my life relatively late, though. My first instrument was the violin.

Along with his artistic outlets in woodworking and painting, my father was very musically inclined. I can recall him playing guitar, violin, ukulele, harmonica, and recorder around the house, and it's possible he knew how to play other instruments that we didn't happen to have on the premises. Music lessons seemed like a logical choice for his children, but our family didn't own a car at that time, so extracurricular activities had to be on a bus line or within walking distance. We had a supermarket, a drug store, a Kentucky Fried Chicken, and a camera specialty shop all within a few blocks of our urban Detroit duplex, but unfortunately, no music school.

Then, a few years after moving to the neighborhood, my mother happened to meet a Bulgarian immigrant named Luben Haladjoff, who taught orchestra at a local high school and lived just down the street from us. He didn't take many private students, but she convinced him to see Dorothy and me at his house once a week for violin lessons. It was mostly a coincidence that this was also one of my father's instruments—had Mr. Haladjoff been trained as a trumpeter, no doubt that's what we would have learned instead. At just five and six years old, we were a rarity among his students, and at one point Mr. Haladjoff even arranged for us to be guest performers during the high school's formal concert. Unfortunately, something happened in the middle of the piece that caused us to get out of sync with the older kids, and the rest of the song was a disaster. We were not invited back.

My enthusiasm for the lessons was minimal at first, though I acquiesced politely enough—my mother was determined to inject some culture into our lives, and I knew that if it weren't this it would be something else. But over time, I grew to love playing the violin. Our concert bookings temporarily stalled after the debacle at Mr. Haladjoff's school, but my sister and I would perform duets for our parents and their friends, and after a few years I joined a small community orchestra. Eventually, Mr. Haladjoff suggested I should audition for the Youth Orchestra, a program run by the Detroit Symphony to groom future performers.

The piece I prepared was *Concerto for Two Violins in D Minor* by Johann Sebastian Bach, and with it began one of the longest-lasting obsessions of my life. The "Double Concerto," as it's commonly known, was a step up from anything else I'd ever played, and I was entranced with its beauty. More than anything else, I was fascinated by the way in which Bach's music seemed simultaneously surprising and inevitable. There was clearly a secret, and I wanted to understand it.

Around that same time, I found a music theory textbook in our house called *Harmony*. It was written by a Harvard professor (and celebrated composer, though I didn't know it at the time) named Walter Piston, and had appeared on the bookshelf as part of a collection that a family friend had been disposing of. I'm not sure my father even read the titles before rescuing them; he believed in the inherent value of books no matter what the subject was.

Piston's *Harmony* was a revelation. Suddenly my two worlds

became one, as page after page explained how music could be understood mathematically. Of course I had understood early on that rhythms are fractional parts of a whole, but *Harmony* taught me that pleasing chord combinations were as easy to calculate as ratios. Concepts were illustrated with real examples from eighteenth- and nineteenth-century composers, including many from Bach, and I was happy to see that my instincts about him had been correct. Bach's harmonies were some of the most effective in all of music.

The violin, however, is not a chord-based instrument. It's possible to play two-note combinations across multiple strings, or to progress quickly from one pair to another up a chain of notes, but to play three notes precisely at once requires too much pressure to sound very pleasing, and many of Piston's examples used four or more. So in order to try out the principles I was learning, I bought an electric Wurlitzer piano from a friend at school. The $200 price tag was hefty for a teenager, but as with my first Atari computer, I tended to save my money for the important things.

Between the *Harmony* textbook and my existing knowledge of violin music, I taught myself how to play the piano pretty well over the next few years. I even managed to fit the Wurlitzer into my dorm room at the University of Michigan, though the thin walls prevented me from playing as much as I'd have liked. Shortly after that, my studies became filled with circuit boards and punch cards, and my musical tastes skewed decidedly modern as well. In the same way that I took coding very seriously, but used it to create entertainment, my obsession with understanding Bach's brilliance deepened, even as I directed that knowledge toward the wonderful new world of polyphonic synthesizers.

A few months before graduation, I traded in the Wurlitzer for a Polymoog. Used by everyone from ABBA to The Moody Blues, the Polymoog analog synthesizer came with a pitch controller ribbon, three-band equalizer, self-oscillation, and independent volume control for different sections of the keyboard. Most importantly, it featured a "variation" function that allowed the musician to hand-modify its eight preset voices into almost any sound imaginable. It wasn't just a way to make beautiful music; it was a way to create entirely new forms of music that had never existed before. Learning this system would one day help me program audio on the Atari POKEY and Commodore 64 SID chips, but for now, I put it to the more traditional use of rocking out with my new coworkers, Andy Hollis and Grant Irani.

A few months after I started hanging out with the basement band, Andy approached me with an offer to join his other, professional, band. They called themselves Fragile, and played a variety of popular cover tunes for nightclubs, weddings, and the occasional bar mitzvah. They even had a recurring gig at the local Moose Lodge, one of those charitable fraternal organizations. Armed with a cheat sheet of chords for "Celebration" and about twenty other radio hits, I technically became a professional musician only a few months after becoming a professional programmer, though of course one paid considerably better than the other.

After the band split up, I had rechanneled my musical interest into composing game soundtracks for several years, until sound design was politely pried from my hands—rightly so, like I said before, but still, I missed it. Now, as I cast about helplessly looking for a game that wasn't a game, music emerged once again to offer safe harbor.

The thing that makes Bach's work so extraordinary is the degree to which it manages to be both predictable and stunning, like the pattern of a snowflake. He routinely used something called invertible counterpoint, in which the notes are designed to be reversible for an entirely new, but still enjoyable, sound. He also had a fondness for puzzle canons, in which he would write alternating lines of music and leave the others blank for his students—often his own children—to figure out what most logically belonged in between.

Bach even went so far as to hide codes in many of his works.

Substituting place values for letters creates a numeric total of 14 for his last name, and this number is repeatedly embedded in the patterns of his pieces, as is its reverse, 41, which happens to be the value of his last name plus his first two initials. His magnum opus, *The Art of the Fugue*, plays the letters of his name in the notes themselves (in German notation, the letter B refers to the note we call B-flat, and H is used for B-natural). At the top of one famous piece, *The Well-Tempered Clavier*, he drew a strange, looping flourish that scholars now believe is a coded set of instructions for how to tune the piano to play in every possible key, opening up new possibilities for variation and modulation.

Today, we recognize these and many other signs of genius, but when he died, Bach was not especially revered. He spent the last twenty-seven years of his life as the cantor at St. Thomas Church in Leipzig, composing music for weekly services attended by only a few hundred parishioners. His handwritten originals were worth something as music, but only at prices comparable to any church cantor of the era, and unfortunately, his descendants were more often in need of money than legacy.

Bach's widow, Anna Magdalena, still had a number of younger children to care for, so after his death she traded her portion of her husband's music back to St. Thomas Church, in exchange for an extra six months in the cantor's residence. The church made formal copies for republishing, so most of the songs themselves survive, but they had no particular use for the originals, and eventually began selling them as scrap paper to wrap fish and other market goods in.

Another collection of Bach's music went to his adult son, Carl Philipp Emanuel, who was already one of the most respected performers of his day—much more so than his father, at the time. C. P. E. Bach, as he was known, was personal chamber musician to Frederick the Great, and his work was praised by no less than Mozart, Beethoven, and Haydn. He had the financial stability to protect what he was given, and the wisdom to recognize his father's greatness when no one else did. Nearly all of the pages bequeathed to C. P. E. Bach are held in museums today.

The final stack of compositions, however, went to Bach's eldest and least reputable son. Like his brother, Wilhelm Friedemann Bach was a talented musician, and he taught many pupils who would go on to be famous composers in their own right. But a string of conflicts with his employers and alleged problems with alcohol left him perpetually in debt and on the move. Some of his inheritance was sold for cash, while other pieces were lost, accidentally destroyed, or even given away to his students. No one knows exactly how many he disposed of, but Bach's obituary referred to five seasonal cycles at St. Thomas Church, which would imply a total of four hundred cantatas composed during his tenure. Only about two hundred of them survive today. Meanwhile, other records indicate the existence of several masses, concertos, fugues, and other works that have never been found.

When I learned this bit of history, I was genuinely devastated. Hundreds of musical pieces from the greatest Baroque composer in all of Europe, gone forever. Just imagining what the seventh Brandenburg Concerto might have sounded like, and knowing we would never hear it, was deeply painful.

It's a little hard to explain why I find Bach's music to be so transcendent. The sense I get when I listen to his work is that he's not telling me his story, but humanity's story. He's sharing the joys and sorrows of his life in a more universal sense, a language that doesn't require me to understand the specifics of his situation. I can read a book from eighteenth-century Germany, and find some amount of empathy with the historical figures inside, but there will always be a forced translation of culture, society, and a thousand other details that I can never truly understand. Bach isn't bogged down in those things—he's cutting straight to the heart of what we already have in common. He can reach across three hundred years and make me, a man who manipulates electromagnetic circuits with my fingertips on a keyboard, feel just as profoundly as he made an impoverished farmer feel during a traditional rural celebration. He includes me in the story, just as I wanted to include my players in my games; we make the story together. Bach's music is a perfect illustration of the idea that it's not the artist that matters, but the connection between us.

I couldn't bring back Bach. But what if I could harness artificial intelligence to generate more music like his, calculating harmonies and rhythms and contrapuntal phrases with the same ruleset that he would have followed? If he could create a puzzle canon with only one right answer, then so could a computer.

This was, admittedly, dangerous territory. People take it personally when you suggest computers can create art, let alone art that rivals our best. They see it as a reduction of humanity, rather than an elevation of technology. But Garry Kasparov didn't cease to be a human the day the Deep Blue* computer beat him at chess, and the beauty of Bach's work wouldn't diminish even if I did manage to mimic his style.

Besides, I think time has proven that the "humans are special" folks don't have much to worry about. We've made so much progress in the confluence of art and technology over the last twenty-five years, and yet are still so far from completion. Every time we solve a problem like chess, we find three more impossibly fuzzy and human-dependent problems like humor, love, or running on two feet without falling over. So, I don't think we're in any danger of making either art or humanity obsolete. In fact, I'd say that creating a computer that creates art counts as a form of artistic expression itself. It's participation, not hubris. Regardless of whether my musical experiments were successful, or even passable, nothing could be more human than the act of trying in the first place.

Plus, it was about as orthogonal to *Civ* as I could get.

I started with the fugue, since it was one of the more rigid for-

* *Achievement Unlocked:* Watson's Pals—*Discuss Deep Blue and Sherlock Holmes.*

mats that Bach wrote in. Like a sonnet in poetry, there are rules to what a fugue is, no matter who's composing. It gave me a good benchmark to see how close I was getting, first to a fugue at all, and then hopefully to a Bach fugue.

I enlisted my coworker Jeff Briggs for advice. He had been hired at MicroProse as a composer—the third member of our growing sound department—for a game called *Sword of the Samurai*. ("Like *Pirates!*, but with samurai.") But he also had a background in board game design, and functioned as a kind of everyman on a number of projects. He did playtesting and documentation for several games, including *F-15 Strike Eagle II*, and was a project leader on various ports of *Pirates!* and *F-19 Stealth Fighter*. He wrote music for *Railroad Tycoon* and *Covert Action*, among others, and most recently he had worked with me on *Civ*, composing music and contributing to the massive Civilopedia reference tool that Bruce had started.

While I may have read Walter Piston's textbook, Jeff could have written a version himself. He helped me break down the obvious rules, the secret rules, and the broken rules of Bach's music. We talked about what made him unique and stylistically recognizable from other composers, and I resisted Jeff's attempts to convince me that some of those other composers might, in their own way, be as talented as Bach himself. Maybe that was true, I thought, but I wasn't interested in anyone else's music.

Jeff also helped me file the patent for the game's algorithm, which stretched to 12,000 words by the time the lawyers were done with it. The idea of a computer generating music was certainly not new—our patent referenced fifteen similar claims, as well as technical books from as far back as 1956, and was subsequently mentioned by 117 others, the most recent from Yamaha in 2016. But the way in which we did it was different enough that we felt it might be a nice thing to commemorate. We included a dense, three-page flowchart explaining the program's logic tree, and outlined major acceptance rules, like "Leaps of more than a fifth are always followed by a step back" and "A step followed by a leap in the same direction, if the first note is a sixteenth note, is prohibited." I also programmed statistical tendencies that would discourage things like dissonance, but not prohibit them entirely—in other words, rules on how and when to break the rules, just like Bach did.

I named my creation *C.P.U. Bach*, as a portmanteau of his most responsible son and the central processing unit of a computer. The melodies might not have been inspired by numerology or emotions, but it worked well enough to convince a layperson. Even a Cornell University music professor acknowledged that it was, at least on occasion, "uncannily plausible." MicroProse agreed to publish it, though I'm not entirely sure why. Mostly, I think I was being given a free pass, since I had just made them a whole ton of money with *Civilization*. And hey, they hadn't thought that game would be a big success either, so who knew? Maybe I was about to prove them all wrong again.

I wasn't.

The obscure subject matter and minimal interactivity definitely played a role, but those weren't the only reasons *C.P.U. Bach* was a commercial failure. The other major pitfall was the console we chose for the game's release, a new machine called the 3DO.

For the most part, the 3DO was simply ahead of its time. The early 90s were full of technological optimism, fueled by the upcoming turn of the millennium—everyone just knew that once the years had twos in front of them, we'd be living in a science fiction paradise. Things like virtual reality and internet connectivity were barely in their infancy, but advertisements and news profiles promised us that they would completely infiltrate our lives any day now. What had previously been thought of as merely inevitable suddenly seemed imminent, and everyone agreed that a comprehensive media center was at the top of the innovation list. Music, movies, games, telephone calls, and more would come from a single, universal box—along with a propeller function to blow everyone's hair back, if you believed the ads.

Electronic Arts founder Trip Hawkins strongly supported this noun-not-adjective dream of "a multiplayer," and when the EA board was hesitant to enter the hardware market, he stepped down to pursue it on his own. Supposedly, he chose the machine's name as a reference to the new rhyming triumvirate of media: audio, video, and "3D-o." It would serve all your needs, and replace all your devices, with better graphics than your PC, and better speakers than your stereo. The 3DO wouldn't even play common floppy disks, only CD-ROMs, a move which prodded developers to either take advantage of its cinematic capabilities, or else waste 99 percent of their disk space.

Like *C.P.U. Bach*, a number of factors contributed to the 3DO's ultimate failure in the market, including a high price tag, inconsistent manufacturing quality, and a lack of support from game developers. Without games, even the greatest console in the world can't amount to anything. But all of this was only evident in hindsight, and as of 1993, there was not yet any writing on the wall. The only thing everyone agreed on was the size of the 3DO's impact, which one stock analyst described to the *New York Times* as "a binary event." It would either be the biggest hit, or the biggest failure, the industry had ever seen.

As usual, I tried to stay away from decisions based on money, and consider only what was best for the players. *C.P.U. Bach* was a music generator, and it didn't make sense to release it on a platform with substandard audio output, which unfortunately included the vast majority of consumer PCs. High-quality audio cards existed, but they weren't common, and I didn't want people listening to our music in eight-bit mono and thinking it was the best we could do.

All of the evidence, not to mention the heavy marketing, pointed toward the 3DO as the best choice for an artistic, media-centric project like ours. Plus, it came with an algorithm that could generate colorful, abstract visuals in time with the beat, in case users got tired of watching our little animated Bach accurately playing the harpsichord. My friend Noah Falstein, who worked for 3DO at the time, has ruefully admitted to "convincing" me to release my game with them, as has Trip Hawkins, but I don't remember getting a hard sell from anyone in particular. I went with the 3DO because it seemed like the best format for the game, and for all I know, the sales for *C.P.U. Bach* would have been the same on a different platform anyway. My only regret is that the game is essentially unplayable today, now that the physical console has become a lost relic.

But I still have a 3DO at home.

14

SEQUEL-ISH

Sid Meier's Colonization (1994)

*

Sid Meier's Civilization II (1996)

CIVILIZATION MAY HAVE LEFT ME burnt out for several years, but other designers in the building were just getting started. We'd made the world safe for strategy games, and there were plenty of ideas that we hadn't had the time or wisdom to fit into ours. Some of the best belonged to a young designer named Brian Reynolds. He had been hired for a strange project called *Rex Nebular and the Cosmic Gender Bender*, which was apparently MicroProse's answer to the *Leisure Suit Larry* franchise of adult-comedy adventure games. Though I wasn't personally involved in its development, we still have a number of gaudy red baseball caps from this game floating around the office— unlike today's cornucopia of flash drives, fidget toys, travel mugs, and reusable grocery bags, promotional merchandise back in the early nineties was almost always clothing—and we wear them for good luck when a project is going through its final testing phases. I don't know how this marketing swag from a bygone era came to be seen as lucky, but it probably has something to do with the idea that if we released that game, we can release anything.

Fortunately for everyone, Brian's heart was in the strategy genre, and now that he had his foot in the door, he was eager to

prove it. Without being asked, he created a working prototype of a game he called *Colonization*, which he pitched to the executive team as a narrower, deeper version of *Civ*. Set during the European discovery of the Americas in 1492, the game would focus less on expansion and more on resource gathering within the player's society, testing its robustness primarily through the economic challenges of the era. Any colonist could grow tobacco, for example, but a Master Tobacco Planter would do it twice as fast, especially if your colony bordered on the proper grassland. Meanwhile, a separate colonist might be trained to convert that tobacco into exportable cigars, and an Expert Farmer could grow enough to feed all three of them. Once you established a sufficient population and achieved dominance over the other colonizers, the game ended by staging an alternate version of the American Revolution,

allowing you to rebel against the king of whatever nationality you had originally chosen and secure your independence.

The corporate suits had seen the error of their ways, at least to a certain degree, and were willing to support a strategy game that might continue the recent sales numbers of *Civilization*. I think it was expected that I would help Brian on his fledgling project, maybe even taking over if it turned out he'd bitten off more than he could chew. But he didn't need it, which was fortunate, because he was flying without a net whether anyone knew it or not. I was not about to end up coding another strategy game so soon after *Civ*. I gave guidance early on, mostly of the "here's how you figure that problem out for yourself" variety, and then checked back in at the end to help him tweak a few final details, but the eighteen months in between I spent as a committed disciple of Bach.

Colonization and *C.P.U. Bach* actually released at the same time, but the last few months of my game were taken over by a programmer named Kerry Wilkinson, who did the work of converting the finished PC code onto the 3DO. Both games were on display at CES that year, but while Brian's was in its final, almost-bug-free stages, the conversion of *C.P.U. Bach* was not a gradual process. Either it was done, or it wasn't—and when the day came, it wasn't. So instead, we put a decoy 3DO on display, then hid a PC inside the cabinet underneath to actually run the program. We didn't lie about it if asked, but we hoped we wouldn't get asked too many times.

Even after I started offering more concrete direction at the end of *Colonization*, I worked very hard not to alter the spirit of the game Brian had created. I was willing, for example, to suggest cutting the radius of the cities in half—something we pulled off at the last moment, just as we had with the world map in *Civ*—because it further highlighted the job-specialization mechanics that Brian had developed. But I didn't argue against ending the game with the American Revolution, even though it was a grandiose, win-or-lose proposition with the potential to invalidate hours of successful gameplay. Generally speaking, I would never risk alienating the player to that degree. It was historically accurate, however, and Brian saw it as a satisfying boss battle rather than a last-minute bait and switch, so I deferred to him. Good games don't get made by committee.

The question of how much influence I'd really had on the game brought us to a major crossroads, both for MicroProse and the future of my career. I'm not sure if they'd planned it from the beginning, or held off until I crossed some imaginary threshold of hours spent, but at some point marketing began floating the title *Sid Meier's Colonization*.

Truthfully, my name had already gone on one game I didn't do much for, *Railroad Tycoon Deluxe*. But that had been a mostly cosmetic upgrade to my original code, and there were no new designers whose contributions were being diminished. *Colonization*, on the other hand, was not "Civilization Deluxe." It was a unique world that had drawn only loose inspiration from mine, and Brian had written every line of code—I'd made sure of it. Yes, I made suggestions along the way, but it had been up to Brian whether to accept them. *Colonization* was not Sid Meier's game.

From a marketing standpoint, though, none of that mattered. Over the course of five games and one remake, my name had somehow become a brand. My entire philosophy of gaming was that the player should be the star and the designer should be invisible, yet I was the guy who kept ending up on the box. I should clarify that no one was trying to maliciously exploit me—the marketing team's position was purely utilitarian. And I couldn't deny that selling more copies would mean a stronger company, which I did still care about even if it wasn't technically my company anymore.

Ultimately, the decision was up to me. They didn't ask, per se, but I could have put my foot down. I reached out to Brian to gauge his feeling on it, and he surprised me by being strongly in favor of putting my name on the box. After all, it was his first major venture as a lead designer, no matter what the packaging said, and if the game sold poorly he might not get to do another. Like me, Brian wasn't much concerned with accolades; he just wanted to bring his ideas to life with minimal obstruction.

I'd helped him a lot, he pointed out. He'd been in my office asking questions more times than either of us could remember. And I had to admit, there was nothing about the game that I would change—the ending might not have been to my personal taste, but it was a valid design choice, and Brian had executed it flawlessly. *Colonization* was a great product, built on all the same principles I would have built it on.

So I conceded. "Sid Meier's" now meant "Sid Meier mentored and approved" instead of "Sid Meier personally coded." I think some part of me probably knew it was inevitable. I'd seen enough promotional decisions by now to understand that they inched relentlessly forward as long as you let them. To refuse at this point would be an overt rejection of Brian's work, which would have been both unfair and inaccurate. The situation was good for him, good for the company, good for me, and arguably good for consumers, who were being bombarded with bandwagon strategy titles in the wake of *Civ*'s success, and deserved some guarantee of the quality inside.

But I also knew it was time for a hard line, in my own mind, of what I would and wouldn't accept in the future. I would never put my name on something I didn't truly approve of, for a start. I would never put my name on a game if the lead designer didn't want me to, and I certainly wouldn't let them sell my name to the highest bidder. I hoped I'd never see the day where I'd have to fight the issue, but I resolved that I would if I had to.

The discrepancy didn't go unnoticed in the press, but only a few were cynical about it. One argued that since I had created a new genre, it made perfect sense that it should be named after me, just as it would have been if I'd discovered a species or a new disease (a parallel some addicted *Civilization* players found especially relevant). Fortunately, the gaming writer Alan Emrich soon coined a more permanent name for the genre, "4X," representing the four main objectives of exploration, expansion, exploitation, and extermination. I don't know what I would have done if my name had become generically synonymous with all strategy games, but I'm grateful to Alan for stepping in. Not only was it a clever and succinct way to summarize the essential elements of strategy gaming, but as a programmer in the era of limited disk space, I couldn't help but appreciate a descriptor that could be shortened to just two characters.

The day after *Colonization* went gold, meaning the final product had been approved and stamped onto its gold master copy for distribution, Brian boarded a plane for England. His wife had been awarded a Fulbright Scholarship in Yorkshire, and she'd gone overseas at the start of the semester to begin her studies, while he'd been held hostage in America for months by the final testing and approval process for his game. From what I understand, *Colonization*'s gold date was also his birthday, so it was a double celebration. Now that he was free, he couldn't pack his bags fast enough.

Fortunately for us, Brian's leave was only temporary; fortunately for him, we had a project he could work on in relative isolation for the next nine months. If you're old enough, you may recall—and if you're not, just consider the horror—that in 1994 you had to buy an account through providers like CompuServe or Prodigy to access their curated version of "computer information services," i.e., the internet. One ad from *Popular Science* magazine listed the many desirable features of a CompuServe membership, such as sixty emails a month and the ability to talk to "twice as many people" about parallel universes, all under the headline that users could "never outgrow" this comprehensive service.

For Brian to connect to our office directly across the Atlantic would have involved by-the-minute international phone charges. So instead, the plan was for him to dial in to our UK office through a local number first, and then use their corporate network to send updated versions of the game over email. Attachments had size limits, but then again, so did the final game. England's hardware market didn't overlap well with ours, so MicroProse also shelled out for a state-of-the-art "portable" Compaq computer for Brian to personally carry overseas. It was roughly the size and weight of a briefcase full of bricks, and the receipt he used to declare its value to the customs officer listed a retail price of $8,700, or over $14,000 today.

The game, of course, was *Civilization II*. Again, management assumed I'd be involved, and for a little while I was. While Brian worked on updates to the main game, I prototyped a new battle system that would drop players into a separate, detailed battlefield screen during conflicts, then return them to the main world map once the tactical winner had been determined. But I wasn't pleased with the results, and after several months I emailed Brian to let him know that it wasn't happening, and he should stick with the current battle system. I think it was the right move for the series, and not just an extension of my burnout phase—being king is the heart of *Civilization*; slumming as a lowly general puts the player in an entirely different story (not to mention violates the *Covert Action* rule). Win-or-lose battles are not the only interesting choice on the path to good game design, but they're the only choice that leads to *Civ*.

Brian sure changed a lot of other stuff, though. To be honest, I hadn't been keeping a close eye on the builds he was sending back from England each week. Or any eye at all, really. With *Colonization* under his belt, I trusted Brian even more than before, and figured the in-progress deliveries were mostly just for the art and sound guys to get started on. But I knew he'd want to pick my brain once he was back in person, so shortly before his return, I sat down and fired up the latest version.

The first thing I noticed was that he'd added a sixth difficulty level called "Deity," and the ability to adjust the aggressiveness of the barbarian tribes. Nice. Then, I was given the option to declare a gender. I made a mental note to watch for personalized text and graphics later on.

Time to select my tribe—wow, twenty-one choices. The original *Civ* had maxed out at fourteen. It wasn't difficult to add them from a programming standpoint anymore, thanks to improved technology, but the historical research would have taken Brian some time. I was impressed.

One more dialog box to select the aesthetic style of my cities, and we were finally on the main screen.

My stomach dropped. Surely this was a joke.

Civilization II was built on a fancy new operating system called Windows 3.1, which kept a permanent line of menu options along the top of each program. Game, Kingdom, View, Orders—these all made perfect sense. But there, second from the end, was the word Cheat.

Cheating was an inherent part of the game now, right on the main screen? This was not good. For one thing, modifying the rules doesn't really count as cheating anymore, it's just an accepted form of gameplay. But the faster and easier gameplay becomes, the less it starts to count as a game at all. Like all storytelling, gaming is about the journey, and if you're actively finding ways to jump to the end, then we haven't made the fantasy compelling enough. A gripping novel would never start with an insert labeled, "Here's the Last Page, in Case You Want to Read It Now." Players who feel so inclined will instinctively find their own ways to cheat, and we shouldn't have to help them out.

In fact, it's our job to stop them when they succeed. Most bug fixes are not about broken code, they're about closing design loopholes that players refuse to ignore. The first revision I sent out for *Civ* came after someone discovered you could blanket the land with a checkerboard of tiny cities, thus eliminating the cost of roads and irrigation. Alternatively, you could choose to play the right way—but the temptation was there, and the complaints

made it clear that players wanted us to protect them from themselves. So we introduced the concept of corruption, which favored
fewer cities by increasing your people's misery with each new set of
local politicians. Normal gameplay was essentially unaffected, but
now the city-spamming strategy resulted in a populace so unhappy
that they could barely be bothered to grow food for themselves.
Shortly after that, players found an even more complicated way to
break the game, this time involving the Mongols and chariots, and
a second revision had to go out. The original cheaters in that case
needed a page and a half just to explain the strategy on the bulletin
boards, so their creativity and determination were evident. There
was no need for us to hand it to them on a silver platter.*

But Brian quietly ignored my advice, as he'd always been able
to do, and *Civ II* shipped with a Cheat menu. Players could steal
money directly from their enemies' treasury, wipe out civilizations
with a single click, reshape the land beneath their feet, and more.
It didn't inherently spoil anything about the core game, I just felt
like it was shooting ourselves in the foot with regard to replayabil-
ity. Once you have a foolproof way to win, there's no reason to try
again. Personally, I could choose to enhance my own enjoyment by
ignoring the cheat option right in front of me, but I wasn't sure the
players could. We were the designers for a reason.

A few years later, I happened to watch over my son Ryan's shoulder as he gleefully spawned a legion of tanks into the Middle Ages
to squash a few pikemen, and I realized that there might be some
level of fun behind cheating after all, at least once it becomes suffi-
ciently gratuitous. I still wish the option had been two or three lay-
ers deep in the menu, just to make the player work a little harder
for it, but I did eventually see the appeal.

The other thing I had to admit was that the cheating function
directly inspired the most important part of *Civilization II*, which
was its modification, or "modding" capability. In the very earliest

---

* **Achievement Unlocked:** Too Long for a Tweet—Read 240,000 characters.

days of the industry, the guts of our games were wide open, right there on the disk for anyone to play with. Programs in general were so small that magazines often published pages of code for readers to copy by hand onto their own computers. Eventually, though, compiled programming languages bundled up the individual line commands and made them inaccessible. Knowledgeable hackers might be able to slice out certain chunks of code, such as after-the-fact copy protection routines, but the content of the game was now protected—they couldn't go in and change the map, or switch out the main character with a picture of themselves.

But modern computer languages like C and C++ allowed the program to pull active game data from text files outside the compiled code. Essentially, this meant you could set certain values to be flexible, even after the program had been finalized. Few designers had ever seen a reason to do this, but when Brian first made *Colonization*, he decided to leave many major parameters open to the educated player. Weaken your enemies, lower the cost of buildings, force your king to trade favorably with you—all with a few simple keystrokes inside an easy-to-understand text document.

In retrospect, Brian's editable text files were a clear philosophical precursor to his Cheat menu, but at the time they were a small back door buried deep within the *Colonization* disk, not a flashing billboard inside the game itself. Now, with cheats out in the open for *Civ II*, Brian unlocked the back end even further. He made it possible for players to alter graphics, replace sound effects, modify rules, and basically create an entirely new game for themselves around the skeleton of our code.

I could not be convinced this was a good idea. Like I said, the actual game that we had created was great, and I was happy to put my name on it, which Brian was again in favor of. But this idea of handing everything over to the players was just baffling. They would probably be terrible at it, I thought, and blame us for their uninspired creations. And if by chance they did happen to be good at it, then all we were doing was putting ourselves out of a job.

Either way, I knew that modding was a great way to ensure that *Civilization* never saw a third installment.

I was so wrong, on all counts. The strength of the modding community is, instead, the very reason the series survived at all. Our audience had been clamoring to modify the game since the first fan letter, but I was protective—not of it, but of them, afraid that they would damage their own experience. Their story was important, and the only way to guarantee that was for the setting to feel real and important, too.

What I didn't see at the time is that imagination never diminishes reality; it only heightens it. Just like a fantasy can awaken you to new possibilities in the real world, letting the fans play in the sandbox with us only brought them closer to the universe we had created, the one that had made their fantasy possible. Every alteration, from the smallest AI tweak to the wildest comedic parody, functioned as a kind of tribute that kept *Civ* fresh, rather than pushing it aside. I'd thought they were tearing the house down, when in fact they were only remodeling because they liked the neighborhood and wanted to stay. Fortunately, Brian had the wisdom to give away the construction materials.

To say the fans ran with it would be an understatement. Stunningly creative mods of *Civilization II* began appearing online within weeks of the game's release. The simplest ones made only cosmetic changes—adding leaders we'd left out, perhaps, or renaming military units and buildings to their liking. More complex mods included a set of progress data, allowing the player to jump into the middle of a complex scenario as if it were a saved game. Some of these laid out real-world conflicts, like *The Conquest of Britain* or *Persian Gulf War,* including historically accurate distributions of wealth, population, and military firepower. Others took a turn for the whimsical, such as *Battle of the Sexes* (pitting the lush and economically prosperous "Womyn" civilization against a ruggedly hostile continent of over-weaponized "Manly Men") and *Santa Is Coming* (in which players took down rival elf workshops within a toy-based economy). Some of them swapped out so much art that they were virtually unrecognizable as *Civilization* mods. The best of these fan-created scenarios were eventually released alongside our own in-house scenarios in the official *Civ II* expansion packs, and some of their creators even secured jobs in the industry on the strength of their mod portfolios.

Others in the mod community took a more experimental approach, pushing the game to its technical, rather than creative, limits. It was popular to set up oversized maps with as many civilizations as the player's computer could keep track of—or else cram them all into the smallest possible map, and watch the chaos unfold. This eventually culminated in a *Battle Royale* mod containing sixty-one simultaneous civilizations, spawned in their real-life locations on an accurate world map. Unfortunately, a winner could never be determined, because the scenario kept crashing after a few hundred turns. But others in the community were so intrigued that they offered to write automated scripts and efficiency tools for a potential remake, and their team effort continues to this day.

Meanwhile, another young man made headlines by simply ignoring the clock. A typical game of *Civ II* was expected to last about ten hours, maybe fifteen with heavy diplomacy. Experienced players could sometimes assimilate every competing nation by the turn of the twentieth century, but as often as not, the game would reach a complex stalemate of democratic superpowers in the modern age. When that happened, accomplishments were tallied, and the tiara was awarded to whomever had the highest score when the year struck 2050 AD.

As with *Pirates!*, however, the game never actually forced you to quit. Numerically triumphant or not, you could keep up the struggle for as long as there were opponents left on the board. Such stubbornness usually led to a late-stage loss, because declaring war in a world dominated by peace treaties was a great way to turn everyone else against you. But for some reason, one particular game started by fourteen-year-old James Moore never escaped the era of nuclear saber-rattling. Instead, the Vikings, the Americans, and James's own Celtic civilization somehow rose to the top in perfect aggressive equilibrium, continuously pelting one another with warheads while never losing or gaining substantial ground.

Other games grabbed and lost his interest over the years, but James was fascinated by the odd little dystopia he had stumbled into, and continued running the simulation long after he'd been declared the nominal winner. As he graduated from high school, went to college, withdrew from college, got a job, got a better job, and eventually returned to college, James continued to transfer his saved game file from city to city, and computer to computer. Each week, he would spend a few hours nursing his post-apocalyptic world, still hoping for a resolution even as centuries of conflict killed 90 percent of the population, and nuclear fallout melted the polar ice caps more than twenty times. (We'd programmed it as an abstract consequence whenever global warming reached a certain level, never expecting it would be triggered more than once. After 1,700 years of nonstop thermonuclear bombing, the rising oceans in James's world had covered all but the highest mountain regions with swamps.)

Perhaps he was emotionally attached to it because *Civ II* was the first computer game his family could afford, or perhaps the notion of dystopia holds a similar fascination for all of us. Maybe the thing that makes *Civ* so compelling is that it illuminates our deepest fears about ourselves—it's hard to play out a fantasy of worldwide domination without occasionally wondering whether you're really the best person to put in charge after all.

"Every time a ceasefire is signed," James lamented, "the Vikings will surprise attack me or the Americans the very next turn. . . . I was forced to do away with democracy roughly a thousand years ago because it was endangering my empire." Detonating a nuclear bomb on civilians was usually a sure path to defeat in the game, because every other nation would immediately declare war on you.

"But this is already the case," he pointed out, "so it's no longer a deterrent to anyone. Myself included."

In 2012, James went public with his now ten-year-old game, which he nicknamed *The Eternal War*, and asked the community for help.

"The military stalemate is air tight," he warned them. "You want a granary so you can eat? Sorry; I have to build another tank instead. Maybe next time." Winning was still on his mind, but he'd also grown weary of the virtual suffering. "I want to rebuild the world," he said. "But I'm not sure how."

James posted a copy of his current save file so that others could experiment, and to his surprise, the message went viral. Thousands of players wrote back, some to offer advice, but many just to marvel at this supposed insight into human nature. The parallels to George Orwell's* *1984*, they said, could not be ignored. Humanity was doomed, and *Civilization* had proven it.

The whole thing garnered enough attention that a journalist contacted me for a quote, and I quickly dispelled the notion of any hidden social commentary.

"There's no way we could have tested for this," I assured them. The vast majority of games didn't play out this way, and such a perfectly balanced state of war was about as likely as a flipped coin landing on its edge—remarkable, but not completely impossible, and certainly not evidence of any deeper meaning. The only insight on display here was how much fun James must have been having, since he could have ended the war himself at any time if only he'd been willing to lose. In the real world, James would have been assassinated or died of old age long before the polar ice caps figured out how to melt for a second time.

Though he'd developed it organically, the scenario functioned like a mod once James posted the data. He had created a very

---

* *Achievement Unlocked:* Dystopian Dinner Party—Hang out with Orson Scott Card, Aldous Huxley, Robert Heinlein, and George Orwell.

unpleasant, but nonetheless fascinating story, and was able to share that experience with thousands of people as they all struggled to find a way out of the mess he'd offered up to them. One player did eventually work out a strategy to defeat the Vikings in "only" fifty-eight turns, but most were not interested in following his instructions to the letter. They wanted to win it in their own way, and create their own dramatic, back-from-the-brink story.

In this, and all the other mods they crafted and shared with one another, the *Civ* community revealed more about human nature than the chance outcome of a few algorithms ever could. When faced with the opportunity to dismantle all challenges, most players chose instead to devise endlessly clever new ones for themselves, and banded together to support one another in their efforts. They were stronger than I initially gave them credit for—and I've never been so lucky to be wrong. Because while we didn't know it yet, the strength and loyalty of our fanbase was about to be tested like it never had been before.

15

THE DISPERSING

Sid Meier's CivNet (1995)

*

Magic: The Gathering (1997)

MAGIC: THE GATHERING WAS
more than just a game. It was a phenomenon that owned a generation, as surely as *Minecraft* owns this one. Designer Richard Garfield published his original deck of cards in 1993, long before Pokémon, Yu-Gi-Oh!, or any of the hundreds that followed. It was the very first trading-card game, purchased in collectible packs like baseball cards, but played head-to-head like gin rummy or war.

By the time MicroProse was in talks with Wizards of the Coast to create a digital version, Magic had replaced nearly all of the other board games in the company break room. I never played it much myself, because I spent most of my time testing the games I was already designing, but I had seen it demonstrated enough to know that the rules were complicated, and winning strategies were not always obvious. Developing an AI routine that could challenge the serious player would be intriguing, and it might make a nice stepping-stone back to more game-like games, now that *C.P.U. Bach* was out of my system. The break from pure strategy had been a worthwhile indulgence, and one I was still enjoying. But I agreed, hypothetically, to take on the project, and several of the more ardent fans in the office convinced management that a Magic: The Gathering computer game was a great idea.

It was a mostly good idea.

I hadn't done a licensed property since *Red Storm Rising* nine years earlier, but we seemed to be taking on a lot of them these days, thanks to some new corporate overlords. The arcade market had been a flop, as I'd feared, and Bill had been forced to sell MicroProse to a larger developer named Spectrum HoloByte in 1993. Shortly after that, around the time *Colonization* and *C.P.U. Bach* were shipping, Bill had stepped down as head of the studio. MicroProse really wasn't ours, anymore.

Spectrum HoloByte was based in California, and didn't seem to care much what was going on in our little office. Their darling at the time was a license for the movie *Top Gun*, which already had six published games from four different companies. Meanwhile, *Civilization II* was given low priority despite the record-breaking success of its predecessor, and official corporate estimates anticipated sales of just 38,000 copies. Even after Brian's game surpassed a million, we were hard pressed to get any support from the bigwigs on the West Coast. "Mainstream and marketable" was their thing, not "interesting and nuanced." The pressure to acquire licenses might have been explicit, or else the remaining MicroProse executives might have been currying favor on their own—but either way, it probably seemed prudent for us to choose the kind of license we liked, before they assigned one to us.

These days, *Magic* would be a multiplayer game by default, with the AI opponent tacked on for those rare times when, heaven forbid, you couldn't get Wi-Fi. But this was still the mid-90s, when the word "Wi-Fi" hadn't even been invented yet. Hardcore nerds sometimes connected directly to one another over a local area network, but the average user was not willing to load up their computer and drive to a central location with a bunch of cables. Major universities had broadband connectivity, but everyone else was still stuck on dial-up.

Not that dial-up made online games impossible. Multiplayer text adventures had been garnering small audiences for a decade, and some bulletin boards offered simple rounds of chess or low-resolution shooters. MicroProse had recently published a (slow and buggy) multiplayer version of *Civilization* called *CivNet,* and while we were developing *Magic: The Gathering*, a young man named Richard Garriott was writing his code for the massively multiplayer revolution known as *Ultima Online*. His game would eventually be released in the same year as ours, so clearly the technology was out there.

The difference in our situation was twofold. First, Garriott's company had invested in the infrastructure to handle thousands of active *Ultima Online* users, with racks of servers running twenty-four hours a day, and full-time employees to maintain them. MicroProse, perhaps remembering the sting of all that unsold arcade hardware, was not willing to host dedicated servers. *CivNet* users had to forge their own connections through a LAN or other service provider, and even then, the game routinely performed worse than open-source copycat versions written by fans. What's more, some *CivNet* customers hadn't realized that *Civilization II* was due for release just a few months later, and felt they'd been tricked into buying two products back-to-back. Needless to say, *CivNet* was not a success, and did nothing to inspire executives' confidence in the value of online play.

But more importantly, the design of *Ultima Online* was tailored for multiplayer from the start. They could dump anywhere from five to five thousand users into one world, while *Magic* would have required a matchmaking service to pair off available players. Plus, *Ultima* was in real time, so there was no need to wait on anyone else to take their turn. *Magic* was not only turn-based, but the rules frequently gave the option to play a card or not, and an online version would have been constantly popping up dialogue boxes asking whether each player intended to pass.

To counteract the letdown of a multiplayer game that would

offer no multiplayer, we fabricated an adventure game framework, which would also substitute for the physical pack purchasing in the real world. Collecting rare cards and building your deck was a significant part of the fun, and we quantified it with a mystical realm where you could hunt for such items. The whole thing turned out to be pretty engaging, and soon we started to hear the strongest praise of all: the sound of the game being played up and down the hallway after hours.

That's when things started to go awry, in the same way that all licensed products eventually do. Wizards of the Coast had been incredibly supportive in general, but at the end of the day, they were beholden to the success of the card game above all else. They determined that some of the rarer cards we were using in our game were over-powered, and too easily available compared to their frequency in the real world. In order to preserve the integrity of the card game experience, they told us, we had to remove these special items from our version.

While it was genuinely the right move from their perspective, it hamstrung the player's motivation in our game. It just wasn't as fun to go traipsing through dungeons for mediocre rewards. In a social setting, it was fine to know only one friend who had found an incredibly rare card—you had proof the item was out there, and were excited to imagine that you might find one someday, too. But in a computer game, you were supposed to be the star, and isolation had to change the scale of what rarity meant. If only one in five strangers on their own computer found a particular card, it might as well not exist for the other four.

I was frustrated. *Magic* was a good computer game, but not as good as it could be. I didn't like doing licenses, and I didn't like the corporate structure that had been slowly but surely building up around me for years. Oddly enough, Spectrum HoloByte had determined that MicroProse had better name recognition than they did, despite our reversed market positions, so they'd recently adopted our name for their business as a whole. "MicroProse" would be releasing even more licenses, now.

I just wanted to make interesting games. Bill and I may have had different definitions of interesting, but at least we'd always agreed on making products that were special, and valuing the creative process. I had a suspicion that he'd gone to bat for the design team more than once behind closed doors, and now that he was gone, we were getting even less support from the executive side than we were used to. Meanwhile, Bruce Shelley had left for Chicago after his wife got a unique job opportunity there, Andy Hollis had gone to work on a series of flight simulators for Electronic Arts, Arnold Hendrick had joined Bill in his new business venture called Interactive Magic, and many other early folks had moved on as well.

It was time for me to do the same.

Fortunately, there were others who shared my vision of small-town game design. Brian Reynolds didn't want to find out what they'd do to *Civilization* now that it had a two-game track record, and Jeff Briggs wanted to compose original music, not rehash popular movie soundtracks. The three of us decided that we would form our own studio, and run it the way we wanted.

It was not an easy extraction, but we tried to make it as painless as possible. Each of us had different contracts to fulfill, so while Jeff could start establishing our new enterprise in May 1996, Brian couldn't join him until June, and I was the last to make it over in July. Even then, I consulted part-time at MicroProse for many months after, in order to help them get *Magic: The Gathering* out the door. I had no desire to leave the game in an unfinishable state, and both sides were nervous enough as it was. On the one hand, active recruitment of our former coworkers could have put us in deep legal trouble; on the other, the executives knew we could probably obliterate their workforce if we tried. They could sue us, of course, but by the time they were done both companies would be out of business. If it got ugly, it would be ugly for everyone.

So we backed away slowly with our hands in the air, and they didn't make too much of a fuss. I continued to have a presence in the MicroProse office several days a week, handing over the last of my code and explaining how it should be implemented. I even have a vague memory that we were supposed to pretend I was taking some kind of sabbatical, instead of starting a new company. In return, I was allowed to take with me all of the code libraries and programming tools I'd written over the years. Technically they were property of MicroProse, but again, a legal fight would have halted everyone's use of them until we sorted it all out. Both sides got what they needed to stay in business, with the understanding that we'd each keep to our own corner of the market—they didn't want to be making detailed strategy titles any more than we wanted to be making *Top Gun* flight simulators. Fortunately, the question of whether they could put my name on *Magic: The Gathering* was moot, since it was already someone else's property. *Sid Meier's Wizards of the Coast's Magic: The Gathering* would have sounded ridiculous.

We named our new company Firaxis, after a piece of music that Jeff had once written combining the words "fiery" and "axis." It was only meant to be a placeholder, but we liked it and it stuck. Our office was situated in the middle of several factories owned by the McCormick spice company, and it was fun to come into work each day and find out by smell what they were dry roasting that morning. Once, we had some guests from China visiting the offices, and no one ever explained our proximity to the spice plant. I'm sure they figured it out on their own, but I like to imagine they went home believing that Americans were so decadent, we perfumed the outside air with cinnamon for no reason at all.

Meanwhile, my personal life was starting a new chapter, as well. Gigi and I had separated amicably a few years earlier, and I had recently begun dating a friend of my sister's named Susan. Vicky and Susan had originally met in a choir group near Washington, DC, but hadn't been able to see each other much after my sister changed jobs and moved back to Michigan. My house in Baltimore was only about an hour north of DC, so when Vicky and my mother happened to come visit me, Vicky took the opportunity to invite her friend up to have dinner with us. I'm not sure whether my sister intended to play matchmaker, or to what degree my mother was colluding with her, but I found out later that Susan had apparently earned my mother's approval that evening, most notably by her eagerness to help with the dishes. I was enchanted by her sweet sense of humor and unshakeable kindness, myself.

Though we had many things in common, Susan wasn't especially into computer games. During one of our early dinners together—we discovered a lot of restaurants halfway between Baltimore and DC, that first year—I mentioned something a fan had written in a letter, and she frowned curiously.

"How do they know who to write to?" she asked.

"Well, my name is on the box," I said.

She looked me up and down. Apparently, I did not match her mental image of some famous celebrity who gets his name on things. "Oh yeah?" she said.

"I can show you," I promised.

As soon as we finished eating, I took her to the nearest video-game store. As expected, there on the shelf was *Sid Meier's Civilization*, still selling strong after three years. *Colonization* was there too, and possibly *Railroad Tycoon Deluxe*, though I don't think poor *C.P.U. Bach* made the cut, at least not for eye-level display.

Okay, she admitted with a smile. She was impressed.

After we founded Firaxis, Susan agreed to handle the company's administrative tasks, since she was one of the very few people we knew who had no connection to MicroProse. Some people might have raised an eyebrow at working all day with their significant other, but we had our own domains, and everyone was kept very busy. It wasn't so much that we worked well together, but that we worked well separately. By now, we've been going on more than twenty years in the same office—spoiler alert, we even-

Sid Meier's Railroad Tycoon screenshot.
© 1990 MICROPROSE, WWW.MICROPROSE.COM.

tually got married, in full Baroque costume with Bach playing in the background—so I think it's safe to say the experiment was a success.

Separately is probably how I work best with everyone, to be honest. I'm an introvert who likes people: I want to collaborate on the whole, but do my part individually. There are so many things in the world to be good at, and I get a thrill every time I come across someone who excels in their field. The dichotomy between someone else's talent and your own is a cause for celebration, because the further apart you are, the more you can offer each other. But the opposite is also true. I know where my own talents are, and I find that sharing those duties usually falls somewhere between inefficient and frustrating. I want to combine other people's unique expertise with mine, and create something that none of us could have made alone—not compromise on the same task until it's less than the sum of its parts. It had been a long time since I'd had that flexibility at MicroProse, but Firaxis promised both the freedom to do my best work, as well as the community of talent to make it even better.

In some ways it felt like starting over, but we grew quickly that

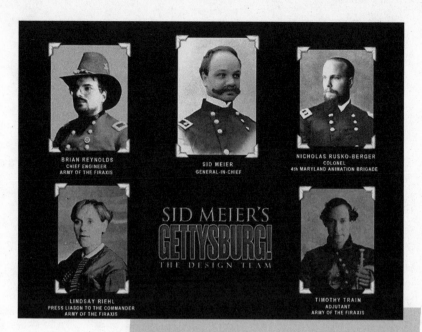

BRIAN REYNOLDS
CHIEF ENGINEER
ARMY OF THE FIRAXIS

SID MEIER
GENERAL-IN-CHIEF

NICHOLAS RUSKO-BERGER
COLONEL
4th MARYLAND ANIMATION BRIGADE

SID MEIER'S
GETTYSBURG!
THE DESIGN TEAM

LINDSAY RIEHL
PRESS LIASON TO THE COMMANDER
ARMY OF THE FIRAXIS

TIMOTHY TRAIN
ADJUTANT
ARMY OF THE FIRAXIS

Sid Meier's Gettysburg! instruction manual.
© 1997 DAVE INSCORE/FIRAXIS GAMES.

first year, and dedicated more people to fewer games in order to make the best products we could. The original team for *Railroad Tycoon* was so small that we turned the credit screen into a portrait, with Bruce Shelley in engineer's overalls, Max Remington carrying a railroad spike hammer, and myself as an industry magnate with white gloves and a top hat. By comparison, my first game at Firaxis, *Sid Meier's Gettysburg!*, pictured five of us in stoic, sepia-toned Civil War garb, and named quite a few more in the traditional credits list. Of course gamers' expectations have continued to grow along with the industry, especially when it comes to animation and art, so these days at Firaxis it's more like eighty to a hundred people per team. But the creative spirit has remained strong, and for the most part, I can still go off and make what I want, when I want, with the assurance that people I trust will be ready to do their part when the time comes.

16

INTERESTING DECISIONS

> *Sid Meier's Gettysburg!* (1997)
> *
> *Sid Meier's Antietam!* (1999)

IT WAS NO SECRET THAT I DIDN'T

want to go to Switzerland that summer. My parents may have had multiple—and somewhat conflicting—rationales for the trip, spanning everything from broadened horizons and familial duty to emotional shielding and medical necessity, but the question of their eight-year-old son's approval didn't seem to be a factor. My father wasn't indifferent to my feelings, however, and just before we left, he handed me a present.

"Don't open it until you are on the plane," he said.

It was shaped like a book, but if so, it was the heaviest one I'd ever seen, except maybe for the dictionary. I felt its weight in my bag all the way to the airport, then on the plane to New York with my father, then on the tram to the Swissair gate. I felt it even when it wasn't on my shoulders. By the time my father hugged me goodbye and sent me down the narrow gangway, anticipation had triumphed over homesickness. There would be time for tears and angsty diary entries later, but in that moment, all I wanted was to get on that plane.

As soon as I was in my seat, I tore open the wrapping to reveal *The American Heritage Picture History of the Civil War.*

"When the Civil War began," read the introduction, "photography was only twenty-two years old; only twelve years had elapsed since the first photograph was made of a U.S. President in office; and only ten since the invention of the wet-plate process." It went on to describe the "combat artists" who had documented the war, not just with photography but "in the fading twilight with freezing or fevered fingers, making their sketches in ambulances and field hospitals, in trenches and on decks over which shells crashed and bullets whined."

The book contained no fewer than 630 pages of drawings, photos, paintings, political cartoons, diagrams, and maps from this tumultuous time in American history. There was the 1851 Railroad Jubilee on Boston Common, with a jaunty Millard Fillmore greeting the Canadian governor general in a carriage drawn by six white horses. There were advertisements for farmland along the Illinois Central Railroad line, and a depiction of the very first election in my hometown of Detroit. There was the iconic publisher William Lloyd Garrison, who once publicly burned the Constitution and called it "a covenant with death and an agreement with hell" for its allowance of slavery. There was the cousin of Senator Andrew Butler, bursting onto the Congress floor and striking Senator Charles Sumner with a cane on his kinsman's behalf. Under the photo of Lincoln's inauguration, there was the caption describing "sharpshooters . . . at the Capitol's windows, and a flying wedge of artillery" to maintain order. And there were, of course, many immortal quotes from the man himself.

"In *your* hands, my dissatisfied fellow countrymen, and not in *mine*, is the momentous issue of civil war. The government will not assail *you*. You can have no conflict, without being yourselves the aggressors. *You* have no oath registered in heaven to destroy the government, while *I* shall have the most solemn one to 'preserve, protect, and defend' it."

There were sheepish boys in oversized uniforms, not yet aware of what was to come. There was the shallow pool alongside the Battle of Shiloh, where wounded men from both armies drank fresh water side by side. There was even some dark humor from the era, including a gag photo of a soldier pretending to light a "Quaker gun"—a tree trunk carved into the shape of a cannon and painted black—which troops would sometimes set up at a distance to appear fearsome when they had no real artillery.

Most of the pictures were originals from the late 1800s, but a handful of recent illustrations had been commissioned to describe infantry movements over the course of the largest battles. One in particular caught my eye, detailing the second day of the Battle of Gettysburg. The sweeping overhead view filled both pages from edge to edge, and was labeled with names that sounded like they'd come out of a fantasy novel: Spangler's Spring, Plum Run, Devil's Den, Sickles' Salient. Hundreds of tiny, exquisitely drawn figures engaged at every major skirmish point across the map, and close inspection revealed a terrain that was just as intricate. Planks were knocked out of fences, wagons overturned, branches torn from trees—the level of detail was mind-blowing. I had always imagined battles to be laid out in clean, wide-open fields, with the two sides charging each other at full force. But this one had farmhouses, creeks, orchards, and even a cemetery scattered through the middle of it. Small clumps of soldiers advanced on each other from every direction, flowing around natural rock formations and coming up behind one another to retake positions they'd already lost once. They practically swarmed across the page, as if the battle were a living organism.

For years I would return to this book, studying its minutiae again and again. We had a telescope in the house that my father had built from a kit, and at some point I discovered that the removable eyepiece worked as a magnifying glass on everyday objects. I would hold it to my eye and lean close to the pages for hours, like a jeweler examining rare diamonds. The Civil War was, in my mind, the turning point when historical characters suddenly became real people. Other wars had dates and facts, but the fighters on these pages were fragile, and brave, and dutiful, and flawed. The art collected by *American Heritage*, not to mention all the surviving letters and firsthand accounts it inspired me to seek out, gave their story a sense of immediacy and humanity that I had never felt before.

Like many of my childhood interests, this one persisted in various forms over the years, and the map of Gettysburg in particular was at the forefront of my mind as my career matured. So many of the skirmishes had turned on chance, and a redirection of any one of them might have affected the entire course of the war. It was an obvious topic to build a game around, and during my time at MicroProse I probably made twenty different Civil War prototypes. None of them were bad, necessarily, but they all felt insufficient—I could see in my head exactly what I wanted, and it couldn't yet be re-created on the screen. Streamlining military encounters until they were digitally feasible was my bread and butter in the early days, and it wasn't like me to rail against what we weren't capable of. I generally saw technology in terms of progress, rather than limitations, and lived in a nearly perpetual state of excitement over what we *could* accomplish. But in this case, my emotional connection to the subject made it impossible to settle for less, and I found myself repeatedly shelving the idea until the technology could catch up.

Now, a decade and a half later, I could finally do those beautiful illustrations justice. *Sid Meier's Gettysburg!* re-created every major skirmish of the three-day battle, allowing the player to take charge of either side's regiments and match their skills against some of history's greatest generals. Since the advantage had shifted many times during the real battle, we decided that the player should be allowed to win or lose each stage independently—and in fact it was nearly impossible to win them all. Instead, we created branching scenarios depending on the total state of your army, and like real military strategists, the best players had to learn the art of judicious sacrifice and retreat in order to win. But to me, the real centerpiece was the technology. In addition to smooth maneuvers and independent AI for each soldier, the overhead view was no longer top-down and flat, as my previous strategy games had been. Instead, it was isometric, or what developers refer to as "two-and-a-half-D"—that is, two-dimensional, but from an angled perspective, with stretched diamonds instead of squares. Tiny soldiers marched, rotated, kneeled, aimed, and reloaded across a detailed terrain at exactly the same angle as I had first seen them on a plane to Switzerland.

Before we could release our first game at Firaxis, though, we had to figure out who was going to publish it. Distribution and marketing was an entire industry now, and Jeff, Brian, and I felt strongly that the lack of quarantine between departments at MicroProse had contributed to its downfall. Business and creativity were both necessary components, but they ought to keep their distance.

Of the many offers we received, Electronic Arts was the largest and most stable. We wanted a company that would be safe (or as safe as possible, anyway) from the endless cycle of bankruptcies, buyouts, and property transfers that still plague parts of the industry even today. As the publisher for Maxis and its flagship game *SimCity*, EA had also proven that they understood our gaming philosophy, and wouldn't be pressuring us for platformers or first-person shooters. The idea of, say, *Railroad Tycoon* conductors aiming at each other from passing trains might sound preposterous to our side of the table, but Sega had once rejected Dan Bunten's *M.U.L.E.* unless "bombs and guns" were added, so anything was possible.

One of the other things we liked about EA was their executives actually played and enjoyed videogames. Our liaison in their offices was a man named Bing Gordon, who would eventually become one of only two Americans to ever win a non-developer award from the Academy of Interactive Arts & Sciences, and the first endowed chair of game design at a university. He began in marketing when EA was founded, and directly managed a few development teams in the early years, but mostly he traveled around giving short, brilliant bits of advice to nearly every project under the company's umbrella. In addition to his formal credits, he's named in the "Special Thanks" section of over sixty games, while at Firaxis we once listed him as our "EA Godfather."

Gettysburg! was a success, and a sequel called *Antietam!* soon followed. Since we knew it was on topically safe ground, we took the opportunity to test our audience's boundaries in a different way. Internet connectivity had finally become the norm by 1999, and EA was willing to let us try the revolutionary concept of direct-to-consumer sales through our website.

Alas, we were ahead of our time. PayPal had only been founded a few months earlier, Walmart wouldn't launch a website for another year, and Amazon wouldn't be profitable for another four. The idea of going to Firaxis.com instead of a brick-and-mortar store was still too weird for most people, especially since the game wasn't available for download—all that convenience of online ordering was spoiled by waiting a week or more for your CD-ROM to arrive in the mail. *Antietam!* got good reviews, but almost certainly sold less than it would have through traditional routes.

Still, I felt like there was room for one more in the series, this time based on the battle of Waterloo. The French Revolution didn't quite reach Civil War levels of fascination for me, but I thought it had some unique military tactics worth exploring, namely the interaction between cavalry and infantry formations. Rifle technology had made cavalry obsolete by the time the Union and Confederacy were marching against each other, because bullets could take down a soldier on horseback long before he got close enough for a counterattack. But during Napoleon's reign, firearms couldn't reliably hit anything more than a hundred yards away, and with a reload time of at least half a minute, the cavalry could quickly close the gap. So while the tactics of the Civil War had been mostly terrain-based—moving artillery to the high ground, and using cover to one's advantage—battles like Austerlitz and Waterloo had been waged with the expectation of close combat, and soldiers had been trained to march and fight in strict, defensive formations.

All of this was interesting from a gaming standpoint because the balance of artillery, cavalry, and infantry created a classic rock-paper-scissors scenario. Cavalry beats artillery, because horses can shift position faster than cannons can be re-aimed; artillery beats infantry, because people can't move as fast as horses; and infantry doesn't strictly beat cavalry, but depending on the formations used, it could. This kind of three-way standoff is one of the major pillars of game design, and anywhere you can find such a proportionate layout of strengths and weaknesses, you have the potential for strategic choices.

And, yes, the Battle of Waterloo also tied back to an episode in my youth. That's what happens when you're a kid at heart; the fun stuff just keeps bubbling to the surface. The must-have technology item for the creative family man in the 1970s was the Kodak Super 8mm home movie camera, so of course my father had one. While it was best known for creating short, flickering snippets of children's birthday parties, the camera also included a setting for exposing a single frame at a time. So as part of a school project, I used the map and army pieces from my board game Risk to create a dramatic stop-motion animation of Napoleon's final defeat. It wasn't exactly up to the standards of Russell Crowe in *Master and Commander*, but the class was suitably impressed.

The other fun thing I remember doing with that camera was filming segments of a football game on TV, then playing them back in slow motion until I could understand all the different patterns the receivers ran. I loved football, but my parents weren't fans, and it was a long time before I was allowed to watch three hours of television all at once. So I used the camera to be a little more efficient with my analysis during the short windows I was given.

I suppose if I had become a filmmaker, or a football player, these anecdotes would be given more emphasis, and others less. As it is, I never even got to make my Waterloo game—EA wanted something new, so we moved on. But the one thing all these memories have in common, including those that actually did affect my gaming career, is the complexity of choice. The quarterback has to choose among open receivers; Ulysses S. Grant has to choose which ridge to storm; Napoleon has to choose the right balance of horses, cannons, and soldiers—and each choice sends these guys careening down completely different paths. It's maybe even fair to say that games weren't the defining theme of my childhood after all. Rather, it was their precursor: the interesting decision. I've always been fascinated by every type of interesting decision, and a game just happens to be a well-curated series of them.

I've been saying variations on this theme for my entire career, but I didn't realize I'd become famous for my definition of games until relatively recently. Sometimes, I'm quoted as saying "choices" instead of "decisions;" other times they're "meaningful" instead of "interesting." No one can agree on what I said, let alone when or where I might have first said it, and unfortunately, I can't be much help in that regard. My earliest public paraphrasing was most likely at CGDC in 1993, as one of twelve important lessons that *Civilization* had taught me. No one recorded the presentation—which was officially titled "How I Almost Screwed Up *Civilization*"—but a staff writer for *Computer Gaming World* summarized my second bullet point that day as, "Meier prefers games where the player has all the fun (where all the vital information is presented and the gamer has the ability to make meaningful decisions)."

Prior to *Civilization*, I wasn't getting nearly as much publicity, so while I may have had the idea sooner, it's doubtful anyone was asking. Then again, my foreword to the *F-15 Strike Eagle* strategy guide, published in 1990, includes the dramatic line, "Decisions. Decisions. Decisions. Just like in real life." So there's no way of knowing when, exactly, this insight became fully developed in my mind.

Part of finding out that I was famous for this "series of interesting decisions" line was the revelation that a number of people disagreed with me, some quite vehemently. I thought it was a little strange to be both exalted and maligned for something I'd never really elaborated on, so in 2012, I formally codified all my thoughts on the matter into a new hour-long presentation at GDC. The whole thing's online for those who want to get into the nitty-gritty of game theory, but the overall takeaway is that my definitions of both "decision" and "interesting" are probably broader than expected.

Consider the hit game *Guitar Hero*, in which players use a special guitar-shaped controller to match the rhythms of their favorite rock 'n' roll tunes. This is probably the most commonly cited counterexample to my assertion that good games are a series of interesting decisions: it seems to demand only dexterity from the player, yet its popularity clearly establishes it, to the reasonable individual at least, as "a good game." Perhaps, they suggest, I only meant to describe good *strategy* games . . . ? But in fact, *Guitar Hero* has multiple interesting decisions subtly built in.

To begin with, there is the game's concept of "Star Power," in which some sections of the music offer a bonus prize—players must choose whether to attempt a perfect game throughout, or abandon lesser notes in order to secure the reward for harder ones. Having filled their Star Power meter, players then have the opportunity to "spend" their popularity later in the song. Some will take advantage of the doubled scoring by activating Star Power during the easiest sections, while others will rely on the increased notoriety it brings in order to skate through harder sections of the music that might otherwise turn the audience against them. Some will use a combination of strategies. All of these are interesting options that rely on mental discretion rather than physical agility, and they multiply exponentially once the player enters career mode, where each instrument in a four-person band is given unique scoring abilities that can be applied in different ways to achieve group victory.

Interesting decisions are not about the specifics of what you let the player choose between, but whether the investment feels both personal and significant to the outcome. If you present players with options A, B, and C, and 90 percent of them choose A, then it's not a well-balanced set—an interesting decision has no clear right or wrong answers. If players are evenly distributed among A, B, and C, but they all chose within three seconds, then it's not a very meaningful decision. Any answer would have worked. Ultimately, the most fundamental characteristic of an interesting decision is that it makes the player think, "I wonder what would happen next time, if I did it differently?" Of course, the best way for them to find out is to play your game again. But with enough reinforcement, players may even find themselves asking the same question in the real world, where the choices are less clearly delineated. In the right context, a game is not just a vehicle for fun, but an exercise in self-determination and confidence. Good games teach us that there are tradeoffs to everything, actions lead to outcomes, and the chance to try again is almost always out there.

17

BACK TO
THE FUTURE

Sid Meier's Alpha Centauri (1999)
*
Sid Meier's Civilization III (2001)

WHILE I WAS MAKING GETTYS-
burg!, Brian was working on another title players had been begging for, called *Alpha Centauri*. One of the nonmilitary paths to victory in *Civilization* was to win the space race by landing a small ship of colonists in the nearest star system before anyone else. The parallels to the lone settler at the beginning of the game were deliberate, and it was the most satisfying way to end the story, in my personal opinion. To anyone familiar with the series, *Alpha Centauri* was a clear sequel—created by the same people, operating with the same game mechanics, and picking up precisely where the original had left off. It was the "*Civilization* in Outer Space!" title that our fan letters had always demanded.

In a legal sense, however, it was not part of the *Civilization* canon. MicroProse still owned the franchise, and Firaxis didn't dare use the word anywhere in the title or promotional materials.

The history of the *Civilization* copyright was long and tortuous. It started in England in 1980, when a designer named Francis Tresham published his Civilization board game through a company called Hartland Trefoil. Tresham's design was based primarily on trade and cooperation among the players, and like many foreign titles, it was soon licensed for US release by Avalon Hill. (Tresham's first creation, a railroad board game called 1829, served as the foundation for Avalon Hill's 1830, which Bruce Shelley had worked on before coming to MicroProse.)

When Bruce and I started developing our "entire history of human civilization" prototype several years later, we informally called it "Civilization," but only in the same way that *Gettysburg!* had once been "the Civil War game"—it was a placeholder that we expected to change later on. Marketing would surely want to call it *Government Tycoon*, or perhaps *Sid Meier's Latest: The Revenge*, and there was no point in trying to pin down an official name before they had their say. As a former employee at Avalon Hill, Bruce was of course aware of their Civilization board game, and we might have even had a copy of it somewhere in the Micro-Prose "Fun Zone" (also known as the break room)—but I had never personally played it before embarking on our project.

This is not to say that my version of *Civilization* had no outside influences—far from it. Aside from the general "creating not destroying" concept I had first encountered in *SimCity*, there were two games that I very much respected, and blatantly took ideas from to use for my own purposes. The first was *The Seven Cities of Gold*, written by Dan Bunten in 1984. It was a land-and-sea exploration game that had very clearly shaped *Pirates!*, all the way down to the menu-driven interface. But even now, six years after its release, Dan's brilliance was still compelling me to build upon it. *The Seven Cities of Gold* would randomly generate a new continent for each round, and gave you the option to behave honorably or cruelly with the natives you encountered, something I had never seen in a game before. *Civ* would later be classified as "edutainment" for its loose embrace of history, but in fact, that term was first invented by Trip Hawkins to refer to *The Seven Cities of Gold.* The game was a cloud-parting, shackle-removing, mind-blowing masterpiece for me, and there were elements of it in nearly every game I made thereafter.

The other game that directly influenced *Civilization* was called *Empire: Wargame of the Century,* by Walter Bright and Mark Baldwin. It, too, had a randomly generated map that was slowly revealed as you marched your armies across it, but unlike *Seven Cities* and the board game called Civilization, *Empire* had a significant military component. It also extended the timeline from the ancient into the modern era, and differentiated the types of units available as the clock progressed. Ironically, Walter Bright had submitted an early version of *Empire* to MicroProse back in 1985, but Bill apparently gave the pitch a form-letter rejection, saying that we were only looking for "action oriented real time strategy simulations." I suspect he didn't even play the demo, and I know I didn't, or I would have pushed for us to publish it. The game was captivating, and at one point I asked Bruce to make a list of ten things he would improve about *Empire,* so it obviously played a large role in my thinking. (Incidentally, this is a great strategy for revising your own game mid-development as well. It's important to step back and view your work in terms of concrete opportunities for improvement.)

As our development progressed, however, Bruce and I grew more and more attached to the "Civilization" nickname, and eventually came to the conclusion that no other title could be as suitable. Even though Avalon Hill's product wasn't a direct precursor to ours, they had the name we wanted, so Bill approached them to work out a deal. We agreed to share the rights to the name in exchange for a small fee and a cross-promotional flier in every box.

A few years after *Civilization* exploded, Avalon Hill released an official computer version of their board game, which they called *Advanced Civilization.* Though we were now competing in the same format with nearly identical names, everyone took great care to distinguish the two products. *Computer Gaming World* opened their review with, "No, it isn't *that Civilization*," and Avalon Hill wrote in their own self-published circular, *The General*, "The MicroProse version had nothing in common with our boardgame other than the theme and the name. . . . To put down [*Sid Meier's Civilization*] is to insult the Holy Grail." When we released *Civilization II* shortly after, no one was confused about the lines of succession.

But a couple of years after Jeff, Brian, and I headed to Firaxis, things got kind of dicey. Avalon Hill licensed their rights out to Activision for a game they dubbed *Civilization: Call to Power*, and at the same time, the two companies jointly sued MicroProse for copyright infringement. Avalon Hill couldn't have afforded the suit on their own, and Activision had no legal standing without Avalon Hill, but together they hoped to gain control of one of the most successful names in gaming history.

The executives at MicroProse responded with an equally winner-take-all attitude. Instead of countersuing, they went overseas to Hartland Trefoil, the original owner of the British board game, and bought the company out entirely. MicroProse now owned the ongoing licensing deal that had been granted to Avalon Hill in the first place, and judiciously rescinded it—along with every other Avalon Hill contract.

During the tense negotiations that followed, Activision secured the right to finish their game under its current title, as well as make future *Call to Power* sequels without the word *Civilization* attached. But Avalon Hill lost everything to MicroProse, including their 1830 railroad series, which had grown into quite a successful franchise by then. To avoid bankruptcy, they were forced to sell their company to the toy maker Hasbro.

Eight days after buying Avalon Hill, Hasbro also bought MicroProse.

Safe in our offices at Firaxis, we watched these corporate shenanigans with mild bemusement. Business maneuvering could probably make for a fun prototype, if the rest of it weren't so boring all the time. At any rate, our hands were clean and they were going to stay that way. Whoever the name belonged to, it definitely wasn't us, and we'd made peace with this slow, public strangling of our once-beloved title. All we could do was keep making good games, and trust that quality would be more important than branding in the end.

Hasbro made one attempt to do something with the name on their own, releasing *Civilization II: Test of Time* through the MicroProse label in 1999, the same year as both Activision's *Civilization: Call to Power* and our own *Alpha Centauri*. Again, the fans were not fooled. Our game was the only one that didn't contain the word "Civilization," and yet it was widely considered to be a more legitimate member of the series than either of the others. It didn't hurt that the full title was *Sid Meier's Alpha Centauri*, a name no company could buy.

Then, the real surprise happened. When Hasbro had acquired MicroProse, they also acquired at least one employee who had been around since the beginning of the *Civilization* series. Now a senior vice president of research and development, Tony Parks had a strong nostalgia for those early days, and had apparently been as sad as we were to see the treatment the game had received in our absence. After the failure of their *Test of Time* release, Tony somehow convinced executives at Hasbro that they couldn't fight public sentiment: *Civilization* belonged with the folks at Firaxis, and it would never make any money anywhere else. The fans were demanding it, and the best thing Hasbro could do would be to license the name back to us, and take their cut where they could.

Thus, against all odds, we were handed the opportunity to make *Sid Meier's Civilization III* without even asking for it.

It might seem hard to understand, but I really didn't resent all the other versions that had cropped up over the preceding nine years, insofar as they were willing to stand on their own merits. The first thing Bruce made when he left MicroProse was called *Age of Empires*, which was basically *Civilization* in real time, and it was wonderful! *Rise of Nations*, *Age of Wonders*, *Europa Universalis*, *Imperialism*, they're all fine. It's a philosophy I learned from the best: one of the things Dani Bunten Berry told me later in her life was how happy she was that I'd made *Pirates!*, because it had included all of the things she'd wanted to do with *Seven Cities of Gold* but couldn't at the time—and now that someone else had taken up the mantle, she was free to leap ahead and pursue multiplayer. Dani understood that game design is an evolutionary process that we take part in together, and the growth of the industry is something we all benefit from. The ideas didn't start with us, and they can't end with us either.

One of my favorite anecdotes about "stealing" ideas comes from my friend Noah Falstein, who worked for Lucasfilm Games before taking the doomed position at 3DO. Noah had greatly enjoyed the sword fighting minigame in *Pirates!*, and when he was later tasked with creating a boxing minigame for *Indiana Jones and the Last Crusade*, he couldn't see doing it any other way. As he wrote many years later, "I stole . . . that is, lovingly paid tribute to Meier's interface." To be honest, they don't look all that similar to me, but apparently he felt a fair amount of guilt over it.

Then, after *Indiana Jones* shipped, Noah was assigned to a new project that would soon revolutionize the adventure game genre called *The Secret of Monkey Island*. Though the comedic mishaps of their main character, Guybrush Threepwood, had nothing in common with my game, he *was* technically a pirate. This came back to haunt Noah when his codesigner tried to use their old *Indiana Jones* boxing code for a new sword fighting minigame in *Monkey Island*.

"I don't think that's such a good idea," Noah told him in a panic. "This is a comedy game, and that's . . . not very funny."

It was, he acknowledged, "a pretty lame excuse." But to put pirate characters back into my sword fighting interface would be too close for comfort, even in an industry that thrived on expropriation. He would either have to admit his original transgression to the team, or else come up with a better idea to replace it. But how do you make a sword fight funny? It seemed impossible. Self-preservation is a great motivator, though, and from somewhere deep in Noah's subconscious, a helpful memory bubbled to the surface.

"You are using Bonetti's Defense against me, ah?" said a thickly accented voice, swords clanging in the background.

"I thought it fitting, considering the rocky terrain," came the suave reply.

Inigo Montoya pressed his advantage. "Naturally, you must suspect me to attack with Capo Ferro."

"Naturally!" cried the Man in Black. "But I find that Thibault cancels out Capo Ferro, don't you?"

"Unless the enemy has studied his Agrippa . . . which I have!"

"In *The Princess Bride*," Noah explained, "and indeed in a lot of old pirate classics going back to Errol Flynn, the sword wielders' physical dexterity ran a distant second to their skills with insults and rejoinders." With this flash of insight, Noah suggested that they build the duels around the combatants' rapier wits instead, offering a multiple-choice selection of biting replies for every mocking parry. The result was indeed hilarious, and *The Secret of Monkey Island*'s "insult sword fighting" ended up being one of the most celebrated features of the game.

I found it especially ironic that Noah would cite Errol Flynn, since Flynn's movies had originally inspired me as well. Games may steal from games, but everything we do is stolen from non-game stuff to begin with. My inspirations were history, art, and science, and those guys stole from each other just like I stole from them. Do enough research, and you can always find an older version of any idea. We're occasionally credited, for example, with inventing the line "Consequences, shmonsequences" in *Civilization II*, but actually, it was first said by Daffy Duck in a cartoon from 1957, and Daffy's creators got the derisive "shm-" format from turn-of-the-century Yiddish immigrants. It's all part of our shared human culture—or dare I say it, human civilization.

Someday, if we're lucky, an entirely new industry will steal from us. They'll transform our work into something so unimaginably different, we'll feel like Errol Flynn confronted with his future pixelated form. The difference between creativity and theft is that creativity adds, and each addition creates potential that wasn't there before. If we don't share our ideas and help one another build, we'll never get tall enough to find out what's next.

Another more general concept that I took from *Seven Cities of Gold* was that the anticipation of each new story line was at least as important as the story itself. Dan didn't just design the game you could see and play, he also designed parts of the game that would take place entirely in your head. While the computer took several minutes generating your world, for example, clever messages spooled across the screen, like "Eroding Canyons," and "Creating Lovely Rivers," thus rendering a whole planet-forging cinematic in your mind without wasting a byte of disk space. Dan taught me that it was more powerful for the player to envision than to see, and for a while, my early *Civilization* prototype included those same kinds of messages, following his example to the letter.

Mine were eventually replaced with a real cinematic—I did have thirty-two times more memory to play around with than he did, after all—but that sense of aspirational hope remained at the heart of the "one more turn" phenomenon that *Civ* is famous for. Whether it's exploring a new area, sparring with a neighbor, developing a fancy technology, or building one of the Wonders of the World, you always have multiple irons in the fire. Winning this battle might be a good stopping point, but then you'll only be two turns away from mastering chemistry, so you figure you might as well wrap that up. By then, Genghis Khan* is marching toward you, and you can't just let that threat sit in limbo, so you go ahead and mobilize your troops. Meanwhile your Wonder is almost half-

---

* *Achievement Unlocked:* Be Excellent to Each Other—*Encounter Beethoven, Lincoln, Napoleon, and Genghis Khan.*

way done, and you really want to get it taken care of, because *after that* . . .

A huge portion of *Civilization* happens in this nebulous "after that" realm, stacking potential paths on top of actual. A bad game strands you in the past (as in, "What just happened?") while a mediocre one keeps you in the present ("Sure, this is cool."). But a really good game keeps you focused on what's yet to come. It's the underlying basis for that elusive "moment to learn, lifetime to master" quality. As with chess, you can teach a young person how to look ahead one or two moves, and she'll have fun, yet an experienced player can be engrossed by the same game, because there are enough variables to project ten, fifteen, or even twenty moves into the future. A game that runs on speculation can expand or shrink to fit any player's comfort level.

It is true, though, that once you get this "one more turn" thing rolling, "no more turns" can become a hard thing to choose. The very first review of *Civilization* called it "one of those 'compulsive-addictive' games that one can easily stay up until 4:00 a.m. playing." In 1992, *Computer Gaming World* held a poetry contest, in which 40 percent of the entries were about my games in particular, including rhymes like "His newborn was eighteen / When he glanced from the screen." Fellow game designer Peter Molyneux once told a reporter that his bladder had almost exploded while playing *Civ*, and in later years, marketing created a fake ad for a CivAnon twelve-step support group, giving me a cameo as the clueless janitor who ends everyone's sobriety by inadvertently revealing the new version's release date. *Civilization* has even made me late to my own meetings about *Civilization*, so it's not like I'm immune to its charms. But I've never been too concerned about the supposedly slippery slope we're on. The spectrum from interesting, to compelling, to addicting is long and nuanced.

Alexey Pajitnov, the creator of *Tetris*, was once asked about the addictiveness of his game, and whether he was disturbed by it.

"No, what else would people be doing?" he scoffed. "They'd read a stupid book, go see a movie? No, playing a game is a good thing."

Of course he only meant "a book that happens to be stupid," rather than "all books are stupid," but in fact, the value of books has not always been taken for granted. Just as this generation has fretted over the perils of gaming, the generation that grew up with the occasional county fair for entertainment considered books to be a genuine danger to their children.

"Compulsive reading," wrote the eighteenth-century historian Johann Gottfried Hoche, "is a foolish and harmful abuse of an otherwise good thing, truly a great evil, as contagious as the yellow fever in Philadelphia."

Later, the generation that grew up with public libraries was horrified by the proliferation of movies, leading the "purity department" of the Woman's Christian Temperance Union to write scathing editorials against this so-called "addictive" activity. Then, the Academy Awards were invented, movies became understood as an art form, and everyone turned their reactionary instincts toward gaming.

In the last several years, I think we've finally crested that hill, which is great news—but I also know that one day, my future grandchildren will sneer at whatever new thing is captivating the attention of their youth. They, too, will call it addictive, and grumble about how kids these days ought to go play a good videogame instead of wasting their time on those newfangled psychogels, or whatever.

No form of media is perfect, and no form has a monopoly on addiction, either. The important distinction is what you choose to convey with your vehicle. Imagination is good, compelling narratives are good, and empathy is good, in whatever form we express them. Addiction is a problem, but it can happen with any type of escapism—leisure, substance, behavior, food, even social approval—and it should be addressed through individual circumstances, not the banning of excellence. We shouldn't fear the things that enthrall us, but instead acknowledge our responsibility to harness them as a tool, and determine what good can be accomplished with them.

For every workplace lunch hour that stretched into three, there's someone who learned career skills through the economic strategizing and political negotiations of *Civilization*. For every student who failed a class after too many late nights fighting Montezuma, I can point to one who read a book about Montezuma because the game made him curious. For every "*Civilization* widow" who feels neglected by her game-obsessed spouse, well . . . I have one story that trumps them all.

A couple of years after the original game came out, we received a letter at the MicroProse office from a young boy, about ten years old judging from the grammar and handwriting. Fan communication was at its peak by then, and we were used to being told on a daily basis that the game was a life-changing experience. But in this case, it turned out *Civilization* had actually saved lives.

The boy's mother was an avid player, he told us, and sometimes stayed up conquering the world long after the rest of the family had gone to bed. On one particularly late night, her game was interrupted by the smell of smoke, and she ran upstairs to discover a large fire already in progress. Thanks to *Civ*, he said, she was there to wake up the family and get everyone out just in time.

My favorite part about that story, aside from the "hooray, nobody died" aspect, was that it was the mom, not the dad, who was playing. Gaming is for everyone—and not just on an individual level, but as a whole. It's for everyone *together*. I haven't always known what appeals to people who aren't specifically me, but I have always been interested in finding out, and when it comes to games I think addiction is usually just another word for the intense connection we feel toward a work of art. As an artist, my job is to foster that connection in a constructive way—and if I'm lucky, to connect people to one another through our shared experiences.

When escapism is done right, it creates a community of escapees that never existed before. The only alternative would be to knowingly create something less powerful, to deliberately dial back that human connection out of fear. That's madness. We're stronger together, and the more universal and effective our games are, the more knowledge, empathy, and ambition we can inspire.

18

EXTINCTION

The Dinosaur Game
(66 million BC)

IF THERE WERE SUCH A THING AS
a quintessential Sid Meier topic, dinosaurs would probably be it.
They have that familiar hook of childhood fascination, yet enough
scientific details to keep an adult interested. Narrative conflict is
easy to establish between predator and prey, but the chronological and emotional distance keeps the game from feeling violent.
There's a built-in system of advancement via evolution, and when
it comes to ticking clocks, a giant meteor strike is about as exciting
as you can get. It should be easy!

And yet it was so hard.

Though I mostly remember working on the dinosaur game in
the early 2000s, it turns out I'd been toying with prototypes since
at least 1991. I've held on to most of my computers over the years,
and just recently, I was persuaded to drag a few of the oldest models out of storage and fire them up. Initial attempts were unfortunately literal—as soon as the first machine was turned on, sparks
flew, and the whole thing went down in a blaze of short-circuiting
glory. The second one we tried was mercifully free of fireworks,
but only because it wouldn't power up at all. Our Firaxis IT guys
love a challenge, though, and after locating an ancient boot disk,
we were finally able to exhume the fossils held within.

Sure enough, there was a dinosaur folder, along with about a dozen others. Some of them were ancestors to games we eventually made, including a spy game, a space game, and of course a Civil War game. They were more like imperfect siblings than a direct lineage, ideas trapped in amber by a turnover in technology. Virtually none of the data would have been useful on whatever computer replaced it, but it wasn't a big loss, because I build most major revisions from scratch, anyway. The coding is the easy part; it's like drawing a picture of something after you've excavated it. The sweat is in the digging, not the documentation.

Other prototypes on this museum-quality computer, like a mystery game and a Wild West game, had turned out to be evolutionary dead ends—at least so far. The truth is I never really give up on anything. The ideas just sit in stasis, sometimes for decades, until I can figure out the right way to make them work. I may have to poke and prod in a hundred different ways, but once I find that perfect angle the rest falls into place pretty quickly. In my entire career, the dinosaur game is the only one I've ever had to declare totally, soul-crushingly, extinct.

The first few versions were turn-based, or what I affectionately thought of as "DinoCiv." Your little herd would wander around the grid, foraging instead of farming and building nests instead of cities. Sometimes you'd run into other herds and have a fight, and if you won, they'd join you and increase your genetic diversity. This is where it got interesting, or so I thought: when it came time to breed, you'd suddenly become an embryonic specialist, able to see which genes were available from the two herd members you'd chosen for the shotgun wedding. Pick a large head from mom and a long tail from dad, and junior would hopefully come out a little smarter and better-balanced than his parents. Keep at it for enough generations, and maybe his distant progeny would one day rule the savannah.

As the game got harder, dominant and recessive gene patterns came into play, as well as gambles on random mutations. It seemed fun at first, but ultimately, it was just Dinosaur Mr. Potato

Head*—the pieces got old very quickly. I added a button to automatically optimize the breeding, but if you have to offload the supposedly fun part of your game, that's a pretty good indication that you're confused about what fun is. Even at its best, this version broke the *Covert Action* rule, because players who took the time to embrace the genetic system would lose track of the main storyline. What's more, randomizing the dinosaur traits eliminated all the celebrity actors like Tyrannosaurus rex and Stegosaurus. Their recognizability was a key part of the emotional hook, and without them, it was just a bunch of lizards.

No problem, I thought, that's what prototyping is for—figure out what's bad, and ditch it. So I transitioned into the second major version of the dinosaur game, which I mentally dubbed "DinoAge" in reference to several *Civ* competitors that focused on just one era. Now, the player was following a set path of evolution toward known dinosaurs, with just a few major choices like carnivore or herbivore, cold-blooded or warm-blooded, and so on. It was simpler, faster, and also hugely boring. There was usually a clear right answer to the choices in any given situation, and it almost seemed as if the computer were playing you instead of the other way around. Simplification helps when there's too much going on at once, but if you're investing the time needed for a turn-based game, you want all of the interesting decisions to be under your control.

Okay, so, what if the game weren't turn-based? *Gettysburg!* had worked out great as a real-time game. Maybe what you really wanted was to be leading your Velociraptor hordes against a phalanx of Brontosaurus heavies, keeping an eye out for volcanic land mines and Pterodactyl air support. Once again, I rewrote the code, calling the new version "DinoCraft" after the popular real-time

* *Achievement Unlocked:* To Infinity and Beyond—Collect a piggy bank, toy soldiers, T. rex, and Mr. Potato Head.

game *StarCraft*. Unlike its namesake, though, this third prototype was just as much a disaster as the first two.

The reason was simple mechanics. A major pillar of real-time strategy games is the use of ranged weapons: some fighters are slow and strong, and spend their time bullying through the front lines, while others are weak but nimble, and mostly hop around at the fringes of the battle doing damage from a distance. The latter can shoot arrows, launch cruise missiles, sling magic spells, or whatever else suits your theme—as long as they have to spread out a little to do it. Otherwise, if all units are equal, it becomes a free-for-all mashup at the center of the screen, like a bunch of five-year-olds trying to play soccer. Good strategic planning can't happen until you spread your team out, and throwing some kind of ranged weapon into the mix forces the player to do that.

But there was no such thing as a ranged dinosaur. The best you could get were a few species who could jump surprisingly far, but that still put them at the center of the fray when their jaws clamped shut. I found myself taking more and more paleontological liberties, until finally, I gave up all pretense of realism and invented a dinosaur that could spit poison. As a friendly nod to our producer at EA, Bing Gordon, I named my new species the Bingosaur. Probably I would have had to change it by the time the game shipped, but I cleverly avoided that by never finishing the game.

If I'd only had to fabricate one dinosaur, it might have been okay. But the rock-paper-scissors axiom meant that roughly a third of the fighters had to be ranged, which meant either a lot more spitters, or a lot less diversity. Meanwhile, the distribution of real dinosaur species was heavily tipped in favor of herbivores. When the goal had been herd evolution, that worked out okay, but now all the gentle species had nothing to do but sit and watch a handful of carnivores chew on each other. The "builder-to-fighter ratio," as we call it, was way off.

Goodbye to prototype number three.

By now, I was getting desperate. Breathless news articles had already been written about the game; fans were actively discussing on message boards what features we might include. I'd even fired up the prototype for a few interview candidates, seeking fresh feedback from anywhere I could find it. We'd had a full team of employees on the project for at least six months, and I still hadn't even figured out what type of game it was supposed to be.

One of the big questions I couldn't answer was, "Who is having the most fun in the dinosaur universe?" That's who you want your player to be: the person with the most power, living the most exciting life. In the history of civilization, it's the king; on the Spanish Main, it's the captain of the pirate ship; in war, it's the general; in the transportation industry, it's the tycoon. But individual dinosaurs don't really have a lot of power. T. rex can eat all the little guys, but he doesn't build an army. Evolution is a useful mechanic, but it's not something the individual gets to experience—you have to take a step back into the role of Dinosaur God to even play around with it. But then, what god would micromanage the daily feeding and fighting of specific animals? There didn't seem to be a unified perspective that could tie in all the best parts of dinosauring.

I'd steered the game left, right, and every angle in between, all to no avail. The only remaining option was to swerve off the road completely. So the fourth and final dinosaur prototype was nicknamed "DinoMon," because, like the pocket monsters sweeping the nation that year, it was a card game. Really it was closer to "Dinosaur: The Gathering" than Pokémon, but that didn't roll off the tongue as easily when it came time to give presentations on why this endeavor had failed so thoroughly.

To be fair, the card game version wasn't bad. It neatly solved the recognizable-versus-evolving debate by dividing those duties between dinosaur cards and mutation cards. You could start with a scientifically accurate Coelophysis card, for example, but then play a horns or feathers card on top of it to make him more powerful in a particular duel. It felt like seeing your favorite celebrity playing different characters. Returning the cards to your deck after each battle also meant that the "I'll do it differently next time" itch could get scratched even faster than usual. Meanwhile, the card format took advantage of the players' imagination, letting them animate the swirling dust storm or splattering mud bath in their own mind instead of using up on-screen resources. Even the sense of collectability seemed to resonate with the theme. The more dinosaur names a kid can rattle off, the cooler he is, as if the fundamental childhood instinct is to mentally collect all of the different species in the first place.

In the end, though, the innovation just wasn't there. First, the way the cards interacted was simply too close to Magic. Stealing ideas is fine if you've put your own twist on it, but I was never convinced that the dinosaur game had enough new material to justify its obvious origins. Second, I could sense a general sort of malaise in both the team and myself. To have spent so much time and energy on the supposedly quintessential Sid Meier game, and ultimately settle on a run-of-the-mill card format . . . it just felt like a letdown.

Then again, so did quitting. It's easy to reject my own efforts when they don't measure up, but much harder to do it to other people. Would Electronic Arts even let us walk away from this game after all the money we'd sunk into it? How many of my team members would be disappointed, and how many would be secretly relieved? Which was worse? I didn't even want to think about all the "Sid Cancels Game!" news articles, which would surely be even more numerous than the ones eagerly anticipating the game in the first place.

In the midst of this growing dread, I took a trip to Los Angeles for the sixth annual Electronic Entertainment Expo, also known as E3. It was a strange time for the industry—videogame sales were now topping $35 billion a year, and Americans had preordered half a million PlayStation 2 consoles before a single one had left the factory. Clearly there was enthusiasm for our work. Yet families of the Columbine shooting victims had just sued twenty-five different game manufacturers for their alleged role in the attackers' behavior, and the US Senate was holding official hearings on "The Impact of Interactive Violence on Children." Later that year, presidential hopeful Al Gore would select Joe Lieberman as his running mate, due in part to Lieberman's long-standing bipartisan efforts to regulate the gaming industry.

The atmosphere at E3 that year was very *Tale of Two Cities*. At the same time that Nintendo was bringing fans to tears with their stunning trailer for *The Legend of Zelda: Majora's Mask*, the city of Indianapolis was considering a law requiring arcade games to be hidden from public view. Inside the Sega booth, attendees were delightedly shaking electronic maracas to the rhythms of *Samba de Amigo*, while out on the street, protestors were shaking their fists at the convention hall in angry condemnation. The denouncements didn't do us any real harm, as demonstrated by the fact that nine years later EA would be caught hiring fake protesters for publicity. But at the time, we didn't know how the politics would play out, not to mention the lawsuits, and everyone was just a little on edge.

The vibe wasn't helping my already discouraged mood over the dinosaur game, and near the end of the weekend, Susan and I took a break to visit the famous Grauman's Chinese Theatre in downtown Hollywood. Strangely enough, Baltimore was going through a heat wave that year, and the Los Angeles weather was considerably nicer than it was back home. Just as I was starting to relax, we were stopped short by a large crowd of people on the sidewalk, all craning to see past a police line. Up ahead I could make out limousines, floodlights, and what looked like a massive Carnotaurus rearing up over the sidewalk. I thought for a moment I had finally cracked.

No one seemed disturbed by the cold-blooded (but possibly warm-blooded!) killer among them, however, nor was there any sense of urgency among the police, who had their backs to the spectacle and their crowd-control frowns turned toward us. Whatever weird celebration was going on, we would not be getting through. So we ducked into the Disney Store, thinking we could pass through and exit on the south side of the building, one street away from the quagmire.

"I'm sorry sir," said a friendly young man in a monogrammed polo. "You can't go this way right now."

"Great," I muttered, somewhat more tersely than he deserved. "What's going on here?"

He smiled, obviously glad I'd asked. "We're having a movie premiere today for *Dinosaur*, a new major motion picture from Disney Studios."

"Wonderful," I replied, almost sincerely. That explained the life-size model of the Carnotaurus, at least. "We're just trying to get down Hollywood Boulevard."

"Where are you folks from?"

As someone who has to engage in convention small talk a lot, I know when someone's really interested, and when they're just asking because it's their job. "Baltimore," I said politely, before getting back to the issue at hand. "So, how are we going to get past here?"

"Baltimore, eh? How's the weather there this time of year?"

"It's fine. Do we have to go around, or what?"

"How about those Baltimore Orioles?"

"Yeah, right," I agreed, trailing off as noncommittally as possible. I had no idea about those Baltimore Orioles, and didn't want to be chatting about them regardless.

After a long, pointed silence, the employee seemed to suddenly remember something. "Hey, I happen to have a couple of passes left to the premiere, are you interested?"

I sighed. "We're really trying to find that theater with the stars' footprints in cement. When does this premiere start?" My tone made it clear that unless the thing was starting in the next five minutes, we weren't going to wait around.

"The movie starts in about five minutes," he said.

"Oh."

"There's free popcorn and soda, and these passes will get you in to the post-premiere party next door, with more free food and drinks, and a chance to meet some of the stars of the movie. Plus, you'll get a free T-shirt!"

Well, who could say no to a free T-shirt? Moments later, Susan and I found ourselves in the upper balcony of the El Capitan Theatre, watching the world premiere of a dinosaur movie while I secretly went through my own dinosaur-themed existential crisis. It was a pleasant but bizarre set of circumstances, and I vaguely pondered whether this was some kind of sign—maybe I should be doing my game in 3D, like the movie. Or maybe the lesson was its wholesome plot, and I should go back to one of the earlier prototypes that hadn't focused so much on combat. One of my favorite bits in DinoCraft had been the little babies that followed the grownups around, and maybe that sense of generational growth had been the right angle to pursue after all. Or maybe this was all just further evidence that a strategy game could never capture the essence of dinosaurs after all.

Before I could decide what this whole weird coincidence might signify, though, I was hit with an even weirder one. After the post-premiere party, which was every bit as good as promised, we finally managed to get across the street to our original destination, Grauman's Chinese Theatre. As the name implies, this 1927 Hollywood landmark is a beautiful, but not exactly subdued, shrine to faux-Asian kitsch. Elaborately carved square turrets flank either side of a courtyard, which recedes far back from the street before rising up into a three-story red pagoda. Stone lions guard the entrance, and dragon motifs cover practically everything. If it were built today, public reaction would probably place it somewhere between gaudy and offensive, but as a relic from the Golden Age of movies, we're fortunately allowed to keep enjoying it.

Over the years, Grauman's Chinese Theatre had hosted hundreds of blockbuster premieres, from *The Wizard of Oz* to *Star Wars*, but its main attraction was the courtyard. Legend has it that either a famous actress, or perhaps one of the theater's cofounders, accidentally stepped in the wet cement during construction, and this gave them the idea to permanently memorialize the hand- and footprints of movie icons in the floor of their entryway. With less than 250 of them allotted after almost a century of operation, some consider the humble concrete blocks to be the most prestigious award Hollywood can offer. Many contain little messages of inspiration or thanks, and a few actors have pressed iconic items into the cement as well, such as Groucho Marx's cigar, or Daniel Radcliffe's wand from the *Harry Potter* movies.

As Susan and I crossed the threshold for a glimpse of all this movie history, I happened to look down at my feet. "Sid Dear," the pavement read, "My wish is for your success."

Once again, I briefly questioned my sanity, but the words were real. Someone named Norma Talmadge had written a message to me all the way back in May 1927. Nor was she the only one: Mary Pickford and Cecil B. deMille had each written "Greetings to Sid" on either side of Norma's block, and just above that, Douglas Fairbanks wished me good luck. Opposite him, Bebe Daniels went so far as to call me "Our King of Showmen," while Barbara Stanwyck declared her outright love. The whole courtyard, it seemed, was rooting for me.

Thanks to some historical pamphlets, we quickly figured out that Grauman's Chinese Theatre had been built by a man named Sid Grauman, who was both an entrepreneur and a close friend to all of the early stars. Nonetheless, I chose to take their messages personally. I mean, there aren't that many people in the world named Sid, and I'm sure he wouldn't mind sharing.

Clark Gable called me a great guy, and both Roy Rogers and his horse Trigger wished me many happy trails. Humphrey Bogart wrote, "May you never die till I kill you," while John Wayne insisted, "There are not enough words." Jimmy Stewart, Bob

Hope, Fred Astaire, Ginger Rogers, and countless more all mentioned me by name, and I took their encouragement to heart.

I had spent most of the weekend coming to terms with the inevitable abandonment of my beloved dinosaur game, and this historical pep talk didn't change that reality. I'd have to pull the plug once we got back to Baltimore, and face the disappointment of my team, my publisher, and worst of all, my fans. It wouldn't feel good at all. But at that moment, walking out of Grauman's Chinese Theatre into the bright California sun, what I felt instead was the conviction that it was going to be okay. If the creative lifespan of an industry was longer than any one person enshrined in this courtyard, then it was certainly longer than a single project. Time kept marching on, and there would always be more cool ideas and fun adventures on the horizon.

19

ARTIFICIAL TURF

Sid Meier's SimGolf
(2002)

MY COWORKER JAKE SOLOMON once asked me point blank, "What's your guilty pleasure?" It should be mentioned that he did this on stage in front of a few hundred people, which is not usually the ideal place to unburden your soul. Fortunately, the answer came easily.

"Excess," I told him with a pained smile. The drawback of being able to isolate the interesting part of any given thing is that you are constantly interested by every given thing. I routinely find myself stumbling into new hobbies almost by accident, and as with my work life, I seem incapable of doing anything halfheartedly.

As an example, I like to play the guitar. I know a fair number of chords, and when I'm playing music with friends I'll occasionally hand over the keyboards to someone else, so I can pretend to be a rock star in short bursts. But I wouldn't consider myself astronomically talented at, or obsessed with, playing the guitar—I'm just interested in it. Therefore, I own about twenty of them.

In my defense, some are for convenience. I keep two at the office and two in our church building, because you never know whether the acoustic or electric mood will strike, and I don't want to haul them back and forth all the time. The rest are either hanging on display at home or in various states of storage, but they do get played, as I keep insisting to Susan.

Then there are the radio-controlled airplanes, and the historical memorabilia, and the golf clubs . . . like I said, guitars are just one hobby of mine. I'm a nerd, and nerds always want to have the latest gadget. I can justify my extensive collection of game consoles as part of my job, at least, but for the most part I have to make a conscious effort to keep the accumulation below pathological levels. I once got to visit George Lucas's library at Skywalker Ranch, which has a ladder leading up to a second-floor balcony where you can access another several thousand books. It's probably a good thing that I've never lived in a house that could hold that many books, but a grand, sprawling library is the first room I'd install if I did.

One important deterrent I've learned is to limit myself to a trickle of information, because it only takes a few minutes with a magazine before I start thinking that *this* set of titanium-alloy golf clubs will finally take my game to the next level, or *that* digitally superior guitar amp will really make my Paul Reed Smith hollowbody sound like it was meant to. A few years back, I canceled all my subscriptions for my own well-being, and since then, I've been doing better. But in late 2000, when we killed the dinosaur game, I was still getting two or three different golfing magazines delivered—and I wasn't even playing regularly.

It was in one of these magazines, hiding among the course reviews and backswing improvement articles, that I discovered a contest for designing golf holes. Apparently there was more to it than just laying down an oblong putting green and digging a sand trap or two. There were even course designers who were as famous as the pro tour players who stood on their creations.

Interesting.

Like *Railroad Tycoon*, my golfing prototype started out as a model builder rather than a competitive simulator, and I again developed it while on vacation to clear my head from a stalled title. Of course, the expectations for a prototype were much higher now, and the length of a vacation was still the same, so what was impressive in 1990 should have transitioned to impossible in 2000. But one of the secrets of being a game designer is that you get to reuse your stuff—writers can't plagiarize their own passages; artists can't add details to a portrait and call it new; but I can rearrange existing pieces of code into a completely different game within just a few hours. *Gettysburg!* already had big grassy fields, and soldiers who could walk around. All I had to do was swap out those Union grays for an argyle vest, and my golfing prototype was halfway done.

The internet offers plenty of hijackable material these days, as well. John Williams unwittingly loaned me his *Jurassic Park* soundtrack for the dinosaur game, while the art came from a series of prehistoric-themed postage stamps. *Gettysburg!* used pictures from my own Civil War books until our artists could replace them. As long as you're talking about a temporary mockup that will never leave the office, anything is fair game. The point of a prototype is just to get across as quickly as possible what the experience could potentially feel like, if we spent the time on it.

"This feels like it could be part of the *Sims* universe," Bing Gordon told me when I got back from vacation and showed him my new golfing prototype. "We should get you guys in touch with Maxis."

In the years since *SimCity*, Will Wright had produced several sequels and spinoffs through his studio, including *SimCity 2000* (released in 1993) and *SimCity 3000* (released in 1999). There had been a brief time, in fact, when *Civ II* was going to be called *Civilization 2000* as an indirect homage to Will's game, but we decided that there was no point in trying to make sequels sound less sequel-y. Maxis eventually came to the same conclusion, truncating their next title to *SimCity 4*. But like me, Will had handed his series over to fresh talent by then, and in the actual year 2000, he had released his latest triumph, *The Sims*. It had been a monumental hit, of course, and as the publisher for both our studios, Electronic Arts was hungry for crossover products.

So we consulted with Will a few times, and ended up with *SimGolf*, which had a reasonable blend of both *Sims* and *Tycoon*-style elements. The menu was a traditional *Sims* interface, and the golfers spoke that curious string of nonsense syllables that Maxis had labeled Simlish. (After several months of development, we were practically fluent in it ourselves, and would regularly shout "myshuno!" to get each other's attention in the office.) But the way to keep your customers happy in *SimGolf* was through environmental design, rather than manipulation of their behavior, and you still had to watch your bank statements no matter how happy the people were.

With the basics in place, I was now brought back to the central question inspired by the magazine contest: what makes a "good" golf hole? How do you score the aesthetics of fun? If the beauty of Bach could be analyzed and mathematically described, then the psychological appeal of golf surely could be, too. Unlike music, however, I didn't have years of experience on the putting green to draw my own patterns from. I had to talk to some real golfers.

Fortunately, my Firaxis cofounder Jeff Briggs had a brother-in-law named Jonathan who was a member of a prestigious club up in New York. Somehow, Jeff convinced him to come down to Maryland along with one of his professional golfing buddies. Presumably, the focus of their trip was to play a few rounds at Caves Valley or one of the country clubs in Bethesda, but they generously took the time to meet us for lunch one afternoon to discuss what made these courses superior.

"It needs to be easy," someone declared. "Nobody actually likes a hard course."

"Then why not make the green into a giant funnel?" I asked. "Anywhere you hit, the ball goes in."

"Right," he said thoughtfully. "Yeah, okay. So, you want it to *look* hard, but still play easy."

Over the next hour, we narrowed it down even further. What these guys really liked best, it turned out, was when a hole was easy for them, but hard for others. If Jonathan were especially good at chip shots, for example, then he had the most fun on holes that relied heavily on them. Golfers wanted to be the star in their world just as much as gamers did.

Slowly a scoring system began to form in my mind. We would run four hypothetical players through each hole. One would be completely average, and each of the three others would have a special talent—accuracy, distance, or curving their shots. At the end of the hole, we would compare how the three unique players performed against the average guy, and rate your hole design based on the difference. So if the average player could hit the ball around 200 yards, and the distance player usually went for 250, then you would ideally build a hill at 225 yards out. The distance hitter would make it over the top, while the average one saw his ball roll backward, and the bigger deviation meant a higher score for you.

The interesting thing about this system was there was essentially no AI involved. We had to lay out the complicated assessment algorithms, but the computer was never tasked with creating a good golf hole itself. There were no competitors encroaching on your land, and no calculated setbacks in the form of weather or financial upset. It was my first project without any element of antagonism since *Solo Flight*—and even that had come with a demo mode that could fly the plane without input, despite not being utilized in the main game.

Railroad Tycoon had come close to shipping without AI, but near the end of development we decided that the added urgency would be an improvement. This was around the same time that its working title, *The Golden Age of Railroads*, converted to the more aggressive *Tycoon* descriptor. Unfortunately, because we implemented the code less than a month before the game's release, I didn't have time to fully develop it. So rather than creating progressively smarter versions of the AI, each increasing difficulty level was defined by how much the computer was allowed to cheat. Robber barons like Cornelius Vanderbilt and J. P. Morgan lived up to their job titles by taking on more debt than the player could, building stations in unsuitable terrain, and apparently blackmailing their rivers into behaving even when the player had been flooded directly upstream. But the game also came with an option to turn the competition off, and very few players griped about it. Generally speaking, people who like trains *really* like trains, so most of them were just thrilled to have their fandom acknowledged.

Even if we had taken the time to create more-nuanced algorithms, the truth is it wouldn't have changed much. Highly realistic AI gets accused of cheating even more often than its dishonest brethren, because on some level, all players are unnerved by the idea that a computer could outsmart them. Part of the fun is learning the patterns of the AI and successfully predicting them, and when computers don't act like computers, the only psychologically safe assumption is that they must have accessed information they shouldn't have. AI isn't allowed to gamble, or behave randomly, or get lucky—even though humans do all of these things on a daily basis—not because we can't program it, but because experience tells us that players will get frustrated and quit. The same phenomenon doesn't happen when both opponents are humans, because they've already tempered their expectations for the possibility that the other guy is crazy. Computers are too smart to be crazy, so if they start acting that way, we can't shake the suspicion that they know something we don't. Thus, from the designer's perspective, brilliant AI is usually not our highest priority.

Even the AI in *Civilization*, which was more involved than most, is nothing compared to what real AI can accomplish. In 2011, an MIT professor used a machine-learning algorithm to teach a computer to play *Civ II* without any underlying instructions. Starting with random clicks and feedback from the game on whether an action was successful, the computer eventually picked up enough patterns to win the game 46 percent of the time. Once it was provided with a text version of the manual for word association—searching for passages that contained the same words displayed on the screen, and making educated guesses about what to do next given the words surrounding them—the success rate went up to 79 percent. Though I dreamed about this sort of thing early in my career, it's frankly a little terrifying now that it's here, and I'm happy sticking with the simpler expectations of our players instead.

SimGolf was well-received, though nearly every reviewer noted with surprise how whimsical the game was. One called it "warm, fuzzy, and pastel—a world sprung straight from the pages of a JCPenney catalog." I suspect they based their impression on my name, rather than any kind of objective cuteness index. Users tend to pigeonhole me into the hard strategy genre despite my varied résumé. But even if *SimGolf* were a little more playful than my last few titles, that was the best reason for me to be doing it. Something new is always more interesting than something I've already done.

By the time I'd finished the game, in fact, golf was ready to take a back seat to other interests, and it was only by accident that I got back into playing the live version many years later. It started after Susan returned home from a fundraising event with what she thought was wonderful news.

"I bought you a golf foursome!" she declared proudly.

"What?" I asked, certain that I'd misheard her. Those words didn't even make any sense.

"The PGA Champions Tour is in Baltimore this year," she said, "and they're having a pro-am golf tournament the day before. I bid on the package, and I won, so now you and two friends get to play a round of golf with a famous player on the Tour."

"But it's been years since I played," I protested, probably setting down a golf magazine while I said it. "You realize there's going to be people there, right?" Never mind the public embarrassment; I could easily see myself shanking the ball into the crowd. "I could kill someone!"

She had been so pleased to present this gift to me, though, and I didn't want to disappoint her by refusing. So I started taking lessons every week, to avoid both humiliation and potential manslaughter charges, and by the time the tournament rolled around, golf had grown from a latent diversion into a full-blown hobby. The irony was that a few weeks before the tournament, I pulled a muscle and couldn't play after all. We gave the tickets to our golfer friend Jonathan, his son, and a former artist at MicroProse named Murray Taylor, and they had a great time. But as soon as I was healed, I was back out on the putting green with my newest set of high-tech golf clubs.

And while it does mean I'm perpetually short on closet space, I think having a slightly obsessive personality is a useful thing. On the one hand, it keeps me focused on the quality of my work, but on the other, it provides critical sources of outside inspiration, which often contribute in surprising ways. My game devoted entirely to Bach's music might have been ahead of its time, for example, but his work influenced several other projects, and even made a notable appearance in *SimGolf*. Testing had revealed that when laying down tiles of fairway, the confirming sound effect of each square quickly escalated from helpful to annoying. So I replaced the ordinary clacking sound with the notes to a well-known Bach cantata called "Jesu, Joy of Man's Desiring." (The title may be unfamiliar, but you've almost certainly heard it at a wedding or two.) With this tiny change, the most repetitive part of the game suddenly became one of the most endearing. Fans felt smart for recognizing the piece, amused by its presence, and subtly motivated to keep building so they could complete the tune. *SimGolf* wouldn't have been as good if I hadn't maintained an interest in music—and wouldn't have existed at all if I hadn't maintained an interest in golf. A designer who's only interested in games will find it very hard to bring anything original to the table, and I'm sure this is true in other fields, too. Whatever it is you want to be good at, you have to make sure you continue to read, and learn, and seek joy elsewhere, because you never know where inspiration will strike.

20

INTO THE WIND

Sid Meier's Pirates!
Live the Life (2004)
✳
Sid Meier's Railroads! (2006)

CIVILIZATION III SEEMED TO ACT
as a falling domino, and over the next several years, nearly all of
the loose MicroProse properties would be returned to us one by
one. The next to come home was *Pirates!*, which Hasbro had sold
to the French company Infogrames, who had then begun calling
themselves Atari after those naming rights went up for sale. I'm
sure it was mostly a financial decision on "Atari's" part, just like it
had been for Hasbro to let us make *Civilization III*, but it still felt
really good to be acknowledged as the rightful caretakers of the
Pirates! legacy.

With the seventeen-year gap, it made sense for a new *Pirates!*
to look and feel very different from the original, but I found the
transition surprisingly hard to cope with. *Civilization* had evolved
gradually, but catapulting an old title into the modern age required
both a technological and an emotional overhaul. I was especially
resistant to the idea of 3D graphics, which were once again the hot
new thing.

"It's a flash in the pan," I told the team. "It's not going to stick."
The only thing 3D reminded me of was chunky old flight simula-

tors and their attendant coding struggles. Years of successful 2D titles had convinced me that it was just a marketing gimmick, not to mention a huge resource hog—with so much processing power dedicated to that beautiful 3D environment, the rest of the game inevitably suffered. It didn't matter how much everyone oohed and aahed in the first 30 seconds if there weren't enough substance beneath it to keep them coming back for more. No, two was plenty of dimensions for me.

The team's protests made it clear that I was alone in this line of thinking, but I held firm. We were talking about *Pirates!*—my first adventure game, my first break from company tradition, my first namesake—and it had to be done right.

All projects ebb and flow to a certain degree, and at some point most will reach "the Valley of Despair." It's that moment when it seems nothing is working, no one understands your vision, the interface is ugly, the gameplay is boring, and you can't imagine how you'll ever finish it. Usually it happens about halfway through the project, when the game gets too big to hold in your head all at once, and the days fill up with meetings, and every adjustment throws eight other variables out of whack. But occasionally, it happens earlier, when it turns out that the plan you were stubbornly clinging to wasn't as good as you thought it was.

"Fine," I thought miserably. "Let's see what 3D would look like, just for the heck of it."

We had all the latest tools at the office, but so far they'd only been used on some introductory cinematics for *Civ III*, plus one Firaxis logo screen that looked like a giant blimp flying by. I hadn't fiddled around much with the technology, but it wasn't my style to stand over someone else's shoulder dictating what I wanted to see. So I spent a long Fourth of July weekend at the office, teaching myself how to use our new 3D engine just enough to create a ship battle prototype.

When I was young, my father and I used to go sailing on Cass Lake, which is right on the thumb knuckle of Michigan's mitten shape. Though the majority of the shoreline is private property, the northern bank is within the scenic Dodge #4 State Park (the first three in the series being strangely nonexistent). In addition to sandy beaches and a few fishing spots, there is a wide public boat launch, and on pleasant weekends, you'll find everything from canoes to small yachts easing their way down the shallow concrete ramp into the water.

Ours was a simple but convenient craft, easily strapped to the roof of our recently purchased gold station wagon. My dad had ordered a do-it-yourself kit called the "Go" that included a premade hull, mast, and sails, and required only a few sheets of plywood and some labor to complete the deck and make her watertight. Small boat kits were fairly common in those days, but this one was unusual because it had no rudder, and we would frequently get hailed by other recreational sailors as we carried it to shore.

"Hey, ah . . . there's something wrong with your boat, buddy."

"No, it's fine," my father would say, waving back cheerfully. In confirmation, he and I would climb into our little dinghy and deftly maneuver into the open water, using only the wind and a hard-earned familiarity with the physics of sailing.

The boat really wasn't meant for two, especially not with the constant moving back and forth one has to do to keep the rigging pointed in the optimal direction. So once my father was satisfied with my navigation skills, he let me take the boat out by myself, standing on the ramp with his hands on his hips and giving occasional advice at the top of his lungs until I was too far out to hear him. Fatherly pride quickly gave way to boredom as I refused to return to shore, and soon he had to build a second boat for himself, this time entirely from scratch. We would sail side by side for hours, racing for short distances and admiring the fancy houses along the opposite shore, until my sense of the wind was second nature.

I had tried to bring a little bit of this experience into the original *Pirates!* by making the player contend with wind direction during battles. The way to move forward into the wind is by tacking, or sharply angling your ship back and forth, like a road winding up a steep mountain. I had assumed everyone knew this, but many players found the process counterintuitive, and it was generally considered one of the more frustrating aspects of the game. With 3D, however, I was able to include so much more nuance. The ship tilted with your turns, and steered from the helm in believable arcs rather than rotating from the middle like a dial. The sails billowed and twisted as they caught the wind, and fluttered helplessly when aimed too directly into it. For the first time, the maneuvering felt true enough for non-sailors to grasp what was going on.

Plus, it was a ton of fun to animate all the little pirates jumping off the enemy ship before it sank. We'd bent the "no one dies" rule a few times over the years, but I wanted *Pirates!* to retain its sense of innocence, and if 3D could help us do that, so much the better.

Of course in retrospect, *Pirates!* had been the perfect instrument for 3D even without the swimming scallywags. It was the most story-based game I'd ever made, ideally suited for both picturesque environments and full-scale cinematics. The original's main breakthrough had been an extravagance of still images on the screen, and now the remake could once again showcase the latest graphics technology.

Once I'd finally seen the light, the team was reinvigorated and the rest of the game fell easily into place. But to be honest, I'm still wary of 3D cinematics even today. Certainly there are appropriate uses for it, but 3D has an almost hallucinogenic ability to convince game designers that they're moviemakers. Stephen Spielberg* can't react in real time to the twitch of your wrist, or change the ending to suit your mood. His interaction with you, profound as it may be, is strictly one-way, and the worst thing we can do is subordinate our unique two-way abilities beneath a jealous imi-

---

* *Achievement Unlocked:* **This Belongs in a Museum—Go on a raid with Indiana Jones, George Lucas, John Williams, and Steven Spielberg.**

tation. Beautiful is nice, if you can swing it, but we don't need to look any further than *Minecraft* to prove the modern-day value of gameplay independent from graphics.

Even with our priorities firmly in place, the new *Pirates!* had to contend with the constraints of added graphics more than once. In the opening 3D cinematic, for example, we introduced an overarching nemesis who could be hunted throughout the game. In keeping with the spirit of the original, Marquis Montalban's nefarious story line remained optional, but simply assigning him a nationality—which we had to do, in order to animate his clothes and accent—caused problems for players who wanted to stay on good terms with the Spanish. Attacking a criminal within an ally's borders wasn't an impossible scenario, and we wouldn't let it damage your friendship too badly. But if the player went so far as to court the governor's daughter in Havana, she would soon be kidnapped by Montalban's subordinates and whisked away to his home country—which is to say, the cantina next door to the governor's house. We acknowledged the plot hole with a little humorous dialogue and moved on, but it illustrates how even a single cinematic cutscene can harden the story structure, and end up removing more plot than it adds.

Shortly after the modernized *Pirates!* was released, I found myself in Germany with a few hours to spare between press interviews. We decided to visit a tourist attraction in Hamburg called Miniatur Wunderland, home of the largest model train in the world. At the time, they had just finished their fifth major section, with a total of 560 trains pulling nearly 6,000 cars behind them. Several hundred other vehicles rolled freely on magnetic pathways hidden beneath the city streets, and each hour the model's twenty-six computers ran a full day's worth of drama: police cruisers pulled over speeding civilians, firetrucks responded to flickering windows leaking tendrils of real smoke, and a space shuttle periodically launched in search of tiny, tiny aliens.

It was both an adorable and perfectly timed experience. Fans had begun asking for other classic remakes almost as soon as the new *Pirates!* had been announced, and this little side trip to Hamburg was just the thing to get my creative juices flowing for an update to the original *Railroad Tycoon*.

There were ownership issues, as always. Immediately after my departure, MicroProse had sold the license to PopTop Software, who had later been acquired by Take-Two Interactive. Coincidentally, we were already in talks with Take-Two after they had purchased the *Civilization* license from Infogrames in late 2004, though the buyer's name wasn't made public for several months in order to keep the development of *Civ IV* under wraps. In just eight years, Firaxis had already had relationships with four different publishers—Electronic Arts, Hasbro, Infogrames, and Atari— and while some of these were technically the same group of people under a different name, there were always new executives to answer to, and the disruption to the workflow was the same. In the case of Hasbro, we didn't even get the chance to release a single game before the corporate moniker had to be changed once again. Now, we were looking at a fifth relationship with Take-Two, and more than anything, we just wanted stability.

So, instead of signing yet another licensing contract, we came to a much bigger agreement. Take-Two would first buy up all of the remaining MicroProse properties from Infogrames and elsewhere, and then acquire our studio outright. It would take a lot of paperwork, but the lawyers assured us that Humpty Dumpty could be put back together again.

The decision was dramatic, but relatively easy to make. We'd always suspected that Firaxis would end up with a permanent publisher at some point, and if it were inevitable, certainly this was the best way for it to happen—with everything handed back to us, and no more piecemeal negotiations over properties we'd invented in the first place. Take-Two considered our games to be a good counterbalance to some of their other franchises, like *Grand Theft Auto*, and they were happy to let us do our thing with minimal interference. So in January 2005, they unveiled themselves as the buyer of the *Civilization* license, revealed the upcoming release of *Civ IV*, and announced the acquisition of Firaxis all at once. It was a hefty press release. Two months later, we added *Sid Meier's Railroads!* to the roster as well.

It was a little ironic that, after all that effort, we didn't end up using the *Tycoon* brand. Owning the license was still prudent, since our game was clearly related, but we decided that we wanted a little distance between ourselves and the genre as a whole. PopTop's sequels had been solid, but the last fifteen years had seen an absolute glut of "tycoon" titles, from studios of every size and quality. Players could be fish tycoons, toilet tycoons, moon tycoons—and that was just back in the early 2000s. These days, we can lord our business acumen over beard trimmers, Dairy Queen franchises, or even game development studios (who are presumably making their own tycoon games, like an entrepreneurial nesting doll). Not all of them were bad, but some were downright terrible, and the genre had evolved enough that what we were making just didn't belong.

With *Civ IV* only a few months away from release, I knew I would be alone on the *Railroads!* design team for a while. Rather than wait around for an artist to become available, I installed a copy of our modeling software on my computer, and started learning how to use it. I'd mastered our 3D physics tools during *Pirates!*, but my early ship models had been swiped from somewhere— probably the *Civ IV* artists, now that I think about it—and I guess they didn't have any useful train graphics to steal. So I had to make my own.

Obviously, I didn't expect my art to stay in the final version of the game, but I made it anyway, because it's important as a designer to sit in all the chairs. Understanding the needs of each department and learning their requisite tools will improve your output, ease communication with your coworkers, and provide a critical perspective when it comes time to admit you were wrong about an idea. But most importantly, it will make you more self-sufficient.

When I wanted to put a ballroom dancing minigame into the new *Pirates!*, for example, not everyone thought it sounded fun. I had to give them a demonstration, which meant creating, among other things, a tool to mark the beats of the music so the computer would know whether the player had nailed the rhythm. If I'd had to rely on someone else to put that together, it likely never would have happened—some still wished it hadn't, but that was mostly due to a bug that made the timing harder than it was supposed to be. I still maintain the dancing was one of the neatest innovations in the remake.

Likewise, I doubt I could have sold a publisher on the idea of a golfing strategy game without a functioning prototype, and you can pretty much forget everything I made prior to 2000. Ideas are cheap; execution is valuable. When people used to ask me how to get into the industry, I'd say, "Get a copy of DPaint and a C++ compiler." These days it's more like, "Get a copy of Photoshop and a Unity tutorial," but the principle hasn't changed—there's no guarantee your talents will be discovered, but they certainly won't be if you never make anything. The best way to prove your idea is a good one is to prove it, not with words but with actions. Sit in the programmer chair until you have something playable, then sit in the artist chair until you have something crudely recognizable, then sit in the tester chair and be honest with yourself about what's fun and what's not. You don't need to be perfect at any one job, you just need to be good enough to prove your point, and inspire others to join you.

21

HIGHER EDUCATION

Sid Meier's Civilization IV
(2005) * Sid Meier's Civilization
IV: Colonization (2008) * Sid
Meier's Civilization V (2010)

OF ALL THE THINGS *CIVILIZATION*
taught me, I never expected one of them to be empathy for politicians. It's easy to criticize leaders for their choices, but it only
takes a few rounds of nation-building before you begin to appreciate that it's not as easy as it looks. Everything comes with a price—
and if playing a game of *Civ* gives you a bit of perspective, then
designing one gives you a whole wagon train of it.

This is part of the reason why each version of the game gets a
new lead designer. After Brian's sequel, Jeff Briggs stepped in for
the third game, programmer Soren Johnson took the helm on *Civ*
IV, and a designer named Jon Shafer rose to the challenge for *Civ*
V. It's good for the series to have a steady turnover of ideas, but it's
also a function of self-preservation in the face of utter, but loving,
exhaustion. Previous *Civ* designers are like grandparents: we made
our major sacrifice when we were young and full of energy, and
now we get to enjoy all the good parts of raising the new generation, while their caretakers handle all the diapers and tantrums.

Aside from art and audio, which are fully replaced with each new technology cycle, *Civ* designers traditionally follow a rule of thirds. One-third of the previous version stays in place, one-third is updated, and one-third is completely new. These days, "updated" is a synonym for "scaled back to make room for the new things," because we don't want the game to become too complicated for someone who's never played. On the other hand, we don't want to alienate existing fans with cookie-cutter sequels, either—and our designers themselves are existing fans, so there's always a strong impetus to add more features. *Civilization III* tried out a new espionage system, *Civ IV* added major mechanics for religion and culture, and *Civ V* overhauled the board itself, by implementing a "one unit per tile" rule and switching the terrain layout from squares to hexagons.

Most of these were ideas that I had considered at some point for the first game in the series, but either the technology couldn't handle it, or it wasn't right for the audience of the era. Hex grids, for example, had been a mainstay of board gaming for decades, and were clearly superior to squares because they eliminated diagonal moves. Visually, diagonals seem fine, but mathematically, they cover significantly more ground than straight moves, and throw off the balance of the game. Designers either have to accommodate for the irregular speed, or else put directional constraints on the player that seem arbitrary and frustrating—no one likes being cut off from a square that's physically touching the corner of their own. Unfortunately, math rarely triumphs over popularity in a head-to-head battle. Despite being better from a design standpoint, hexes were considered too nerdy for the average computer user when *Civ* first came out, so we had to fall back on the familiarity of squares in order to get a strategy game into their hands at all. Like I said, everything comes with a price.

Other new components, like slavery, were left out of the original because of their potential to offend. Here, again, I learned that public figures are doomed no matter what we choose. *Civilization*'s popularity brought it to the attention of professional academics, and it wasn't long before I was being hammered in peer-reviewed journals for "trafficking in tropes" and generally glossing over the sins of Western expansion. Yet, when *Civilization IV* tried to address the issue of slavery for the first time, the complaints were even louder. Shortly after that, we built a remake of *Colonization* that once again removed slavery, and it caused the biggest uproar of them all.

Once the seal was broken, this philosophical analysis quickly spread to my older titles—or as one paper described them, my "Althusserian unconscious manifestations of cultural claims" with "hidden pedagogical aspirations." *Pirates!* wasn't about swashbuckling, it turned out, but rather "asymmetrical and illegal activities [that] seem to undermine the hierarchical status quo while ultimately underlining it." Even *C.P.U. Bach* was accused of revealing "a darker side to the ideological forces at work behind ludic techniques."

Oddly enough, my military titles weren't subjected to any real scrutiny, despite being chock full of "hegemonic assumptions." I suspect it had to do with their stated intent. *F-15 Strike Eagle* was never about anything but military dominance, while *Civilization* was clearly trying to accomplish something more. It's only once you start aiming for a universal, apolitical theme that you begin to be judged by that metric, and inevitably fall short of the ideal.

All I can say is that our motives were sincere, and maybe these guys have a little too much time on their hands. I don't deny that the earliest version of *Civilization* had a predominantly Western perspective—it was a time of pervasive Cold War rhetoric, which tended to oversimplify all narratives into good guys, bad guys, and unfortunately no one else. Americans in the early nineties were brand new to the concept of international diversity in games at all, and at least we can claim that we were at the forefront of a movement that still had a long way to go. We've achieved a much better balance of South American, Asian, and African cultures as the series has matured, with each game striving to be more inclusive than the last. We worked so hard at it, in fact, that we eventually encountered the opposite extreme: due to their taboos about photography and idols, the All Pueblo Council of Governors in New Mexico objected to the inclusion of the ancient Pueblo leader Popé in *Civilization V*. Fortunately, this was discovered during development, and we were happy to respect their wishes and replace him with Chief Pocatello of the Northern Shoshone tribe instead. We might have been occasionally ignorant of other perspectives, but we were never dismissive once they were brought to our attention.

The accusation that we embrace a "progress" model of civilization is also a fair one, and realistically, that's not going to change. Games must involve accomplishment. It's certainly not the only way to look at the world, but it's the only way that makes sense in the context of what we're trying to create. Likewise, the revelation that our historical figures and events have been caricatured to some degree is not an earth-shattering one. All games are inherently reductive. But we strive to be reductive in a balanced and polite way, and always with the goal of improving the overall experience for the player. As Dr. Tonio Andrade of Emory University once put it, "History's not just about the past. History's about the present reflecting on the past." He was talking with Dr. John Harney on the *History Respawned* podcast, where guests dissect the cultural and historical implications of various videogames. Regarding the latest incarnation of *Civ*, Dr. Andrade said, "There's a bunch of assumptions in it that maybe aren't entirely realistic, but that's exactly the point. As historians, no matter how many texts we look at, how careful we are, we're still making models and assumptions . . . and this is just a sort of tangible and fun model."

In our line of work, everything must be in service to fun, and it happens that learning history often is fun. But sometimes, it's also super depressing. We have to offer a moral clarity to our players and eliminate the painful quandaries, because unlike other forms of storytelling, they are personally standing in for our main character. Their ego is on the line, and we have to be gentle with it. Our version of Genghis Khan doesn't beg for his life when he's near defeat, because that puts the player in the uncomfortable position of questioning whether winning is worth it—which is effectively the same as asking whether the game itself is worth it. What we offer instead is the ability to play as Genghis Khan yourself the next time around. An engaging comparison of two positive, yet opposing experiences is always going to be more effective than shaming the player until they walk away entirely.

Generally speaking, though, I don't mind philosophical hair-splitting and constructive feedback. Our critics have helped us find some legitimate blind spots, and the end result has been a better game. Even when they're totally wrong, that's good too, because it reminds us that we can't make everyone happy all the time, and we have to answer to our own conscience above all. Not everybody appreciated the presence of global warming in the original *Civilization*, for example, and one early reviewer called our implementation of women's suffrage "another brick in the wall of political correctness." So I can confidently say that, at least on occasion, we're only unpopular because we're ahead of the curve.

I'd even venture to claim that the whole conversation is a creature of our own making. The earliest academic commentary on videogames was sparse, and intellectually removed from the people who actually played the games. Nearly every discussion made some kind of reference to age: in 1997, one author coined the term "screenager" to describe our audience, while in 2002, an anthropologist scorned the (supposedly token) inclusion of nonmilitary victories in *Civ* by comparing them to "five members of a boy band" for naïve young girls to swoon over. Whether the industry's youthfulness was seen as a negative or a hopeful aspect of the industry, the implication of immaturity was always there.

What none of the critics seemed to realize was that teens were our least-established demographic. Gaming had begun as an adult nerd activity, with no connection to children at all. When I brought

Hostage Rescue home with me to Michigan in 1980, my mother was the only one who tried to defeat the Ayatollah. My siblings Vicky and Bruce were about ten and eight years old at the time—what we would consider prime videogame age today—yet it didn't occur to anyone to call them over. Computers, and therefore any activity that happened to take place on them, were for grownups.

But by 1994, Disney had entered the market, and it was perfectly normal for four-year-old Ryan to be sitting on my lap playing *Dick Tracy: The Crime-Solving Adventure*. The Entertainment Software Rating Board was formed that same year, partly because of parents' false assumption that all games were meant for young children. It wasn't a complete demographic takeover, but in the ESRB's inaugural round of ratings, games marked for "Early Childhood" and "Everyone" outnumbered "Teen" and "Mature" by roughly two to one. This ratio held steady until the year 2000, just as the generation that had grown up with games began to move away from home. The rebalancing was swift, and by 2003, kids' games had lost their lead entirely.

Since then, the split has remained roughly even, as it is for movies and books. But our new, late-teenage cohort didn't just wander off. They kept playing games through college, and then during master's degree programs, until finally, around 2010, the first lifelong gamers started earning PhDs—right about the same time that nuanced academic debate on the societal effects of gaming (and, yes, the specific ways in which we could do better) really exploded into the mainstream.

Scholars talk about us, and critique us, because they know us. Gamers didn't magically gain credibility with academics; they grew up and *became* academics. We created our own watchdogs, and when they complain, I know it's only evidence of how much they care.

A few years back, we held our own little gaming convention in Baltimore called Firaxicon, and I was truly unprepared for the number of parents who brought their children. These adults weren't acting as reluctant chaperones, but as native guides. Mothers and sons, fathers and daughters, even a few grandparents and grandchildren—all wanted to express their love of games by passing on the traditions. They weren't embarrassed, but deeply proud. What's more, they were living proof that gamers aren't just shut-in teenagers. They have careers, and relationships, and families. There is life after *Civ*! It was enough to bring a tear to your eye.

These days, signs of our legitimacy can be found everywhere. The musical theme to *Civilization IV*, "Baba Yetu," won a Grammy, and a concert series called Video Games Live currently travels the world playing fully orchestrated versions of game music. Their opening night sold 11,000 tickets, and they've played over 400 concerts since. I once received a call from the *Wall Street Journal* wanting to know how we so perfectly captured the essence of tax policy, and which parts of Adam Smith's economic theories we found most relevant. (The answer was none in particular, because I'd never read his works, and I didn't think *Civ*'s tax system was nearly as profound as the reporter was making it out to be.) In 2016, an article appeared on the AARP website extolling the virtues of gaming for senior citizens. And though there are still professors who dislike our simplification of history, they've been balanced by a not-insignificant number who assign *Civilization* to their students for academic purposes. Our game is an official part of the curriculum at universities in Wisconsin, Pennsylvania, Kentucky, Oregon, Massachusetts, Colorado, Georgia, and more.

We're in high schools, too. Back in 2007, a Canadian company made a *Civ III* mod called *HistoriCanada*, which included extra Civilopedia entries, accurate maps, and aboriginal art and music. It was distributed for free to 20,000 schools and another 80,000 individual students, to help them experience the birth of their country firsthand.

Though the educational overlap is entirely logical, I've always been uncomfortable with the label "educational software." I've always preferred the word "learning," myself. Education is somebody else telling you what to think, while learning is opening yourself to new possibilities, and grasping a concept because you understand it on a personal level. To chastise us for our lack of historical accuracy is fair in the educational sense, but misses the point entirely when it comes to learning. Are Aesop's fables meaningless because real mice can't talk? What we encourage is knowledge-seeking in itself, and ownership of one's beliefs. We want you to understand that choices have consequences, that a country's fate can turn on a single act of diplomacy, and that historical figures were not black-and-white paragons of good and evil—not because we've told you, but because you've faced those complex dilemmas for yourself.

When games are done right, players don't even realize they're learning. Of course one could also argue that when teaching is done right, students don't realize how much fun they're having, either. As Marshall McLuhan famously quipped, "Anyone who tries to make a distinction between education and entertainment doesn't know the first thing about either." But technology gives us an undeniable advantage over traditional teaching methods, because we're able to reach more students, and offer a broader range of topics, than could ever be contained in a single class.

One married couple reported that their monthly finances had been brought under control with a household budget based on *Civ*'s economic system. A professor at the University of Colorado praised *Railroad Tycoon* for teaching him about the pitfalls of debt and bankruptcy in third grade, and more than one *Pirates!* fan has told me they aced a geography test thanks to their encyclopedic knowledge of Caribbean coastal towns (though I imagine their teachers might have been less thrilled to hear which towns were easiest to sack and loot). A journalist for the website Kotaku credited gaming for his precocious vocabulary as a child, including words like "ziggurat," "aileron," "épée," and "polytheism," and his readers chimed in with dozens more. My own son learned how to read almost entirely through computer game hint books.

None of which is to say that our games are designed for children—nor are they *not* designed for children. Our belief is that a really good game covers all the bases. Bruce Shelley used to joke that we do our research in the children's section of the library, and it's not entirely a metaphor. Kids' books skipped the details, and got right down to the important themes. Their simple illustrations usually translated well to the limits of graphics cards at the time, and the information inside was a solid baseline for what our players would already know coming in. We could layer our own fantasy, humor, and drama on top of it, while remaining confident that everything underneath would resonate with that foundation of joy that adults tended to forget was inside themselves. Certainly the world is more complicated as an adult, but children aren't dumb, and if the fundamental essence of an idea isn't enough to capture the interest of a child, then I would argue that it's not really as interesting as you think it is.

22

FUZZY MATH

Sid Meier's Civilization
Revolution (2008)

MY OWN FIRST EXPOSURE TO
videogames was, like most people my age, the venerable black-
and-white tennis match known as *Pong*. There was a small restau-
rant down the street from General Instrument where some of us
would hang out and have dinner after work, and at some point
they installed this weird little table in the lounge with a television screen facing upward underneath the plexiglass surface. The
idea was you could set your drinks and bar snacks on it while you
played, but it seemed irreverent to eat on the surface of a TV, so
most evenings we would just wander over to play a few rounds
before returning to our normal, wooden tables. The most memorable thing about it was that one side of the cabinet had somehow
ended up wired backwards, sending the little white line to the left
side of the screen when the player turned the knob to the right. So
we had always agreed that whoever was more skilled had to sit on
the broken side to compensate—perhaps my earliest experience in
balancing gameplay.

Rotating dial controls were sometimes called "spinners" in
arcade hardware terminology, and truly inveterate nerds recognized them as either potentiometers or rheostats, depending on
their function. But to the general public, they were incongruously
known as "paddles," due to their original table tennis associations.

A year after *Pong*'s release, the first four-way gaming joystick—a word which, oddly enough, had its roots in early airplane controls—made its debut in the arcade game *Astro Race*. It caught on quickly, and by 1977, the Atari 2600 home console offered a standardized plug that could support a potentially limitless number of third-party controllers, in addition to the five different styles produced by Atari themselves.

The market responded. A 1983 issue of *Creative Computing* magazine included a 15,000-word hardware review comparing sixteen different joystick brands and eight unique paddle sets, plus eight converters for the less-common plugs those accessories might be required to fit. Some of the products were surprisingly forward-thinking, like Datasoft's "Le Stick," which detected motion through a set of liquid mercury switches that triggered whenever the freestanding cylinder was tilted more than twenty degrees in any direction. It's easy to see why it didn't last, but toxic metals aside, Datasoft deserves credit for predating the motion sensor craze by a quarter of a century.

Soon, however, the third-party manufacturers fell away, and an evolutionary split emerged. On one side, the traditional knobs, buttons, and joysticks of arcade cabinets consolidated into a single proprietary controller for each console system. On the other, the personal computer industry began to drift toward more established business peripherals, namely the mouse and alphanumeric keyboard. Major gaming companies tried to straddle the gap for as long as they could, but in late 1983, the North American console market crashed, with previous annual revenues of $3.2 billion plunging to just $100 million by 1985. The drop was so devastating to Atari in particular that the whole event was simply known as "Atari shock" in Japan. For various reasons, the Japanese market remained stable, and with every console company in America either bankrupt or pivoting sharply to the PC, Japan emerged as the home console champion for the next twenty years.

Of course there were still regular computers in Japan, too.

MicroProse had released translations of nearly every game since *F-15 Strike Eagle* onto Japanese machines like the MSX, FM Towns, and PC-98. Likewise, there were console owners in America who played English translations of games like *Super Mario Bros.* and *The Legend of Zelda*. But the culture of each format was firmly rooted in its respective country, and very few games successfully crossed over. It was like baseball versus cricket: you'd find fans of each worldwide, but rarely individual fans of both, and never professionals who played both, despite the relative similarity of their athleticism.

Mechanical differences did play a partial role in the divide, at least from our perspective. It was hard to replicate the subtle movement of a computer mouse with a console's directional pad and floating cursor, or to fit as much text on the screen when console players typically sat several feet away. Personally, I don't feel like the problem was mutual—we had more keys than they had buttons—but that's probably not surprising given which half of the industry I work in. Plenty of people have argued that certain console games could never feel intuitive on a PC, and given our processing and graphical differences at the time, maybe they were right. Both have their strengths and weaknesses, and I've already acknowledged that I own at least as many consoles as computers.

But the embargo between the two formats couldn't all be chalked up to controllers, as even games with simple interfaces often failed in their opposing market. It wasn't until 1989 that MicroProse first attempted to convert *Silent Service*—which was by that point thriving in thirteen different computer formats—to the Nintendo Entertainment System. Western console owners were considered such a long shot that we didn't even bother with a Japanese version, despite having translations readily available from the PC-98. If any Japanese fans were broad-minded enough to accept our game on the console, we would just have to hope they spoke English as well.

I don't remember whether the NES version made any money,

but my guess is that it didn't, because we went back to ignoring the platform for the next several games. Even *Gunship*, which was successfully ported to five different computers in Japan alone, didn't get a console release in any language. We eventually dipped our toe in the water a few more times—*Pirates!* saw a pretty successful conversion to the NES, and *F-15 Strike Eagle II* made a respectable appearance on the Sega Genesis. But meanwhile, the Super NES version of *Railroad Tycoon* was cancelled mid-development, and *Covert Action* went in the opposite direction and became our first port to Linux on the PC instead.

Only *Civilization* was successful enough to be ported everywhere, including the Super NES, PlayStation, and Sega Saturn. Yet still, universality eluded us, as Nintendo required several changes to the game in order to bridge the chasm between our worlds. We knew by now to expect a handful of tweaks concerning their tightly guarded reputation as a family brand, like when they replaced "tobacco" with "crops" in the *Pirates!* merchant system. No arguments there. And when they wanted to sub in the Japanese as a playable civilization, that made perfect sense, too. But then, things got kind of wacky.

In a normal game of *Civilization*, the opening screen was a swirling animation of astrophysics and volcanic activity. "In the beginning," it read, "the Earth was without form, and void. But the sun shone upon the sleeping Earth, and deep inside the brittle crust, massive forces waited to be unleashed."

Pretty epic, right? Nintendo did not agree.

"Long, long ago," began the Super NES version, "humankind was divided into many tribes who wandered the Earth."

Well, okay. That's good, too, I guess. The lilting fantasy music was no match for the driving, suspenseful beats of our original theme, but maybe they were building up to it.

"One starry night, however, a very strange thing took place."

Um . . . was it the first settler arriving on a 3 × 3 grid?

"A beautiful Goddess appeared before Tokugawa, the young

leader of Japan. 'Oh Tokugawa, I have a mission for you. Build great cities, and cause civilization* to flourish throughout the Earth . . .'"

Whoa.

The rest of it was fairly harmless, just a kind of bonus tutorial about how irrigated land grows more food, and people like roads. But I was baffled by the localization team's insistence that this bizarre animation of a blonde lady in an evening gown somehow improved the game. How can you claim "It's good to be King" if you're only doing it at the behest of some celestial being? Besides, I'd thought I was dodging controversy by leaving religion out of the game, and now they were trying to artificially insert it.

In the end, we took their word for it—mostly because we had no choice—and sure enough, none of the console reviewers thought the vignette was the least bit out of place. If a thirty-second wrapper of mysticism made the rest of the game more palatable to this particular audience, then I guess we could live with it. But the whole experience really underscored the fact that the cultural gap between console and PC users was about more than just buttons versus keyboards.

So, in mid-2007, when I made the announcement that I was going to design a console-only game called *Civilization Revolution*, the horrified outcry from our fans was not exactly surprising. *Civilization II* had made it to the PlayStation several years after we left MicroProse, but every *Civ* title at Firaxis—including *Alpha Centauri*, *Civilization III*, *Civilization IV*, the soon-to-be-released *Colonization* remake, and the secretly-already-in-development *Civilization V*—had all been exclusively for the PC. According to certain portions of the internet, we were betraying our fans, dumbing down the series, and/or pandering to the obviously inferior platforms of an obviously unenlightened group of gamers.

* **Achievement Unlocked:** Expected Territory—Read the word "civilization" 125 times.

They were furious. They were skeptical. But mostly, they were just afraid of losing something they loved, which made the whole ruckus seem kind of sweet.

They were also used to having their opinions taken into account, from the simplest fan letter to the 600-page "Official Suggestion List" that a diehard group of players printed out and mailed to us in anticipation of *Civ III*. The nature of our game inspires fierce ownership, so when faced with something new, our fans never hesitate to make their voices—and especially their displeasure—heard. But once it became clear that the console version was just another kind of *Civ*, and not the only kind of *Civ* that would ever exist again, everybody settled down.

"In fact," admitted one reviewer, "because it caters directly to its platform rather than trying to shoehorn an unwieldy PC port into a console, it succeeds where others have failed."

This was exactly what we'd been aiming for. It was, as we described it at the time, *Civilization* in an evening. Not everyone has eighty hours to devote to a single game, and there was no reason folks with greater work and family obligations should be left out in the cold. Cities were easier to build and expand, technologies developed sooner, opponents attacked earlier, battles were over quicker. The whole thing was actually developed on the PC, and we could have easily flipped it over to that side of the market—but it wouldn't have been a success, because the gameplay wasn't designed for the PC any more than the originals had been designed for consoles. Addressing an entirely new audience had given us more freedom than we'd had in years to determine what was and was not "supposed" to be in a *Civ* game. Did players really need an entire economic system of trade routes to manage between cities, in addition to everything else? Some of them certainly enjoyed it. Others got bogged down in that level of detail. Now, both types of player had a *Civ* game that met their needs.

The other feature that set *Civilization Revolution* apart was that we finally managed a robust, workable multiplayer experience, thanks to those same simplifications we'd set out to pursue. Officially, every version of the game since *CivNet* had offered multiplayer, usually as an expansion several months after the single-player version was released. But the truth is none of them ever worked very well. Between different types of PCs, different encoding methods, and different online services that fans could connect through, there were too many variables to provide anything consistent. One early review noted that their multiplayer test had been conducted over "a distance of about 40 miles," because the length of the wires actually mattered in those days. When players did manage to connect, the game's complexity dragged the pacing to a crawl, especially during diplomatic discussions that were visible only to the parties involved. We offered multiplayer because skipping it would have appeared lazy, but it was never intended to be the primary experience of the game.

The world of consoles, however, was different. Multiplayer was not only a critical feature for that set of gamers, it was required by the manufacturers. Sony and Microsoft had invested in a hefty online infrastructure for both the PlayStation 3 and the Xbox 360, and they expected game developers to use it.

My first real attempt at programming online multiplayer—not counting a two-person tank prototype at MicroProse that never got off the ground because we didn't want to host the servers—had been during *Gettysburg!*, and actually turned out quite nicely. The gameplay was in real time, so no one was ever stuck waiting for their opponent to finish their turn, and skirmishes were by historical definition always limited to two players. As with our single-player games, we knew the *Gettysburg!* multiplayer was good when everyone in the office kept setting aside their work to play it all afternoon. I'm not hugely competitive myself—the closest I get to trash-talking is a polite reminder that I'm their boss, so they should probably let me win—but when you hear folks gleefully taunting each other down the hall, and office mates cheering them on, you know you've hit on something special. Unfortunately, this set me up with some unrealistic expectations about how easy it would be to program the multiplayer for *Civ Rev*.

There are always two issues to consider when it comes to online play: lag and sync. The first is more recognizable and reviled by players, but the second is more destructive, and trying to improve one often causes problems with the other. In order to keep a game synchronized—that is, both computers agree about what is happening at any given moment—they must constantly pass data back and forth.

"I have fired my gun," says one computer.

"Yes, you fired your gun," replies the other. "You hit my target here."

"Yes, I hit your target there."

If the two games aren't in sync, the data immediately dissolves into youthful sibling squabbles—"I got you!" "Nuh-uh, you missed!"—and the game crashes.

The easiest solution, which we were able to get away with in *Gettysburg!*, is to pass entire game-states from one to the other: "My soldiers are here, your soldiers are there, I'm aiming this way, you're aiming that way, I have this much health, you have that much health, and I have fired my gun."

"Okay, I trust you."

Any disagreements would be overwritten at the very next data transfer. There might be a tiny jump on the screen as a soldier's position was corrected, or someone died from a mystery bullet you never saw fired, but as long as things were resolved quickly, the game would appear smooth and reasonable for both.

But even with its simplified gameplay, *Civ Rev* contained too much data to share everything. There were army positions, economic numbers, happiness levels, food stores, truce agreements, terraforming . . . all multiplied by up to five civilizations at a time. This was why every previous *Civ* multiplayer had been decried as sluggish and unfair—a half-second freeze and a forty-five-degree rotation of a regiment was a forgivable glitch; a ten-second freeze and a cross-continent teleportation of that regiment was not.

The alternative, however, was risky.

"My soldiers are here, your soldiers are there."

"Yes. We've moved one north."

"We've moved one east."

"We've lost one unit of health."

"We've gained two units of food."

"We've moved one west."

"Wait—where were your guys again?"

To share just the changes to the board was more efficient, and allowed the game to run at an acceptable speed. But even the tiniest sync error was a game-ending disaster, because there was no way to recover hours of built-up changes from scratch. To make things worse, *Civilization* has always relied heavily on random number generators to determine everything from battle outcomes to subtle graphical variations. So I spent months and months rooting out sync errors, making sure that the random number generators for every possible scenario were being shared, or isolated, as necessary. The effort ended up being worth it after the game found an unexpectedly persistent following among online tablet players, but I'm still grateful that I've never had to repeat it. I'd like to say that's because some brilliant programmer came up with a more elegant solution to the problem, but really all that happened is data speeds improved to the point that we could send entire chunks of the big games, too.

The interesting thing about random numbers, though, is that they're not really random, or at least not in the same way that we tell you they are. When outcomes are truly random, people lose a great deal more often than they think they should. By definition, most of us are average, but we want to believe we're superior, as proven by the simple fact that we picked up a videogame in the first place. It is not average to be a king, a tycoon, a ship captain, or any of the other delusions of grandeur we offer, yet we read the back of the box and say to ourselves, "Yep, I can do that." This unrealistic but pro-fun narrative of exceptionalism is found in nearly all forms of entertainment. Rambo always takes out the bad guys, and Sherlock Holmes always solves the mystery. Professional sports is the only arena where we expect the majority to lose, and even then, the worst-performing teams are usually given an advantage in the following year's draft. Whether spectating or participating, fans demand a sense of justice in order to feel satisfied, and randomness is the very opposite of justice.

Lessons of this nature had presented themselves throughout my career, but it wasn't until *Civilization Revolution* that my eyes were opened to the full extent of people's irrationality regarding random events.

We had decided it would be neat to display the odds of each battle on the screen, partly because statistics are fun, but mostly to address a particular issue that had turned into a running joke on the message boards. The problem stemmed from the fact that there were no guaranteed wins in any matchup—the odds might be incredibly long, but the underdog always had a shot—and this led to the occasional absurdity like a spearman from an underdeveloped nation defeating a military tank in battle. I maintain that it *is* theoretically possible, in the same way that 1,500 Swiss citizens armed with nothing but sticks and rocks defeated more than twice as many trained Austrian knights at the Battle of Morgarten; or how the outnumbered-five-to-one British triumphed against the Maratha Army at the Battle of Assaye; or when Yi Sun-sin of the Korean Navy defeated 133 Japanese ships with only twelve of his own; or that time when just 1,800 Croatians held off 36,000 Serbians for nearly three months at Vukovar.

It happens. And besides, guaranteed victories are no way to balance a game.

But we thought maybe it would help if we showed the players their odds before the fighting started, so they could understand that there were real numbers behind these unlikely battles, and not just a vindictive, petty AI.

We were wrong. Not only were they unimpressed by the long-odds evidence, they fought back even harder on the short-odds information they could now see.

"Sid, the game is messed up. I had this battle with a Barbarian, right? The odds were three to one—and I lost!"

"Well, yes," I would agree. "Sometimes that's going to happen."

"No, no, you don't understand. Three is big. One is small. I had the big number."

"Sure," I'd say, quite reasonably given the circumstances. "But look over here. This other time, you had the tiny little one, and the other guy had the big gigantic three, and you beat him."

"That's different! I had clever tactics, a solid strategy, clean living, and a healthy diet—there are a lot of complex variables to take into account, you know."

It didn't matter how many different ways this conversation played out, I couldn't convince our testers that it made sense for them to lose a three-to-one battle roughly one-fourth of the time. Past certain odds, people expected to win no matter what, but also to occasionally prevail if they were the underdog in the same situation.

And illogical as it may have been, we had to take their gut feelings into account. Nicholas Meyer, the writer responsible for the even-numbered *Star Trek* movies—the good ones, if you follow *Trek* fandom—once said, "The audience may be stupid, but it's never wrong." Around the Firaxis office, we have a similar saying: feedback is fact. If someone tells me a game was frustrating, I can't possibly argue, "No, it wasn't. You just didn't know you were having fun!" They were frustrated, therefore my game was frustrating. Ultimately, it didn't matter whether the *Civ Rev* players blamed their unlikely defeat on chance, skill, or designer malice. The resulting loss of fun was the same, and we had to fix it.

So we changed the actual odds behind the scenes, and made

sure that the player would win any battle with odds of three-to-one or greater. This might have been unfair to the computer AI, but we never heard any complaints, and once players were given the advantage, they reported having much more fun.

"Sid. There's another problem."

"Uh oh. What happened?"

"Well, I had this two-to-one battle, and I lost. Which is okay, I know we've had this discussion. But right after that, I had another two-to-one battle, and I lost again!"

"Well, when you flip a coin, each flip is unaffected by the previous—"

"No, no, I'm not talking about coin flips. It was Horsemen and Warriors."

"Right. Totally different. Got it."

Again, emotions trumped logic, and we had to accept that. So we started taking into account the results of previous battles, and making it extra unlikely for too many bad (or good) things to happen in a row. We made it less random, so that it could *feel* more random.

"Now are you happy? Anything else?"

"Well, now, here's a really weird thing. I had a battle, the odds were twenty-to-ten, see? And somehow I lost."

"That's . . . the same as two-to-one."

"No, two is only one more than one, but twenty is ten more than ten. I mean, do the math!"

So we added another "correction."

By the time *Civilization V* rolled around, we had decided that the feature wasn't worth the hassle (though it did make a brief reappearance six years later in *Civilization Revolution 2*, which was largely built on the code base of its predecessor). Since then, *Civilization VI* has moved to an entirely new Combat Strength system that compares military units numerically rather than by ratio, and allows them to engage beyond a single skirmish. It wasn't enough to listen to our players when they demanded to know the odds between spearmen versus tanks; we had to intuit what they really wanted instead of what they asked for. Feedback is fact insofar as it reveals how our game makes people feel, but after that, it's our job to come up with the right solution to that problem. There are, after all, a lot of complex variables to take into account.

23

SOCIAL
MOBILITY

AS PAINFUL AS THE FAILURE OF the dinosaur game was, it was made even worse by the birth of social media. Many of the earliest "weblogs" came from the gaming community, starting in 1996 when *Doom* developer John Carmack decided to convert his Unix .plan file—something most programmers used as a public to-do list—into a more conversational status update for his fans. Shortly after that, Rob Malda's *Chips & Dips* tech blog changed its name to *Slashdot*, and by late 1999, it was clear to us that this new medium could be a powerful connection to our audience. Thus, the Firaxis developer blog was born, and the fact that we just happened to be firing up *the* quintessential Sid Meier game right at the same time was a sign from the heavens that we were definitely, absolutely on the right track with this decision.

Clearly, it didn't turn out so well. My first post was full of vibrant optimism, starting with a fond childhood memory of buying tiny wax dinosaurs at the fair, in which I insisted on visiting each coin-operated machine one by one to witness the injection molding myself. But by the fourth entry, I was down to only a few paragraphs, and by the seventh, I was telling the Disney *Dinosaur* anecdote without mentioning the game at all. Then six months of silence, before I had to write the awful "Oops, never mind" announcement, rendered even worse by the fact that I had learned my lesson, and could not talk about *SimGolf* as a worthy replacement until we were much closer to publication.

Realistically, it was a small misstep, and we continued to fill our website with relevant, slightly-less-gun-jumping content from a variety of folks within the company. But I recused myself from any further blogging, as well as most of its later offspring. I'm not one of those people who thinks social media is representative of humanity's downfall; it's just not for me. I need my public spotlights to be kept in short, controlled doses. But it certainly seems to work for others, and by 2011, we thought maybe it was time for us to consider the field in the context of production, rather than communication.

One ongoing issue with even the best multiplayer code was the fact that strangers on the internet tend to behave in weird, antisocial, or downright offensive ways. It's a sad state of affairs when muting the speech channel becomes a given with online play. Most services offered a "friends list" function to help you build a team of coherent, sportsmanlike opponents, but the biggest breakout games in the last few years had been on Facebook, where the social component was the focus, rather than a corrective measure. Facebook's saturation of mobile devices also permitted asynchronous play, meaning users only logged on to take their turn during spare moments in the day, freeing everyone to go off and live their lives in the hours between. This idea of drawn-out, cooperative gaming was unexplored territory for me, and therefore interesting, so I set out to design a version of *Civilization* that would fit into the massively multiplayer, 24/7 connectedness of our modern lives.

Unfortunately, interesting doesn't always mean successful.

CivWorld had a number of problems, the biggest of which was the generally uncooperative nature of real people when put to the test. One of our major mechanics relied on players voluntarily giving gold to one another, which they pretty much never did. Another involved asking for help when you were in a bind, which we thought would foster positive feelings of altruism and community importance, but for the most part everyone chose to let their friends suffer. Worst of all, the centralized nature of the game meant we couldn't just let it fade into obscurity—we had to officially shut the service down, this time with a full press release instead of just a blog post. Single-player games could be set aside or revisited according to the individual's preference, but once an online game falls below certain participation levels, the financial reality dictates that it must be taken away from everyone.

The mobile functionality of *CivWorld* was adequate, though, even if the social aspect had been a dead loss, and by now, we had also ported *Civ Rev* to the iPad with great success. There was something worth salvaging in mobile gaming, I thought, especially with its potential for smaller budgets and bigger risks. I'd acquired a taste for sprawling, blockbuster games almost by necessity, and still very much enjoyed working on the AAA titles that Firaxis produced. But my first love would always be the streamlined process of indie development. I was one of the few who could remember a time when no other way existed, and while I would never want to give up the advances we'd made since then, mobile gaming seemed like a viable way to recapture that experience within the safety of an established studio.

And if I were going old school, I decided, I should go all the way. Before *Civ*, before *Pirates!*, even before submarine combat and wargames, there had been a red and white arcade cabinet with a pebbled plastic seat called *Red Baron*.

Though Bill Stealey had obviously been the bigger plane fanatic, I did have a nonzero level of interest in them. When I'd flown to Switzerland as a child, a particular flight attendant had taken me under his wing, so to speak, making sure I was comfortable and unafraid as I crossed the ocean alone. First, he arranged for me to have a row to myself, so I could stretch out and sleep during the overnight portion of the trip. That was probably the nicest favor in retrospect, but as a kid, I was more impressed by the fact that each time he came to check on me, he would deliver a small piece of foil-wrapped chocolate decorated with a picture of a Swissair jet. I ate the first one, but after noticing that each wrapper featured a different kind of plane, I began saving them instead. The flight attendant was happy to indulge me, and by the end of the trip I had the whole collection, probably ten or more. I could have eaten the chocolate and just saved the wrappers, but it was better to have the whole thing. I had the sense, somehow, that they were useful—that I could accomplish something with them as solid, three-dimensional toys that wouldn't have been possible with wrinkly foil bits. I'm sure I must have eaten them eventually, but I remember holding on to them at my grandparents' house for several months at least.

At one point I'd even had a real job involving airplanes. The summer after my junior year of college, my aunt and uncle in Switzerland told me about a computer programming position at a nearby military contractor named Contraves. The owner's wife was American, they explained, and he apparently had a soft spot for us—especially those of us who could read IBM computer manuals in fluent English. The job was mine if I wanted it. Their offices were in Zurich, which was about a thirty-minute commute from Bülach along the very same train line I'd been obsessed with as a child, and of course I was welcome to stay at the family homestead for as long as I wanted. Contraves focused less on aircraft and more on the antiaircraft systems that shot them down, but it was still within my interests, and their salary offer was surprisingly high for someone still in school. I decided I would look at it as a study abroad opportunity, and asked the University of Michigan to defer my final year of college so I could go work at Contraves through the winter. To be honest, I was mostly working on programs for the payroll department, but it still felt really cool to put a major international military contractor on my résumé, and I enjoyed my time there immensely.

In fact, I might have even considered staying in Switzerland, and seen my career turn out very differently. Contraves would have promoted me to more advanced coding projects soon enough, and Bülach was no less charming to me as an adult. But there was a ticking clock destined to send me home: as a Swiss citizen, I was eligible for the country's mandatory military service. Every male over the age of twenty has to endure a minimum duty of eight months, and remain in the reserves for many years after. Living overseas was a valid exemption, but it would be revoked after one year back in the country. For all that I enjoy simulated military games, I am decidedly not cut out for real ones. I had even heard rumors of a special battalion for *Ausländer*, or foreigners, which was presumed by officers to be both inferior and expendable. So just before my one-year anniversary, I said my official goodbyes and went home to America, where people like Bill could bravely take care of that sort of thing, and I could stick to entertaining them once they were safely back on the ground.

It had been twenty-five years since I'd put an airplane in a game, and I felt like the subject was ready for a comeback. This time, however, I would do it my way. *Sid Meier's Ace Patrol* would be a strategy game from start to finish, which meant, among other things, that the battles would be turn-based. Players would have time to consider each maneuver, and since the height of a plane mattered as well as its coordinates, they'd have to strategize across all three dimensions.

Though turn-based flying was exactly the type of unconventional gameplay choice I had always been fascinated by, I did have one strong outside influence as well: a 1980 game by Alfred

Leonardi* called *Ace of Aces*, which was held entirely within a matched pair of thick books. It was like a graphical Choose Your Own Adventure novel, where each page showed an illustration of the view from your cockpit, along with a list of possible maneuvers and corresponding page numbers. Turns in Leonardi's game were paced, but simultaneous, with each player selecting their move and announcing together the page their opponent should turn to, until eventually, one appeared in the other's crosshairs. It was quite clever, and proved that an aircraft game could be both methodical and exciting at the same time.

I was pleased with how *Ace Patrol* turned out, but as our first exclusively mobile game, it did raise the question of pricing. Specifically, we had to decide whether to charge one upfront premium for the game, as was traditional, or try out the trendy new model of downloadable content, in which a limited version of the game would be given away for free and then subsequent levels would have to be individually purchased. If you were to ask a group of gamers their opinion on these so-called "microtransactions," most would probably respond with a string of rude words. But the revenues tell a different story. Nexon, the company that invented the notion of small purchases within a free game, first used it as a Hail Mary pass for an online server that was about to be shut down for lack of subscribers. Membership predictably skyrocketed once the game was free, but more importantly, the new microtransactions dwarfed previous subscription sales, not only saving the game but increasing total corporate revenue by 16 percent in one year. A full 70 percent of *Candy Crush Saga* users have never paid a dime for the game, which is a higher rate than most free-to-play apps, yet it still brings in several million dollars a day. We say we hate it, but the balance sheets prove otherwise.

I do think the idea of a free demo with the option to purchase the

---

* **Achievement Unlocked:** Share the Credit—Identify *thirty-six* other developers by name.

entire game is a fair one, and coin-operated arcades were engaging in microtransactions long before their current wave of popularity. But there's no escaping the fact that many free-to-play games are predatory, especially when they target young children, or blur the line between upgrades and necessary content. There has to be a worthwhile product underneath, and a respectful, honest relationship with players about what they're getting for their money.

We experimented with different forms of the business model during both *CivWorld* and *Ace Patrol*, but found it hard to hit that three-dimensional sweet spot between player experience, reasonable compensation, and a gameplay design that supported both. When the players purchase the game outright, you can increase the difficulty gradually, adding new elements of complexity at a regular pace. But if you know that players will be forced to a crossroads of paying or leaving after the second mission, you may be tempted to throw in more difficult elements earlier, to prove there's something worth hanging around for. In that case, however, you may lose other players who couldn't be brought up to speed fast enough, because they assume the upcoming levels will be even harder. It's certainly possible to do it right, but after a lukewarm reaction to the initial pricing for *Ace Patrol*, we decided not to drag out our learning curve any further. We released the sequel, *Pacific Skies*, under the classic paid-upfront model, and everyone was happier.

While I was learning to embrace the quirks of mobile gaming, my son, Ryan, had been busy earning a degree in computer science from my alma mater, the University of Michigan, and perhaps unsurprisingly, he was now planning a career in game design himself. Aside from the prominent role computers had played in our home, Ryan had been exposed to the development side of the industry early on, often traveling with me when I had to go on press tours. I never taught him any of the principles of game design directly; I just explained them to interviewers, and he paid attention. He would never hesitate to let them know when their questions were repetitive, and by the age of eight, we couldn't let him stand off-camera anymore, because he would jump in to recite all the answers himself.

During college, Ryan had been president of an organization that sponsored intense competitions known as "game jams," where participants try to create a working prototype within just forty-eight hours. I initially agreed to be a judge for their event, but soon decided it was more fun to participate instead. Game jams are like a mini-vacation: they offer the same freedom to explore any topic or genre, and there's something satisfyingly pure about a no-frills, seat-of-your-pants creation. For the university students, I made a fairly standard maze game called *Escape from Zombie Hotel!*, but I've been known to get a little more bohemian when we run similar events at Firaxis. For the topic "Things Aren't Always What They Seem," for example, I created a colorful, blocky platformer, which eventually zoomed out to reveal that the level you were traversing was a famous work of art. It's the perfect illustration of a rule Ryan probably could have quoted me on by kindergarten: Find the fun. Platformers may not be my specialty, but the idea of a hidden work of art just seemed to cry out for one. As with larger, more serious projects, I never try to cram something into a specific game template—I start with something that's interesting all on its own, and figure out what kind of game it's meant to be.

The other risk in starting with a genre and working backwards, aside from a disjointed or unsatisfying game, is that a designer will end up making an obvious clone of their favorite game. Fortunately, I saw none of that during the University of Michigan game jams—one team used a sound studio mixing board for their controller, while another cast the player as a lion eating zookeepers—but most designers these days have been playing videogames for as long as they can remember, and it's easy to get stuck in a cycle of remaking the same ideas over and over. "Find the fun" doesn't just mean take your topic and figure out what's fun about it; it also means go out into the world and find a topic that's never been turned into a game before. Then, once you find that topic, make sure you give it space to breathe, and keep an open mind about what gameplay style will highlight it best. You may end up hopping across Van Gogh's face, or impossibly hovering midair while another plane makes their move, only to discover that both experiences are loads more fun than anyone would have guessed.

24

FUNNY
BUSINESS

Sid Meier's Civilization VI
(2016)

THERE WAS A CERTAIN AMOUNT

of culture shock when I lived in Switzerland during college, despite knowing the language. Well, I should say *mostly* knowing the language. My Aunt Edith and Uncle Fritz had two elementary-aged kids, and for the first couple of weeks they helped me reignite the Swiss neurons in my brain at a vocabulary level I could handle. But it took at least a month before I realized that I'd been addressing everyone with the informal pronouns reserved for children, rather than the respectful grammar used between adults. It's hard to explain just how inappropriately intimate I was being with my new boss and coworkers, since English has no equivalent distinctions, but think of it like a drunk guy you've never met throwing his arm around you and calling you "bro." Correcting me to my face would have been an even greater social transgression for them, so I remained the barbaric foreigner for much longer than I should have.

In any case, I did crave the occasional dose of American culture, and saw English-language films at the movie theater in Zurich whenever I could. This included, among others, the soon-to-be-classic comedy *Blazing Saddles* (also known by its German title,

Der Wilde Wilde Westen). You could tell who in the audience spoke English, because three or four of us would explode with laughter at a punchline, and then the rest would laugh a moment later as they read the German subtitles on the screen. It was the first Mel Brooks movie I ever saw, and definitely not the last. My Wild West prototype had a frontier family named the Schwartzes in his honor, and it's no accident that *Civ*'s slogan was "It's good to be King."

The thing I like about Mel Brooks, and comedians in general, is that they're actually very analytical. To dig down and figure out what's funny about a particular phrase or story is not so different from isolating what makes a gameplay experience compelling. Both are trying to engage the audience with a sharpened version of reality, and both require an appreciation for humanity's flaws in order to know where the hook fits best. Humor also has the counterintuitive ability to make serious moments more potent, which is why most of Shakespeare's tragedies are peppered with comedic interludes. Especially when your materials are limited— whether by painted theater sets, or eight-bit graphics—humor can acknowledge the lack of grit in a way that ends up drawing the audience further into the fantasy, where the grit can be supplied by their imagination instead.

We can't always get away with silliness. *Gettysburg!* was justifiably solemn in its presentation, and even the modding community usually took the opportunity to make that game more realistic, rather than less. *Conflict in Vietnam* was similarly dignified, and *Magic: The Gathering* wasn't ours to toy with in the first place. But nearly every other game I've made has a comedic self-awareness, from the overdrawn James Bond villains in *Covert Action* to the tiny bridge worker who almost gets left behind in *Railroad Tycoon*.

We thought it was especially important with *Civilization*, because the concept of running the world is naturally a little daunting. We're inviting you to make life-or-death decisions for hundreds of millions of people through six thousand years of history, and the lighthearted bits serve as a kind of friendly wink—a promise that we're here for you, and we're on your side—while secretly investing you even more in your own success. Newspaper headlines would provide regular updates on the status of your nation, but we filled the rest of the page with side stories like "Lions Defeat Gladiators 7–0," and "Marie Antoinette's Diet Secret: Cake!" At one point, we needed a physical representation of citizens' happiness, and after a lengthy discussion with Bruce Shelley about traditional symbols of joy, quality of life, and political empowerment, I went with Elvis. He remained a running joke throughout the series, and in *Civ III* there's an Easter Egg—a hidden piece of code, in player lingo—that turns your King into Elvis himself when the game is played on his birthday, January 8.

Of course it was always popular to insert ourselves into the game, too. I played the Science Advisor in *Civ I* and *III*, leader of a Hidden Faction in *Alpha Centauri*, both tutorial guide and King of the Barbarians in *Civ IV*, and a marble statue in *Civ V*. Jeff Briggs served as the military advisor in *Civ III*, and Brian Reynolds appeared in Union garb on the cover of the *Gettysburg!* strategy guide—an honor bestowed on him as the undisputed champion within the office. My voice also snuck into *Gettysburg!*, although I'm pretty sure that was an accident. We record dialogue placeholders so we can figure out which lines work before bringing the professionals in, and somehow my line "Our flanks are covered!" never got replaced. Meanwhile, nearly every voice and likeness in *Ace Patrol* belonged to someone at Firaxis, because our mobile games were on a budget, and it was cheaper than hiring actors.

No one in the company appears in *SimGolf*, but strangely enough, one of the lakes is named after Robin Williams's son, Cody. There had previously been lakes named after all three of his children, because Bing Gordon told me he was going to let Robin play the prototype the next time they got together, and I thought it would be a funny thing for him to discover. But the other two kids,

Zelda and Zak, had to be replaced before the game was officially released, because both would have looked like copyright infringement. (While the former is probably more recognizable today, the latter had appeared only a handful of years earlier in Lucasfilm Games' *Zak McKracken and the Alien Mindbenders*.)

These days, you don't see as many Easter Eggs, due in large part to the "Hot Coffee" scandal of 2005. A deactivated, but never-completely-removed minigame was discovered within the code of *Grand Theft Auto: San Andreas*, and its reinstatement by the mod community revealed pretty quickly why the studio had decided to cut it. The series was already well-known for its adults-only content, but there was a significant legal backlash over whether the minigame had been intentionally hidden to evade the ratings board, and settlements in the case ultimately totaled over $20 million. After that, publishers were understandably nervous about secret content of any kind, and Easter Eggs became widely discouraged.

Instead, their comedic function has been mostly taken over by the concept of Achievements, or virtual awards for meeting certain game criteria. Standard recognitions include things like winning at a particular difficulty level, but others are a little more silly, like the "Book 'em, Danno" badge that appears after discovering Hawaii in a random-map game. Beating the *Civ V* Mongol scenario earns the achievement called "Khan," but losing it produces "Khaaan!" instead. Some badges are as rare as they are strange, like the Ninja Turtle–themed "Pizza Party," which is awarded when the player activates Leonardo da Vinci in New York City, while possessing Great Works by both Michelangelo and Donatello, plus at least one sewer.

But of all the inside jokes and running gags that *Civilization* has inspired over the years, the funniest to me will always be "Nuclear Gandhi." The reason why, however, is complicated.

The default leader for each civilization was generally their most well-known historical figure—the Americans were run by Abe Lincoln, the English by Elizabeth I, and so on. While this was a great shortcut for characterization, it also caused some problems. Case in point: Mohandas Gandhi was the most recognizable figure from India, but he wasn't exactly the world-conquering type. I decided that was okay, though, because there was more than one way to win the game, and Gandhi could still present a formidable challenge in the race for scientific advancement while remaining mostly pacifist. A well-balanced AI takes all types.

Here's where the story gets interesting (not to mention well-documented online): all of the leaders were given a score from 1 to 12 across a number of variables, and Gandhi's military aggressiveness was placed at 1, as would be expected. A different piece of code, however, called for an automatic two-point drop in military aggressiveness whenever a country adopted democracy, which would theoretically have put Gandhi at a score of negative 1. But since negative numbers were impossible in this type of calculation, an overflow error caused the value to wrap around to the top of the number list, giving him a score of 255. Thus, the moment India became democratic, Gandhi would turn into a vicious warmonger and begin nuking everyone in range. A revision was quickly sent out, but players were so charmed by the hilarious juxtaposition that it became a running joke that has been thoroughly enjoyed and built upon by fans ever since. Images of Gandhi with captions like, "First they ignore you, then they laugh at you, then they fight you, then you cleanse them in atomic fire," and "A nuke for a nuke will make the whole world bow down to me" have been shared far and wide. Other memes needed no words at all, like the photoshopped picture of Gandhi riding the falling bomb at the end of *Dr. Strangelove*.

But it's not the countless callbacks and references that make the nuclear Gandhi story so funny to me. It's the fact that none of it is true. The overflow error never happened at all.

It is true that Gandhi would—eventually—use nukes when India was at war, just like any civilization in the game, and at the time this did strike a lot of players as odd. The real Abraham Lincoln probably wouldn't have nuked anyone either, but the idea was that every leader draws a line in the sand somewhere. It's also true that Gandhi would frequently threaten the player, because one of his primary traits was to avoid war, and deterrence through mutually assured destruction was an effective way to go about that. Since all leaders used the same basic diplomacy script, Gandhi's reminder that "Our words are backed with nuclear weapons!" was identical to Napoleon's or anyone else's, and perhaps came off as a bit of a non sequitur from the humble ascetic. Plus, as a scientifically aggressive civilization, India was more likely to acquire the technology early in the game, meaning Gandhi's threats of atomic annihilation might begin at a time when the player had barely mastered gunpowder. So it's fair to say that Gandhi could, on occasion, seem a little unnecessarily zealous, if only verbally.

But at no point did a democratic score change, or any value approaching 255, come into it. That kind of bug comes from something called unsigned characters, which are not the default in the C programming language, and not something I used for the leader traits. Brian Reynolds wrote *Civ II* in C++, and he didn't use them, either. We received no complaints about a Gandhi bug when either game came out, nor did we send out any revisions for one. Gandhi's military aggressiveness score remained at 1 throughout the game.

Dedicated fans will be quick to point out that Gandhi's preference for nuclear weapons over other forms of warfare was set to 12 in *Civilization V*, as revealed by the game's lead designer, Jon Shafer. But that was nineteen years after the original release, and Jon was only leaning in to the existing amusement over Gandhi using nuclear weapons at all. His was the first game in the series to codify it as an Easter Egg for fans, and he had never heard of the 255-overflow story when *Civ V* was released in 2010.

Where, then, did it come from?

The first reference appeared in July 2012—two years after Jon's game, and more than two decades after the original game's release—when a user named "Tunafish" added the supposed trivia to the website TVTropes.org, which can be edited by anyone. It sat, untouched except for cosmetic changes, until November of that year, when a watered-down version of the same story was added by an anonymous user to Wikia, a pop culture site similar to Wikipedia. No other edits were ever made to Wikia from that IP address, and while TVTropes is not as forthcoming with their user data, it appears that the Tunafish account was never used again, either.

Six weeks later, the spread began. First, two well-established users of a gaming forum repeated the story, with one of them citing the Wikia page after someone asked for a source. A few posts trickled out to other small forums over the next few days, again meeting only a single expression of skepticism, which was this time refuted with the TVTropes link.

Things percolated gently for the next year and a half, with the rumor cropping up every few months on the message board Reddit, and once on the Tumblr page of a gentleman named Chaz. The big break came in October 2014, when a comic called "Real Life Gandhi vs. Civilization Gandhi" was re-posted on Reddit. The comic itself was several years old, and only generically highlighted the humor of putting Gandhi's finger on the button at all, but in the comments that followed, half a dozen users chimed in to share the story they'd heard about the overflow error.

With that many in agreement, it became truth.

Ten days later, the gaming news site Kotaku wrote a story about the bug, which was followed by a similar post on Geek.com a few hours later. Both referenced the Reddit thread as their source. Several other news blogs picked up the story, now citing Kotaku as their source. In February 2015, the circle became complete when an anonymous user, again having never contributed to the site before or since, left a single exasperated post on the Wikia talk page: "Are we not going to mention the Democracy bug with Gandhi's aggression level? It's only been a core part of *Civ* since *Civ 1*."

A week and half later, a description of "Nuclear Gandhi" was added to the massive website Know Your Meme, with the origin being listed as a "confirmed" fact about the series, though for some reason they attributed the bug to *Civ II*, rather than its prequel. Six months after that, it was presented as a real-world example of an overflow error in the curriculum of a computer science class at Harvard University. Today, the story is still being revived on major news sites and message boards on a regular basis—Elon Musk tweeted about it as recently as 2019—and almost always triggers at least a few replies of, "Duh, I thought everyone already knew this."

Obviously, there's a cautionary tale to be heard here about the importance of sourcing your facts. I can't imagine what purpose Tunafish had in making it up, unless perhaps it was an intentional demonstration of the internet's unreliability in the first place. Those who know it best trust it least, and this person clearly had enough knowledge of programming to make the story plausible. Maybe somebody out there is sowing seeds for fun, to find out how many detailed-but-utterly-false stories they can establish in the culture as received wisdom. Or, maybe Tunafish is just a random guy who happened to get nuked one time right after India developed democracy, and he was willing to take any logical leaps necessary in order to blame the AI rather than his own failed diplomacy.

To me, the more interesting question is: What makes this particular story so fascinating that it continues to generate traffic every time it's mentioned? Of course there's the popularity of the *Civilization* series itself, and the particular demographic it serves. Our players are computer literate by definition, and more likely to get their news and social needs met online, where word-of-screen persists far longer than word of mouth ever could. The tale also involves a little bit of technology, which makes people feel smart when they share it, but the explanation is simple enough that anyone can wrap their brain around it. And then there's the humor, which adds an extra jolt of longevity to anything it touches. Gandhi firing nukes is, and always has been, inherently funny, no matter how rarely it actually occurs.

Some have argued that a nuke-loving depiction of Gandhi was

in fact a more accurate one to begin with, since his political beliefs evolved over time, and he consistently expressed a deep resentment of nations that oppressed his own. But that's beside the point. At the end of the day, my job was to create a balanced group of AI characters, and then find shortcuts that might connect players emotionally to those characters. The Indian political leader Jawaharlal Nehru might have been a more authentic choice, but without Gandhi, the game wouldn't have been nearly as memorable, or as fun.

And that, I think, is the biggest reason why the myth struck such a chord with fans, and why no journalist made any attempt to confirm or debunk it. Finding a bug in a well-loved game feels much more satisfying than finding one in a game you don't care about. It's an endearing flaw—the gaming community's equivalent of a candid photo under the headline "Game Designers: They're Just Like Us!" So, in that respect, I can appreciate the sentiment behind its endurance, and I don't mind if it happens to chip away at any pedestals people may have placed me on. I've certainly released my share of bugs, even if this doesn't happen to be one of them, and I'm glad to see players engage with the game, and each other, in whatever way makes them happy.

25

BEYOND

Sid Meier's Civilization:
Beyond Earth (2014)
*
Sid Meier's Starships (2015)

I'D LIKE TO SAY I'M CAPTAIN KIRK,
but the truth is I'm really Sulu. I value quiet competence. Boys in the 1960s were supposed to dream about being adventurous, hotshot astronauts, but I always knew that kind of escapade wasn't for me. I belonged in the background, plugging away at complex calculations and just generally being reliable, while those Captain Kirk types handled the dangerous—not to mention public—interactions.

I can remember watching the Apollo 11 mission on television during the summer of 1969, and Walter Cronkite's steady, reassuring intonations about "the voyage man always has dreamed about." Those four days of nearly continuous news coverage, from the rising of the rocket to the landing of Neil Armstrong's boot in the dust, were the first unified, real-time experience of a nation, the first hint of the constant connectivity that we now live with every day. Up to that point, news was something you watched for half an hour in the evening, and Walter Cronkite was merely a messenger. Now, he sounded like a prophet.

"We almost glibly toss that line away now, 'man on the moon,'" Cronkite said. "But by golly, just think it over."

I had been. The original *Star Trek* had aired its series finale just six weeks before the Apollo 11 launch, and I had watched them all religiously. My friends Chris, Frank, and I had a Friday night ritual of swimming at the YMCA,* then coming back to my house together for the latest episode. My favorite was "The City on the Edge of Forever," in which Kirk and Spock travel through a portal to the 1930s and attempt to rescue their shipmate without altering history. Of course, Kirk falls in love with a woman who must die to maintain the timeline, and to a thirteen-year-old boy this was powerfully thought-provoking stuff. The question of how history could play out differently with just a small change might have come up once or twice during my career.

I suppose it's a little strange that I hadn't managed to make a spaceship game since graduating from ASCII art, but the ever-present Space Game prototype on my hard drive didn't find its voice until *Ace Patrol* proved the concept of turn-based flying. Like its predecessor, *Starships* was primarily a tactical game, with a light story structure to carry the player from battle to battle without becoming so involved that it broke the *Covert Action* rule. But in a new twist, we were able to build on the plot outside of the game by setting it in the same universe as our latest *Civilization* title, *Beyond Earth*. Players could run either game independently, or share data between the two and develop their stories in tandem. Maybe someday we'll be like the Marvel Universe of gaming, and link every new release together in some fashion. (No, we won't be doing that. It seems silly to have to clarify, but better to be on the safe side.)

I find it hard to stop myself from the "maybe someday" ideas

---

* **Achievement Unlocked:** Everybody but the Biker—Visit the YMCA with a soldier, a railroad worker, a police captain, Pocatello, and Blazing Saddles.

because the longer I live, the more of them turn out to be true. In 1997, I wrote a guest column for *Game Developer Magazine* about the growing rift between independent studios and large publishers, and predicted that the industry was "returning to the heady days of the mid-1980s, when a few people with a garage and a vision really could revolutionize the computer gaming industry." It was at least partly aspirational—where I *hoped* the industry was going—and probably also an indirect justification for my recent exit from MicroProse, as I referred to the "suffocating" nature of bureaucracy and pointed out that the top five products of 1996 (*Warcraft II*, *Myst*, *Duke Nukem 3D*, *Civilization II*, and *Command & Conquer*) had all been developed by small outfits, with the exception of our own. But I never could have imagined anything like the current iTunes Store or Steam Workshop, where instead of twenty to thirty indie releases per year, we now see that many per day, or sometimes per hour. Back then, I dismissed "virtual reality headware" and "interactive movies" as buzzwords that distracted from the essence of good gameplay—but I also put the terms "CD-ROM" and "DVD" in the same category, so who knows? Maybe someday I'll find myself converting *Floyd of the Jungle* over to the latest virtual reality gear. I find it unlikely, but so many of our wildest dreams have turned out to be laughably conservative that it's hard to write off anything as impossible.

When it comes to the real world, though, I'm not much of a futurist—what really hooked me about the *Star Trek* universe was that it dealt with themes of humanity. Kirk's crew had a lot of the same problems we did, which were the same problems Bach's parishioners had, and so on. I'm always excited to find out what comes next, but I largely think of it in terms of what those innovations can do to improve what we already have. There's no shortage of problems to solve here on Earth—and for what it's worth, I do think that our industry has contributed to some of those solutions. Videogames have educated, inspired, broadened, and enlightened millions of people. We are translated more often, and into more languages, than the majority of books, and some of our best work has connected individuals across warring cultures and helped them find commonality. Like every art form, there are good and bad examples, but I think the former outweigh the latter. There are now entire museums dedicated to the good ones, like The Strong National Museum of Play in New York, and the National Videogame Museum in Texas, plus countless traveling and temporary exhibits at the Smithsonian and many others.

I'm often invited to participate in publicity events at museums like these, but I prefer to visit them as a spectator when I can, because I'm wary of being permanently associated with the past. I don't mind speaking as a witness to that era, but I'm always careful to root my conversation in what we're doing now, and where we're going next. Once you start talking about your own legacy, you're done—and I'm definitely not done. Most of my games I haven't even played since the day they shipped, because I've already moved on to the next exciting thing. Dani Bunten Berry once said that she looked back on her old games as "alternately wonderful and terrible," because she could never stop seeing things she would have done differently. My habit of avoiding them prevents that kind of regret to a certain degree, but even when I do come across flaws, I don't usually dwell on them. I see them as inspiration for a new game that does things differently.

Of course certain titles from my past are inescapable, but that's something that comes with the territory. I'm the one who reached out and forged this connection with my fans, after all, and I feel like I owe them the part of me that is *Sid Meier!*, as opposed to Sid Meier. Not only is the italicized-and-exclamatory version of me very different from the original model who sits at my desk every day, he's actually a different person for every individual fan, frozen in time with whatever gaming experience stands out the most for them. To some people, I'm a wise old teacher who guided them through their teen years; to others, I'm the secret goofy friend who pretended to be a pirate with them when everyone else said they were too old for that sort of thing. Most people's vision of me isn't about me at all, but about the joy they felt, and I want to maintain that happy memory for them.

It's not that *Sid Meier!* is a falsehood. He's just static, made up entirely of flattering snapshots of Sid Meier on his very best days. He doesn't have to worry about any of the less certain times in between, when regular, behind-the-scenes Sid Meier is stuck on an unsolvable problem, or in a bad mood, or snoring too loudly. And I'm okay with the fact that both guys have to exist, as well as the necessary separation between us. I've been on the other side of the interaction, too, watching an actor or a musician and feeling that connection as if I know them personally through their work. So I get it. The rock star wants to keep writing new music, but his fans want to hear the hits, and I think there's a certain obligation for both to meet in the middle. I can play the hits, and talk about *Civilization* whenever I'm asked, but hopefully fans will consider trying out my new projects as well, and give our relationship the chance to grow more complex. Fan interaction is a part of my job now, and it's not a burden by any means—but it's not the reason I get up in the morning, either.

I feel the same way about awards. I once received a star on the "Walk of Game" in San Francisco, with press photos and speeches and everything, and six years later the whole thing was demolished and turned into a Target. I'm keenly aware of how impermanent popularity can be, and I look at awards only as an opportunity for me to quietly reflect and be grateful for the life I've been given. Making games is simply the best job in the world, and I would never look back and say, "Sure, life was awesome, but I don't feel like everyone thanked me enough."

I'm sure I could find a way to frame my life in terms of struggles, if I wanted to. I could talk about how my father came home with frostbite one winter, but continued walking to his night shift job for another several years until we could afford a car. I could point out that when my friends and I played sports in the park, we were sharing half a set of equipment between all of us, or that my family's first television was a hand-me-down from a neighbor who had upgraded to a better model. I could tell you about literally shoveling coal in the basement of our house to keep the furnace running. I could limit my thinking to deals that fell through, and projects that failed. I could let family tragedies define me.

But I see the world in a positive light. I can't say whether that's a conscious choice I made along the way, or a natural part of my personality, but it's what I do. When I was little, I built a skating rink in my backyard by piling up a ring of snow and filling it with water until the ice was layered thick. Shortly after strapping on my skates, I slipped and broke my leg. But I genuinely don't remember the pain, or the trip to the hospital, or the inconvenience of the leg cast I had to wear for several months. All I remember about the experience—and this part is quite vivid—was how special it felt to be carried by older students from class to class because I couldn't walk. They would put me on their shoulders, and parade me around the school like a king. I can distinctly remember thinking to myself, "I sure am lucky this happened to me."

I have another memory of being on a school-wide field trip in kindergarten, and winning a set of horseshoes in a raffle. "Of all these hundreds of kids," I marveled, "they drew my number." I kept the game for years, not because I had a particular affinity for playing with it, but because it was a warm and fuzzy memory, to think back on how lucky I'd been. I also clearly remember being in art class a few weeks before the first Super Bowl, and correctly predicting the score of the game within a painting I'd made (Packers over Chiefs, 35–10). I'm almost certain that these little bits of serendipity haven't happened to me more often than they do over the course of anyone's life, but they seem to be the only type of memory my brain has any interest in keeping.

I think that in life, as in game design, you have to find the fun. There is joy out there waiting to be discovered, but it might not be where you expected. You can't decide what something's going to be before you embark on it, and you shouldn't stick with a bad idea just because you're fond of it. Take action as quickly and repeatedly as possible, take advantage of what you already know, and take liberties with tradition. But most importantly, take the time to appreciate the possibilities, and make sure all of your decisions are interesting ones.

SPECIAL THANKS!

I HAVE BEEN SO INCREDIBLY fortunate in both my professional and personal life, and there is no question that I've had help along the way. First, immense thanks are owed to my wife, Susan, my son, Ryan, and my parents, August and Alberdina, for all their love and support. My profound gratitude also goes out to Bill Stealey, Bruce Shelley, Brian Reynolds, Jeff Briggs, Soren Johnson, Jon Shafer, Ed Beach, and everyone else who has ever worked at MicroProse and Firaxis—neither the companies nor the games would have been possible without you.

Likewise, this book itself would not have been possible without the dedicated talents of my agent, Myrsini Stephanides, and my editor, Tom Mayer. It wasn't exactly a surprise to find gamers at work in the publishing industry, but it's always nice to collaborate with people who share your passion. Thank you as well to the site managers and contributors at Archive.org, Mobygames .com, CGWmuseum.org, and GDCvault.com, who made historical research considerably easier than it would have otherwise been; and to Daniel Silevitch, David Mullich, Knut Egil Brenne, Jeff Johannigman, and Aaron Nwaiwu for their help in tracking down obscure details and materials. And, of course, many thanks to Jennifer Lee Noonan, who had the patience to listen to many hours of my disjointed ramblings and self-serving pronouncements, then combined them with a boatload of fascinating research to fashion a manuscript which I'm certain will stand the test of time.

Above all, I am grateful to the industry as a whole: the hardware and software designers who provide us with tools, the writers and journalists who keep people informed, the marketing and PR folks who organize events, and most especially, the players themselves, without whom our jobs wouldn't even exist. Thank you.*

Achievement Unlocked: Completionist!—Read the Special Thanks section.

SID MEIER'S
COMPLETE GAMEOGRAPHY!

Tic Tac Toe (1975)

The Star Trek Game (1979)

Hostage Rescue (1980)

Bank Game I (1981)

Bank Game II: The Revenge (1981)

Faux Space Invaders (1981)

Faux Pac-Man (1981)

Formula 1 Racing (1982)

Hellcat Ace (1982)

Chopper Rescue (1982)

Floyd of the Jungle (1982)

Spitfire Ace (1982)

Wingman (1983)

Floyd of the Jungle II (1983)

NATO Commander (1983)

Solo Flight (1983)

Air Rescue I (1984)

F-15 Strike Eagle (1984)

Silent Service (1985)

Crusade in Europe (1985)

Decision in the Desert (1985)

Conflict in Vietnam (1986)

Gunship (1986)

Sid Meier's Pirates! (1987)

Red Storm Rising (1988)

F-19 Stealth Fighter (1988)

F-15 Strike Eagle II (1989)

Sid Meier's Railroad Tycoon (1990)

Sid Meier's Covert Action (1990)

Sid Meier's Civilization (1991)

Pirates! Gold (1993)

Sid Meier's Railroad Tycoon Deluxe (1993)

Sid Meier's C.P.U. Bach (1994)

Sid Meier's Colonization (1994)

Sid Meier's CivNet (1995)

Sid Meier's Civilization II (1996)

Magic: The Gathering (1997)

Sid Meier's Gettysburg! (1997)

Sid Meier's Alpha Centauri (1999)

Sid Meier's Antietam! (1999)

Sid Meier's Civilization III (2001)

The Dinosaur Game (unreleased)

Sid Meier's SimGolf (2002)

Sid Meier's Pirates! Live the Life (2004)

Sid Meier's Civilization IV (2005)

Sid Meier's Railroads! (2006)

Sid Meier's Civilization Revolution (2008)

Sid Meier's Civilization IV: Colonization (2008)

Sid Meier's Civilization V (2010)

Sid Meier's CivWorld (2011)

Sid Meier's Ace Patrol (2013)

Sid Meier's Ace Patrol: Pacific Skies (2013)

Sid Meier's Civilization Revolution 2 (2014)

Sid Meier's Civilization: Beyond Earth (2014)

Sid Meier's Starships (2015)

Sid Meier's Civilization VI (2016)

INDEX!

Note: *Italicized* pages refer to photos or illustrations.